BETWEEN RELATIVISM AND FUNDAMENTALISM

Between Relativism and Fundamentalism

Religious Resources for a Middle Position

Edited by

Peter L. Berger

WILLIAM B. EERDMANS PUBLISHING COMPANY

GRAND RAPIDS, MICHIGAN / CAMBRIDGE, U.K.

Published 2010 by
Wm. B. Eerdmans Publishing Co.
2140 Oak Industrial Drive N.E., Grand Rapids, Michigan 49505 /
P.O. Box 163, Cambridge CB3 9PU U.K.

Printed in the United States of America

15 14 13 12 11 10   7 6 5 4 3 2 1

Library of Congress Cataloging-in-Publication Data

Between relativism and fundamentalism: religious resources for a middle position /
   edited by Peter L. Berger.
      p.   cm.
   ISBN 978-0-8028-6387-4 (pbk.: alk. paper)
   1. Fundamentalism. 2. Religious pluralism — Christianity.
   3. Moderation — Religious aspects — Christianity.   I. Berger, Peter L., 1929-

BT82.2.B48   2010
261.2′6 — dc22

                                        2009042572

www.eerdmans.com

Contents

Contents

Contributors

PETER L. BERGER, a Lutheran layman, is a senior research fellow at the Institute on Culture, Religion, and World Affairs at Boston University.

GRACE DAVIE teaches sociology at the University of Exeter and is a lay canon of the Church of England.

INGEBORG GABRIEL teaches social ethics at the Catholic Theological Faculty of the University of Vienna.

CRAIG M. GAY teaches sociology at Regent College in Vancouver.

DAVID M. GORDIS, a Conservative rabbi, is president emeritus of Hebrew College in Newton, Massachusetts.

OS GUINNESS is a writer and lecturer living in McLean, Virginia.

JAMES DAVISON HUNTER teaches sociology at the University of Virginia.

MICHAEL PLEKON is a sociologist at Baruch College and the City University of New York, as well as a priest of the Orthodox Church of America.

Preface

The papers published in this volume are the products of a project of the Institute on Culture, Religion, and World Affairs at Boston University (CURA). The authors constitute a working group that met twice at CURA over a two-year period. The group originally included Muhammad Kalisch, who teaches Islamics at the University of Münster, Germany. He contributed constructively to the original discussions of the group, but for reason of other commitments, was unable to contribute a paper. We regret this downsizing of the agenda from an "Abrahamic" to a "Judeo-Christian" scope but are grateful to him for his initial participation.

The introduction, "Between Relativism and Fundamentalism," was an attempt at the outset of the project to provide a common focus for the working group. Its members were, of course, free to define their own position as they saw fit. The text first appeared in an article in *The American Interest*, September-October 2006, pp. 9-17. Permission to reprint is gratefully acknowledged.

The papers are organized under two headings. Under "Sociological Descriptions," the three authors give an objective picture of how relativism and fundamentalism play out in the contemporary world. The papers under "Theological Directions" are normative rather than descriptive. Their authors suggest how a "middle position" between the two extremes may be established by using resources of various Jewish and Christian traditions.

The project was almost entirely funded by a generous gift from David Kiersznowski, with some additional funds from the Lynde and Harry Bradley Foundation. We are deeply grateful to both donors.

Introduction: Between Relativism and Fundamentalism

Peter L. Berger

Contemporary culture (and by no means only in America) appears to be in the grip of two seemingly contradictory forces. One pushes the culture toward relativism, the view that there are no absolutes whatever, that moral or philosophical truth is inaccessible if not illusory. The other pushes toward a militant and uncompromising affirmation of this or that (alleged) absolute truth. There are idiomatic formulas for both relativism and what is commonly called fundamentalism: "Let us agree to disagree" as against "You just don't get it."

Beware of concluding too quickly that both can be legitimate components of civil discourse: imagine the first being the response to an interlocutor who favors pedophile rape, the second uttered by someone who favors the mass murder of infidels. Rather, both formulas make civil discourse impossible, because both (albeit for opposite reasons) preclude a common and reasoned quest for moral or philosophical agreement. Relativism is bad for civility because it precludes the moral condemnation of virtually anything at all. Fundamentalism is bad for civility because it produces irresolvable conflict with those who do not share its beliefs. And both are bad for any hope of arriving at valid normative conclusions by means of rational discourse — relativism because there is no will to such a discourse, and fundamentalism because there is no way to it.

For reasons that may not be immediately obvious, relativism and funda-

---

This essay originally appeared in *The American Interest*, Autumn 2006, pp. 9-17. It appears here by permission of the journal.

mentalism as cultural forces are closely interlinked. This is not only because one can morph and, more often than may be appreciated, does morph into the other: in every relativist there is a fundamentalist about to be born, and in every fundamentalist there is a relativist waiting to be liberated. More basically, it is because both relativism and fundamentalism are products of the same process of modernization; indeed, both are intrinsically modern phenomena of going to extremes. What follows is an attempt, by means of a sociological analysis, to show how the two phenomena are related.

This is not to suggest that, having gained a better understanding of the situation, one will know just what to do about it. History is not made by committees of sociologists or philosophers. Truth may set many free, but reason has a mottled track record. Many relativists cannot be dissuaded from their position unless they confront what they are quite certain is a moral outrage — that is, at that point where they are unlikely to say, "Well, there is the victim's narrative, and there is the rapist's narrative, and both are equally valid." At precisely this point they may become a convert to this or that version of fundamentalism. Often the only way to interact with a fundamentalist is by the instruments of violence — at which point the fundamentalist, looking at the shambles of an intended utopia, may lapse into relativism. However, it is probably safe to say that most human beings, busy living their lives, gravitate toward a more reasonable middle ground, though usually without being able to justify or even articulate why they believe and act as they do. They constitute the potential constituency for a much-needed declaration of civil moderation.

The Relativizing Process

In the 1950s many social scientists viewed modernization as a uniform and irreversible process. They believed that every society had to pass through a series of predictable stages that, while amenable to some local modifications, would essentially resemble the development of the Western world. It is in this theoretical context that the über-sociologist of that era, Talcott Parsons, called America the "vanguard society."

This theory of modernization provided many valuable insights, and was much too cavalierly dismissed by the neo-Marxist and "postmodernist" theories that have more recently replaced it. Still, it is fair to say that the theory is much less plausible today. The "local modifications" have been far too many and too basic to be interpreted as minor variations on a dominant theme. It turns out that modernity is not a seamless robe. Social scientists today are more likely to agree with Shmuel Eisenstadt, who suggested the advent of "multiple modernities" (or, if one prefers, "alternate modernities"). Thus, to take one of the most important cases, Japan is a thoroughly modern society by any indicator, but is certainly "alternate" compared with the West.

An important component of the earlier view of modernization has been so-called secularization theory. Simply put, it proposed that the more a society became modern, the less would it be religious. This view, of course, was congenial to an Enlightenment philosophy of progress within which the decline of religion was welcomed as a liberation from superstition and clerical tyranny. However, many of those who upheld secularization theory did not welcome it at all — indeed, many were Christian theologians. They just thought that the evidence, unfortunately, pointed in this direction. Again, it is fair to say that since the 1970s this theory has been massively falsified: far from being increasingly secularized, the contemporary world is the scene of enormous explosions of religious passion.[1] Modernity is not only quite variegated but, in most places, comfortably compatible with religion of one kind or another.

At least in the social sciences, it is prudent not to throw out the baby with the bathwater as one theoretical paradigm follows another. Secularization theory had one thing right: modernization undermines taken-for-granted beliefs and values. But the theory was mistaken in assuming that this process of relativization would necessarily lead to a decline of religion or, for that matter, of other historical claims to truth. In retrospect — and here, frankly, I'm also being confessional in terms of my career as a sociologist — the mistake was grounded in a simple confusion — namely, between secularization and pluralization. Modernity does not necessarily secularize; however, probably necessarily, it does pluralize.

What does this mean? Through most of human history, most people have lived in communities in which there was a very high degree of consensus on basic cognitive and normative assumptions. This consensus is

---

1. There are two exceptions to this statement: one geographical — western and central Europe; the other sociological — a thin but influential international intelligentsia that is indeed heavily secularized, even in strongly religious societies such as the United States. Analyzing these exceptions, though they are key to any sociology of contemporary religion, is beyond the scope of this essay.

dependent on strong barriers of separation, geographical or social, between the member of the community and outsiders. Given such barriers,
worldview and morality tend to take on a self-evident quality. While this
was the usual situation in pre-modern times, one must not exaggerate this
observation. The cognitive and normative consensus was challenged in
various places and at various times by such collective experiences as
intercultural migration, foreign invasion, or natural catastrophe. And one
may suppose that there have always been individuals, such as Socrates or
Spinoza or Einstein, who questioned prevailing orthodoxies and managed
to be heard. But such individuals were rare and very often they were prevented from having their say. Thus, while pluralism is not a uniquely modern phenomenon, modernity has enormously increased its scope and accelerated its impact. Today it is a global phenomenon. Even the most
zealous promoters of ethno-tourism have a hard time finding pristine villages with cultures untouched by the turbulent pluralism of the contemporary world. (And if they do find any, they and their clients will almost
instantaneously destroy the pristine quality! Twixt tribal village and tribal
theme park is a short step, indeed.)

"Pluralism" is a less-than-fortunate term. The "ism" suggests an ideological position, as was intended by the American philosopher, Horace
Kallen, who coined it in the 1920s to celebrate ethnic and religious diversity. I use the term here as it is now commonly used, namely to describe
not an ideology but an empirical fact. "Pluralization" is more factual-
sounding, but it is also more awkward. It usually makes little sense to fight
common usage, so let "pluralism" stand. However, here is a more precise
definition of it: *pluralism is a situation in which different ethnic or religious
groups co-exist under conditions of civic peace and interact with each other
socially.* The latter phrase is important. There are situations in which
groups live side by side peacefully, but have nothing to do with one another — the traditional Indian caste system being a good example. Such
barriers to interaction prevent "cognitive contamination" (a phrase I in-
vented in an earlier fit of terminological enthusiasm), which happens
when the beliefs and values of others undermine the taken-for-granted
status of one's own.

There is no great mystery as to why modernity generates plurality.
Modernity has led to massive urbanization, with highly diverse groups
thrown into intense contact with each other. Unprecedented rates of international migration and travel have had similar consequence. Mass literacy

has brought knowledge of other cultures and ways of life to numerous people. And of course, such knowledge has been greatly magnified by newer information technologies: telephone, radio, movies, television, and now, exponentially, the computer revolution. Everyone now talks about globalization, and the phenomenon is real enough. But it only represents a vast amplification of the modernizing process that began with the great voyages of discovery and the printing press. The information technology of the globalization era has brought the dynamics of pluralizing modernity to all but the most remote corners of the world.

Pluralism relativizes. It does so both institutionally and in the consciousness of individuals. This relativization is obviously enhanced when the state does not try to impose uniformity of beliefs and values by means of coercion. However, as the fate of modern totalitarian regimes illustrates, even when the state makes this attempt, it is very difficult to block out every form of cognitive contamination. There is now a veritable market of worldviews and moralities. Every functioning society requires a certain degree of normative consensus, lest it fall apart. No society can tolerate a pluralism of norms concerning intracommunity violence — say, "I believe in my right to shoot anyone who takes my parking space." But within these limits a wide diversity is possible. The American idiom contains the revealing phrase "religious preference" — a market term if ever there was one. But there are also more — lifestyle, ethnic, and even sexual preferences (and an accompanying cottage industry of counselors and therapists assisting consumers in selecting the preferences that are presumably right for them).

The institutional consequences of pluralism are most clearly evident in the case of religion. Whether they like it or not, and no matter whether this accords with their theological self-understanding, all churches become *voluntary associations* in post-traditional societies. Their lay members become consumers of the services provided by the clergy and, in the process, become more assertive. American Catholic writers have described this process as "Protestantization." The term is misleading if it refers to some doctrinal adumbration of Protestantism, but it accurately describes how the social organization of Catholicism has come to resemble the voluntary character of Protestant denominations in America.

But the same move from taken-for-granted allegiance to freely chosen participation creates voluntary "denominations" in areas other than religion. People voluntarily adhere to this or that moral belief system (that is what the American culture war is about), this or that lifestyle (the cult of "wellness" has all the markings of a church), ethnic self-identification (Michael Novak shrewdly proposed years ago that ethnicity has become a matter of choice in America), and even sexual identity (thus many feminists have embraced the notion that gender — tellingly a term derived from the arbitrary realm of grammar — is a "social construction"). In *this* sense (and in this sense only) — to paraphrase Richard Nixon on Keynes — we are all Protestants now!

But pluralism also has profound consequences for individual life. As ever-wider areas of life lose their taken-for-granted norms, the individual must reflect upon and make choices among the alternatives that have become available. Indeed, modernization can be described as a gigantic shift in the human condition from one of fate to one of choice. This shift has been elegantly described by Arnold Gehlen in his two key categories of "de-institutionalization" and "subjectivization." De-institutionalization refers to the process wherein traditional institutional programs for individual behavior are fragmented — where previously there was one taken-for-granted program for, say, raising children, there now are competing schools of childhood education. Subjectivization refers to the process wherein institutions lose their alleged objective status so that the individual is thrown back upon himself in constructing his own "patchwork" of meanings and norms.

The net effect of this transformation can be summed up thusly: *certainty becomes much harder to achieve.* This means that even if the same traditional beliefs and values continue to be affirmed, the manner of affirmation has changed. Put simply, the *what* of belief may not change, but the *how* does. For many people, at least at an early stage of the process, this change is experienced as a great liberation — as indeed it is. But especially after a while, it may be experienced as a burden from which one wants to be freed. There ensues an often-desperate quest for certainty, and where there is a demand, someone will proffer a supply. This is where the fundamentalists come in.

The Fundamentalist Response

Like "pluralism," the term "fundamentalism" is not a fortunate one, though for different reasons. First, it has acquired a pejorative quality, and that is never a good thing if one wants to understand an empirical phenomenon. (After one has understood it, of course, one can be as pejorative as one wishes.) Second, it comes from an episode in the history of the early twentieth-century American Protestantism where it had very specific meanings, and those meanings are misleading when applied to movements unrelated to that history. One may as well go with common usage, but again with a more precise definition: *fundamentalism is the attempt to restore or create anew a taken-for-granted body of beliefs and values.* In other words, fundamentalism is always reactive, and what it reacts against is precisely the aforementioned relativization process.

It follows that, however traditional its rhetoric may be, fundamentalism is intrinsically a modern phenomenon; it is *not* tradition. At most it can be called *neo*-traditional, but that prefix denotes an abyss of difference. The difference is precisely between what is taken for granted and what is deliberately chosen.

What is taken for granted is by definition never objectified into a genuine question. But every choice can in principle be revoked, and that is what makes every fundamentalist project inevitably fragile — and, for that very reason, inclined toward intolerance. In a truly traditional community, those who do not share the prevailing worldview are not necessarily a threat — they are an interesting oddity, perhaps even amusing. In the fundamentalist worldview the unbeliever is a threat; he or she must be converted (the most satisfying option), shunned, or eliminated, be it by expulsion or physical liquidation. This is not to say that there was no fanaticism or intolerance in pre-modern times. These are most likely to be found, however, in the early stages of a movement — before it has settled down into a taken-for-granted community. When the latter development has occurred, a greater measure of tolerance becomes psychologically feasible.

There is a wonderful nineteenth-century story that nicely illustrates this difference between tradition and fundamentalism, albeit in a context that has nothing to do with religion. The Empress Eugenie, the wife of Napoleon III, was on a state visit to London. Now it so happens that Eugenie's background was rather unsavory and, though empress, she was very much an upstart. Not so, of course, Queen Victoria, her hostess. The two attended Covent Garden Opera together. Eugenie made an appearance, magnificently regal. She entered the royal box, graciously acknowledged the applause, looked behind her, and slowly sat down. Then Victoria entered, just as regal. She too graciously acknowledged the applause and sat down slowly. But she did not look behind her. She *knew* that the chair would be there.

The definition of fundamentalism suggested here, in addition to freeing the concept from pejorative associations and from its particular American context, has the advantage of making clear that it can refer to secular as well as religious movements. All sorts of secular worldviews and value systems can give rise to fundamentalist movements — radical nationalism, political ideologies, "scientism," even "secularism" as the belief that religion should be rigorously excluded from public life. In several countries today, secular and religious fundamentalists are pitted against each other politically — for example in Turkey and in France, and indeed in the United States. Though their political agendas are diametrically opposed, their social and psychological profiles are remarkably similar. Both have a black-or-white perception of society, both tend to demonize those who oppose them, and both would deliver the same underlying message to potential converts: "Come join us, and we will give you certainty as to what to believe, how to live, and who you are." There is a very large market out there for this message.

Fundamentalists of whatever stripe must suppress doubt (in psychologists' parlance, they must avoid cognitive dissonance). I will allow myself a personal anecdote here. Shortly after I came to America as a very young man I had a few dates with an attractive and intelligent young woman. I soon discovered that she was an ardent member of the American Communist Party, which somewhat dampened our relationship. Of course we argued about this. She was unwilling to accept any negative information about the Soviet Union. When I spoke about atrocities in Soviet-occupied Eastern Europe, she asked me whether I had personally witnessed these atrocities. When I said no, she said, "Well, I really would like to meet someone who has." I quickly said, "This could be arranged." Well, arrange it I did, and it was a revealing event.

I was friendly with a young couple recently arrived from Latvia. They invited me and my communist not-quite-girlfriend to supper. After some awkward chitchat, I asked them to talk about the Soviet occupation of Latvia. They told one horror story after another. My date sat quietly at first, then became increasingly agitated. After almost an hour she put her hands to her ears and said, "I don't want to hear any more of this." As we walked away from my friends' apartment, I asked her if she thought that they were lying. No, she replied, these people did not impress her as liars. But then she added, "You know, I think that there is something, if we could only find it, that would completely change what they were saying." Evidently she had found a magical pill against cognitive dissonance. The party was well equipped to provide such medicine. She never agreed to see me again.

To restate the argument: the fundamentalist project is the restoration, or the creation *de novo,* of a taken-for-granted definition of reality in the wake of relativization. This project can be realized in two ways, one more ambitious than the other.

The more ambitious version is to make an entire society the basis (in sociological terminology, the plausibility structure) of a newly taken-for-granted cognitive and normative order. This is what modern totalitarianism sought to achieve. It requires an enormous exercise of violence, not only in establishing the new order, but in maintaining it against the ever-present threat of cognitive contamination. Very importantly, the management of the project (the totalitarian regime) must control all communications with the outside world and all dissident sources of contamination within the society.

The history of totalitarianism in the twentieth century demonstrates how difficult such a fundamentalist project is. If realizable at all, it carries with it not only huge costs in human degradation and oppression, but also the cost of economic stagnation and decline. North Korea is the best current example of this. When a regime is unwilling or unable to bear these costs — and especially when it wishes to modernize its economy and is therefore obliged to have extensive communications with the outside world — cognitive contamination undermines the fundamentalist order. The internal disintegration of the Soviet Union is the best example of this; the recent history of China could be described (so far) as a better-managed version of a similar process.

The religious history of Europe is full of attempts to restore a challenged taken-for-granted order. Sooner or later, they all failed. The last significant Christian version of the totalitarian project was the Nationalist movement in the Spanish Civil War and the Franco regime that resulted from its victory. Blessed by the Catholic Church at that time (such a blessing would be unthinkable today), the movement intended the reconquest *(reconquista)* of Spain from what it perceived as the forces of atheism and immorality. Despite a savage apparatus of repression, the Franco victory turned out to be ephemeral. As soon as Spain opened itself to contacts with the outside world, even though initially this opening was to be lim-

ited to economic relations, the ideological unity sought by the regime dis-
integrated rapidly. No similar project has since been attempted in a Christian vein. (There have been some noises of this sort in Russian Orthodoxy,
but they are unlikely to go very far unless conditions in Russia greatly dete-
riorate.)

Religious totalitarianism, of course, characterizes radical Islam. With
the exception of the short-lived Taliban regime in Afghanistan, there have
been no successes. The Iranian ayatollahs may entertain totalitarian ideals,
but they also want Iran to be economically successful, and these two goals
are sharply contradictory. Under modern conditions, any project of full-
scope territorial *reconquista* is either unrealizable or forbiddingly costly.

There is a less ambitious and somewhat more realizable version of the
fundamentalist project. That is to realize it not in an entire society, but in an
enclave within that society. This could be called the sectarian or subcultural
version of fundamentalism. Within the enclave, a taken-for-granted
worldview is established; the rest of society is, as it were, abandoned to its
path to perdition. The recipe for the maintenance of a fundamentalist subculture is simple enough: control all communications between your members and the outside world, and especially control all social relations with
outsiders. The early Christian movement was just such a subculture or sect,
and the Apostle Paul was practicing good social psychology when he
warned Christians not to be "yoked together with unbelievers." In anthropological parlance: no commensality and no connubium with outsiders —
don't have them for dinner, and certainly don't go to bed with them! This
kind of control is easiest to achieve if the subcultural community is physi-
cally segregated from the larger society — often in remote rural villages or,
less effectively, in compact urban neighborhoods. If physical segregation is
not possible, controls over interaction and information have to be particularly stringent.

Now the history of religion is full of such self-isolationist projects,
and some of them have been successful over considerable periods of
time. But this kind of subcultural fundamentalism becomes ever more
difficult under modern conditions, because the walls of separation from
the outside world have to be kept very strong and in good repair. Allow
one little breach, and the turbulent forces of relativizing pluralism will
come surging in. What has to be maintained, if you will, is a sort of mini-
totalitarianism — not easy to achieve in a modern society. In sum, fundamentalists nowadays inherently have a hard time achieving their ob-

jectives. This is the good news. The bad news is that in the meantime they can cause an enormous amount of damage.

A New Normative Agenda

If one agrees with an agenda of articulating a middle ground between relativism and fundamentalism, several discrete issues need to be addressed. There is the cognitive relativism, most eloquently expressed by so-called postmodernist theories, which denies the very possibility of objective criteria of truth or even validity. In the final resort, this is a philosophical problem that cannot be discussed at length here. What can be said, however, is that in the human sciences, not least in sociology, this type of relativism has done immense harm. It makes science itself an impossible project, since there is no reliable way of distinguishing acceptable and unacceptable propositions about the empirical world. In practice, what still goes under the name of science becomes an unfalsifiable exercise in propaganda, or perhaps, if one is in a generous mood, poetry.

It seems to me that recent debates about the possibility of scientific objectivity repeat in a far less sophisticated way what was discussed in great detail in the social sciences about a hundred years ago, and the methodological writings of Max Weber still provide the best guide through this theoretical labyrinth. Without going into this vast body of materials, let me merely repeat what I often say to students who come braying to me with postmodernist ideas: suppose that I return a term paper to you with a failing grade and a note that reads, "I should give you a much better grade, but I hate your guts, so there." You will scream bloody murder, go to the dean, possibly sue me. What is the assumption behind your outrage? Obviously, you expect me to grade your paper fairly — that is, *objectively* — regardless of my feelings about you. But why do you demand this of me as a teacher while denying my ability to do it as a researcher?

Then there is the issue of moral relativism, again a philosophical problem that cannot be developed here. It can be formulated with great erudition, but in the end it comes down to the philosopher saying to the cannibal: "You believe it is right to cook people and eat them. I don't. Let us agree to disagree." It seems to me that there is an important difference between moral relativism and cognitive relativism. Science can never give us certainty, it only provides probabilities, and it must always be open to the possibility that its hypotheses may be falsified. But there are moral judgments that, even if one understands that they are contingent on one's position in time and space, attain a higher degree of certainty. Slavery and torture provide good examples. I am not prepared to say that my moral condemnation of torture is a matter of taste or that it is a mere hypothesis. I am certain that torture is a totally unacceptable moral evil. And any argument to the effect that I would have a different view if, say, I lived as a magistrate in Tudor England will not move me from this conviction. Moral judgments come out of specific perceptions of the human condition formed in the course of specific historical developments, but this genesis does not explain away their validity. Einstein would not have come upon the theory of relativity if he had lived as a peasant in ancient Egypt, but this obvious observation does not invalidate the theory. Einstein's scientific insights are not the same as his moral beliefs, but neither can be validated or invalidated by pointing out their social and historical context.

There are moral certainties that withstand relativization. There is the episode concerning General Napier who conquered the region of Sind for the British Raj in India. Upon establishing control over this area, he did what the British usually did in their empire — he left local customs pretty much as they were, except for a very few he deemed totally unacceptable. Among these was *suttee* — the burning alive of widows. A delegation of Brahmin priests came to see him and said, "You cannot ban *suttee*. It is an ancient tradition of our people." Napier replied, "We British also have our ancient traditions. When men burn a woman alive, we hang them. Let us each follow our traditions." It seems that Napier was not plagued by moral relativism.

My own interest has been mainly in the religious aspect of the relativist-fundamentalist dichotomy. My presupposition, again, is that both extremes are unacceptable: the relativist view that finally all religions are equally true (quite apart from theology, a philosophically untenable view); and the aggressive and intolerant fundamentalist claim to absolute truth (which even a modest acquaintance with historical scholarship about religion makes very hard to attain). It is possible and desirable to stake out middle positions that use the resources available from within the major religious traditions. The traditions coming out of southern and eastern Asia — notably Hinduism, Buddhism, Confucianism — have never had much difficulty doing this theoretically (but which, by the way, did not stop them from being savagely intolerant in practice from time to time). The Abrahamic traditions emerging out of western Asia — Judaism, Christianity, and Islam — have had greater difficulties. Monotheism does not easily develop an ethos of tolerance, especially when it is institutionalized and literally armed within the context of a state. Yet resources for such an ethos can be found in each tradition. What is more, modern ideas of human rights, including religious liberty, are historically rooted in the anthropological ideas of these traditions and, in recent times, have been explicitly legitimated by these ideas (as, for example, in the unfolding of Catholic social doctrine since the Second Vatican Council).

Why is such a religiously founded middle ground important? First, of course, for the obvious reasons that so much contemporary fundamentalism has religious content (and not only among Muslims): one cannot oppose it without confronting its religious claims. The middle ground is thus politically important as a defense against the highly destructive potential of religious fanaticism. But this middle ground is also important for intellectual and spiritual reasons. It can be the location of those who want to be religious believers without emigrating from modernity.

Protestantism, as Max Weber and Ernst Troeltsch showed in the early twentieth century, has had a special relationship with modernity. Its long struggle with the spirit of modernity cannot be replicated in other traditions, but it nevertheless holds lessons for the latter. One is the readiness to have faith without laying claim to certainty — from the *sola fide* of the Lutheran Reformation to Paul Tillich's "Protestant principle." Another lesson is the importance of coming to terms with modern historical scholarship. Protestantism was the first religious tradition that turned the critical instrument of this scholarship on its own scriptures — a historically unprecedented event, most of it carried on in nineteenth-century *theological* institutions by individuals who did not want to undermine faith but, on the contrary, wanted to strengthen it by showing its historical development.

There is a challenging agenda here, one of great interest both to religious believers and to others concerned with preserving a society in which diverse people can live together in civic peace. It is an agenda we must advance.

SOCIOLOGICAL DESCRIPTIONS

Fundamentalism and Relativism Together: Reflections on Genealogy

James Davison Hunter

No one predicted what is now commonplace. And for several decades, as history has unfolded and evidence has mounted, a generation of intellectuals has been in denial, hoping against hope, that it was a grotesque abnormality and that it would quickly disappear. Even at present, many believe it to be anomalous and thus the best strategy is to just wait it out until it disappears.

Yet now it is plain to see that the emergence and persistence of fundamentalist movements globally is an established reality of our time, unlikely to go away anytime soon. The reason is that the emergence of fundamentalism is intrinsic to the late modern world. In this, fundamentalism does not represent a resurgence of traditional religion but is, rather, a distinct variant of traditional religion; one that emerges out of the dynamics of its encounter with the modern and late modern world and the discontents the contemporary world generates. Fundamentalism, at its core, is defined and shaped by the present world order; it is a natural expression of the very world it rejects.

To be more specific, fundamentalism is a phenomenon that is rooted in the epistemic dynamics of late modernity. Whatever else fundamentalism may be — and it is a very complex and multidimensional phenomenon — it is a defensive reaction to the fragmentation, pluralization, and relativization of knowledge and understanding that are part and parcel of our time. In this way, fundamentalism and relativism are at least partially symbiotic — one feeds off of the other. The central contention here then can be restated this way: the tensions between fundamentalism and relativism are an enduring and perhaps permanent structural feature of the

17

present and emerging global order and as such, the dynamic between these polarizing tendencies provides one of the dominant narratives of culture and civilization for our time. In this essay, I want to explore how and why this has come to be and the quandary it presents for those who are neither fundamentalists nor relativists.

The Conceptual Challenge

As a historical phenomenon, the concept "fundamentalism" should generate some pause. Religious historians and area specialists are rightly annoyed by the cavalier usage of the word. The term originally came to life in the first decade of the twentieth century to describe a movement of conservative Protestants who believed that the core doctrines of their faith were being undermined by higher criticism. They reacted by publishing twelve volumes, written by a range of scholars, all defending the central elements of historic Christian orthodoxy. These were "The Fundamentals," and they contained the arguments by which historic Christian (Protestant) orthodoxy would stand its ground against the corrosive forces of theological liberalism. Those who embraced these doctrines were, naturally, "fundamentalists." Rightly understood, then, fundamentalism is bound by a particular context, within a particular tradition, and given expression by a particular group of social actors. What often goes under the name of fundamentalism in Islam, Judaism, Sikhism, and Hinduism, at best has family resemblances to the original. The word has become a synonym for reactionary religious dogmatism of whatever historical manifestation.

At least Protestant fundamentalism was a recognizable social movement in history. Relativism is not a social movement at all. It is most recognizable as theory of truth, beauty, and the good; namely, a theory that states or implies that these qualities are not in any way grounded or universal but, rather, are dependent upon time, place, context, and other factors. In the history of ideas, it has been implicit in some forms of romanticism, in existentialism, and postmodernism — all of which valorize subjectivity in the apprehension of reality and in the attribution of meaning. Each of these claims, in effect, that relativism is reality; that absence is all there is.

In our own day, then, both concepts have lost historical specificity and analytical usefulness by virtue of being overused or misused. One even finds these concepts employed as shibboleths, the function of which is to caricature and discredit enemies. Even when used honestly and without political purpose, they reflect a social analysis with cleaver rather than scalpel.

Making matters worse, fundamentalism and relativism are also related to a range of other paired opposites in contemporary discourse that range from psychology (authoritarianism vs. libertarianism), lifestyle (rigidity vs. permissivism), aesthetics (traditionalism vs. modernism/postmodernism), and worldview (religion vs. secular), to politics (conservative vs. liberal), cultural politics (orthodox vs. progressive), foreign affairs (Islam vs. the West), and globalizing ambitions (jihad vs. McWorld). Needless to say, these too are all ham-fisted in similar ways.

Thus, we have inherited concepts that at best lack parity and worse, are clumsy and tendentious to the point of uselessness. Still, the concepts survive. They do so in part because they point to something meaningful and enduring about the world in which we live. The question is, in what way might the concepts of fundamentalism and relativism be most useful in cultural analysis?

I would suggest that today the concepts of fundamentalism and relativism may be most useful when descriptive of *epistemic propensities* (or orientations in the way knowledge and understanding are grounded) *that are at the root of opposing and competing cultural systems*. There are several aspects of this conceptual approach that need unpacking.

First, when speaking of epistemic propensities, I am speaking of cultural dynamics that exist within social groups as habits of thinking and practices of moral reasoning that assume that knowledge and understanding are, in character, either absolute in the one case or arbitrary in the other. Needless to say, these propensities can only be thought of as ideal types that, as with all ideal types, rarely exist in perfect form but rather as approximations — people, communities, and religious faiths are more or less oriented by or committed to one or the other.

If fundamentalism and relativism might be best thought of as epistemic propensities at the root of opposing and competing cultural systems, it means that by their very nature they have profound implications for the ordering of both individual and collective life. In this way, knowledge and politics, art, family, and social life generally are inseparable.

Importantly, in social life, neither fundamentalism nor relativism is normative for the majority of people precisely because no social order can be sustained on the terms established by either one. Both extremes depend upon a social world and the cultural systems that sustain it that is less utopian than the fundamentalist's and more grounded in the hard and consistent realities of everyday life than the relativist's. And yet the late modern world is characterized by conditions that evoke and accentuate these polarities.

What follows in this essay is, at best, a rough outline that makes no pretense of being a full-fledged description of the social, cultural, and political relationship between fundamentalism and relativism. This is in part because I am trying to cover too much ground in too little space, in part because I have no formal expertise in intellectual history and comparative religion, and in part because these reflections are only in their formative stages. This is like a sketch an artist would make on the back of a scrap of paper long before committing paint to canvas. First, some reflections on genealogy.

Genealogy

Skepticism has a long and illustrious history in the Western tradition, and even in antiquity it took expression in a range between mere anti-dogmatism and dissolutionist cynicism. Yet the story I want to tell is one that ironically traces the sources of contemporary relativism through the Enlightenment quest for certainty. Needless to say, the modern history of ideas has been told countless times, but it may be useful to review a few highlights for the purposes of bringing into relief dynamics relevant to this argument.[1]

Though often a symbol of the Enlightenment's naïve aspirations, Descartes was struggling to make sense of a world whose fabric was torn and whose future was vague and in doubt. The Reformation had divided Europe in two. Indeed, in the early seventeenth century, Descartes had been a young soldier in the bloody Thirty Years War, a religious war that made him and many others skeptical of the possibilities that religion could completely underwrite a stable social order. A century before, scientists had begun to challenge Aristotelian notions of the universe. Vesalius's *On the Fabric of the*

---

1. This part of the argument draws from "Cultural Briefing," J. D. Hunter and Richard Horner, Unpublished Manuscript, Institute for Advanced Studies in Culture, n.d.

Human Body in Seven Books and Copernicus's *On the Revolutions of the Celestial Spheres* both came out in 1543. When taken together, the stories of political theory, religious understanding, and scientific authority exposed a fundamental philosophical crisis of doubt. John Donne, one of the great poets of the early seventeenth century, wrote, "New philosophy calls all in doubt."[2] Pascal may have summed up the anxiety of the age best when he wrote, "We have an idea of happiness, but we cannot attain it. We perceive an image of the truth and possess nothing but falsehood, being equally incapable of absolute ignorance and certain knowledge."[3]

In this context, thinkers were longing for new certainties; for an absolutely dependable basis of knowledge. Stephen Toulmin has shown how the Enlightenment project was grounded in reaction to these political, cultural, and social uncertainties and the need to find an alternative way forward.[4] Descartes himself embarked on a quest for truth and certainty by way of systematic doubt. As he wrote in his *Discourse on Method,* "Since I desire to pay attention to the search for truth, I thought it necessary that I reject as absolutely false everything in which I could imagine the least doubt, so as to see whether after this process anything in my set of beliefs remains that is entirely beyond doubt."[5] This is, *in nuce,* the quest for certainty. It established the methodological basis for his famous dictum, "I think, therefore I am." Descartes can doubt his body, and doubt the world, but could not doubt his doubting self. There had to be something that was itself doing the doubting. The character of this proof seemed to be incontrovertible. It followed then that any other truth, including the truth of God's existence, needed to be established in the same way.[6]

Leibniz, born a generation after Descartes at the end of the Thirty Years War, also made it his life's work to deduce an entire system of knowl-

---

2. John Donne's poem, "An Anatomy of the World," 1611.

3. Blaise Pascal, *Pensees,* #434.

4. Stephen Toulmin, *Cosmopolis: The Hidden Agenda of Modernity* (Chicago: University of Chicago Press, 1992).

5. René Descartes, "Discourse on the Method of Rightly Conducting the Reason and of Seeking Truth in the Sciences," Part IV.

6. Descartes then moves to the question of God with this method. Since knowledge is more perfect than doubt, Descartes himself must be an imperfect being if he is capable of doubting. But the very knowledge that he is imperfect presupposes that there is something outside of him that *is* perfect. This, he decides, is God. Descartes' philosophical method is thus perfected.

edge starting from a few fundamental principles of certainty. His family had witnessed much of Germany destroyed and nearly a third of the population killed in these wars. It is no wonder that he felt the urgency to create a foundation of knowledge and method of logic upon which all people could agree and no longer need to fight. Within a century, people had gained a great deal of confidence in these methods. The scientism of the Enlightenment worked remarkably well on many levels, and so it only made sense that the astonishing increase of human mastery over nature would be extended to all aspects of society and culture.

All of that said, by the end of the seventeenth century the project was beginning to show fissures. Both Hume and Kant, while still champions of reason, pointed to the limitations of reason and to the emptiness to which it seemed to lead. Kant, for example, demonstrated the inability of autonomous rationality to come to certainties on some of the most crucial matters: God's existence, the efficacy of morality, and other issues central to everyday life. Musing famously about the absence of vitality in reason, Hume wrote:

> But what have I here said, that reflections very refined and metaphysical have little or no influence upon us? . . . The intense view of these manifold contradictions and imperfections in human reason has so wrought upon me, and heated my brain, that I am ready to reject all belief and reasoning, and can look upon no opinion even as more probable or likely than another. Where am I, or what? From what causes do I derive my existence, and to what condition shall I return? Whose favour shall I court, and whose anger must I dread? What beings surround me? And on whom have I any influence, or who have any influence on me? I am confounded with all these questions, and begin to fancy myself in the most deplorable condition imaginable, environed with the deepest darkness, and utterly deprived of the use of every member and faculty.[7]

The Romantics echoed these complaints. Though they shared the Enlightenment's suspicion of tradition, its optimism concerning human possibilities and the priority of the individual, they too argued that the deep things of life could not be grounded in rational reflection or the natural sciences. Kierkegaard, for instance, had pointed out the potential for tyranny in Hegel's attempt at a comprehensive philosophy. Hegel's view of

7. David Hume, *A Treatise of Human Nature*, Book 1, Section 7.

reason, Kierkegaard claimed, actually excluded real human beings from his philosophy. When one's own rationality was equated with reality, Hegel's philosophical method could be dangerous.

The assault on autonomous rationality continued through the nineteenth and early twentieth century. Though Marx and Freud understood themselves as champions of the scientific method, each contributed in their own ways to undermining the confidence in modern rationality. In Marx's case, it was his suspicion of the vested interests underneath the bourgeois remaking of the social order, an order largely underwritten by modern rationality. In Freud's case, it was the recognition of the radical irrationality of the unconscious and thus his skepticism of the Enlightenment idea of the rational subject and the possibilities of rational civilization. Marx and Freud both provided a hermeneutics for understanding the modern world, including the nature and the ends of rationality, through a lens of systematic suspicion.

There were many other players in this drama, of course, but the sum and substance of their inquiry has led us to see an end to which the cultural logic of modernity leads: a place where everything is possible but nothing is necessary and, therefore, nothing certain. This has become apparent not only to a few intellectuals but to many others as well. In short, the modern hope was that by reason alone we could attain truth that was beyond the reach of doubt and free from the prejudices of subjectivity. Yet what was supposed to have been reason's ability to achieve certainty, John Patrick Diggins noted, has turned out to be "the ability to question everything and the capacity to affirm nothing."[8] What was supposed to have been the ability of reason to identify truths that would be necessary and inescapable has turned out to be the ability always to deny necessity and to develop endless possibilities for thinking and living differently. In other words, the quest for certainty has led us to the conclusion that there is only one necessary or essential truth, and it is that there is no such thing as necessary or essential truth. In the end, reason has turned out to be the ability always to negate necessity, introduce doubt, and uncover subjectivity.

Thus, certainty has dissolved into doubt, objectivity absorbed into subjectivity, and certainty into the spinning out of imaginative possibilities fueled not simply by the powers of reason but by the force of passion,

8. John Patrick Diggins, "'Who Bore the Failure of the Light': Henry Adams and the Crisis of Authority," *The New England Quarterly* 58, no. 2 (June 1985): 165-92.

will, and faith. What is more, there is no assurance that any one of these different possibilities actually makes a difference. Where reason has been overthrown and passion or taste enthroned, a rationalist form of individualism gives way to subject-centered emotivism or voluntarist individualism. Where a leap of faith has been embraced, a subjective spirituality follows. In each case the cultural logic of modernity remains intact. All roads of modernity, it turns out, lead into the same subjectivist cul-de-sac, as reason becomes indistinguishable from passion or will, and the notion of a unifying truth about humanity becomes indistinguishable from the opinions, inclinations, and preferences of individuals.

No one has ever captured its significance more clearly than Nietzsche in his account of the death of God. Nietzsche recognized that by the end of the nineteenth century, modern reason had already killed God, and what was needed was for someone to say so, for someone to write God's obituary and work out the implications of his death. To be sure, Nietzsche was glad to have God out of the way. But while many of Nietzsche's contemporaries thought that God would turn out to be a small loss, and that his demise would actually create a clearing in which realities worth taking seriously would come to light, Nietzsche realized that with God out of the picture, a lot of other things would disappear as well. Nietzsche understood that substitutes for a dead God are as lifeless as the God whose place they take. Though they may assume divine names such as Nature, Humanity, Man, Life, the Soul, the self, the other, or the body, and though they may be cloaked in the garb of certainty, objectivity, necessity, meaning, or essence, idols are still only idols, and they must be cleared away. The end of the cultural logic of modernity, then, is a clearing, an absence, an empty space.

*   *   *

If the dilemma I describe were only a matter of ideas, then it would be one experienced only or at least most poignantly by academic philosophers and social theorists. Clearly this is not the case, for in fact, this is a dilemma that almost everyone in the contemporary world faces to one degree or another. The reason is that the genealogy of culture not only traces back intellectually through its dominant ideas but traces back institutionally as well through an evolving configuration of social practices. Culture, of course, always exists within a dialectic between ideas and institutions, between theory and social structure, which means that the ideas and values of the modern age are not only theorized but are also embedded in powerful institutions that encompass, in varying degrees, the lives of individuals and communities. As such, nearly all know its reach. Through the ideals these institutions articulate and the practices they necessitate, the dilemma of uncertainty — of absence, "weightlessness," or "homelessness" — is powerfully communicated to ordinary people who otherwise would not have read Nietzsche or Foucault or Derrida or have even heard of their names.

In this case, the particular social circumstance at the root of the experiences of uncertainty is an intensive pluralism inherent to modernity, a pluralization carried by urbanization, global travel, and the proliferation of communications technologies under these circumstances. As modernity brings together different communities, traditions, and habits of life in close proximity, relatively distinct worldviews, belief systems, and rituals of social life rub up against each other and overlap, creating a multiplicity of voices, perspectives, ideals, commitments, traditions, and the social practices they imply. At least two dynamics are at play here.

The first dynamic has to do with the transformation of what Peter Berger calls "plausibility structures." In Berger's view, ideas and beliefs are not merely the province of intellect and will. There is, rather, a dialectic between consciousness and social structure. In his formulation, strong and consistent belief, therefore, presupposes strong and stable social support. Yet the intensive form of pluralism generated by modernity not only means that any shared culture is thinned out by virtue of the sustained presence of multiple cultures, it also means that the plausibility structures that provide the social support for belief are also fragmented and weakened.[9] In the end, strong belief and conviction cannot be sustained by fragile plausibility structures. Uncertainty is imposed upon us because no belief is protected from the claims of alternative beliefs; no conviction is left unchallenged by other equally held convictions.

The second dynamic concerns the individual choice modernity creates. The metaphysics of choice is reinforced both by technology and a consumer-oriented market that together generate a larger and larger range of options from which to choose. The reality of choice does at least two things to the nature of knowledge and belief. First, it de-objectifies knowl-

---

9. Peter L. Berger, *The Heretical Imperative* (New York: Anchor Doubleday, 1979), p. 19.

edge and conviction so that what was once "known" with certitude becomes one opinion among others with no intrinsic epistemological advantage. Second, choice subjectivizes knowledge and conviction, which means, at the very least, that subjectivity fuses with and destabilizes authoritative sources for truth outside of the self. At most, social circumstances compel one to turn inward to one's own subjectivity to find guidance for what to believe and how to live. Here as well, the average person is led to the end of the cultural logic of modernity where one's own passions, interests, will, and reasoning become the principal grounds for knowledge and understanding, belief and conviction. Once again, certainty devolves into subjectivity.

In short, the very structures of the late modern world undermine the possibility of certainty. Epistemological innocence, by which I mean a disposition of taken-for-granted simplicity, is no longer as possible as it once was for those who live in late modern circumstances and are forced to choose what to believe, if anything at all. As Berger emphasizes, these dynamics play out in pre-theoretical experience — that is, in ordinary, everyday social life. It is experienced not only by the intellectual who puzzles through the mysteries of the universe but also by the proverbial person-in-the-street. Uncertainty is a structural feature of the late modern world and therefore it is an experience common (though in varying degrees) to all.

* * *

The epistemic propensity toward relativism and subjectivism then plays out powerfully in *both* the realm of ideas and institutions. The institutional and the ideational reinforce each other — the institutional dynamics create conditions where relativism seems utterly plausible; the intellectual dynamics explain and justify the relativism experienced in everyday life. The dilemma of uncertainty, then, is not just for the theorist but for everyone to one extent or another. In these ways, the late modern world has created a certain "lightness of being" that is, in the end, a burden that weighs heavily on us all.

Having said this, one must acknowledge extensive and substantial variation here. There is variation in the intensity of the experience. Those whose lives are closest to the carriers of late modernity (e.g., urban residence, higher levels of education, work in the professions, travel, access to technology, etc.) experience these world-disaffirming realities more powerfully that those whose lives are further removed (e.g., rural residence, lower levels of education, working-class and agricultural occupations). So too, there is variation in the degree to which human beings can endure these experiences. Some have a greater psychological and emotional capacity to deal with this than others. There are also some cultural traditions that have greater malleability than others in dealing with these realities. Within the range of possible reactions to these circumstances, it is not surprising that there are those who strenuously and even violently object.

Fundamentalism as Dissent

Fundamentalism, then, emerges as a dissent against these uncertainties and their intellectual, structural, and normative sources. This dissent would seem to have a certain anthropological basis. While it is both prudent and politic these days to resist all sorts of essentialist claims about human nature, one that seems empirically unavoidable is the claim that human beings — in all of their diversity — impose meaning and order upon experience. This predisposition strikes me as congenital; if not an instinct, the need to impose meaning upon reality has the force of an instinct.[10] To say the least, the intellectual and institutional circumstances of late modernity confound and complicate this challenge to live meaningfully, not least when those meanings are rooted in inherited sources. Thus, it is among those "who cannot bear the fate of the times like a man," as Weber famously put it, that are likely to protest.

Dissent, of course, has and will take various forms. The mid-nineteenth-century transcendentalism of Thoreau and Emerson, the eastern mysticism popular among the largely upper-class members of the Theosophical Society, aspects of the romanticist movement in nineteenth-century art and literature, and elements of the counterculture of the 1960s and early 1970s were all various expressions of this dissent. Under certain conditions and typically (though not exclusively) within the monotheistic traditions, fundamentalism represents another form of protest. Consider two different contexts.

In the Western context, the intellectual and institutional changes that have unfolded have taken centuries. Most faiths indigenous to the Western

---

10. Peter L. Berger, *The Sacred Canopy* (Garden City, NY: Doubleday, 1967), p. 3.

world have slowly come to terms with these evolving circumstances, mainly by accommodating to them. Protestant fundamentalism in the early twentieth century was the exception. Catholicism, of course, had a similar reaction that predated Protestant fundamentalism in the mid and late nineteenth century. Pope Pius IX promulgated the *Syllabus of Errors* in 1864 in which he condemned most aspects of modernity, inaugurating an anti-modernist campaign on a platform of ecclesial rather than scriptural "inerrancy." Later in the century, Pope Leo XIII echoed this condemnation in his apostolic letter, *Testem Benevolentiae.* While not exactly "fundamentalist," it was a broad censure of what he and other traditionalists saw as a watering down of doctrine, an accommodation to subjectivism (through the attractions of religious liberty), and a denial of the temporal powers of the church (by the appeal of popular democracy).

Outside of western Europe and North America, by contrast, the predominant carrier of a culture of relativism has been the intensifying globalization through technology and commerce. To much of the Third World, the dizzying realities of pluralization have come as a deluge and have thus been experienced as a torrent of change and challenge to traditional ways of life.

It is clearly true that there were proto-fundamentalist movements in the Middle East and south-central Asia as early as the eighteenth century. In the case of Islam, there was the Wahabi movement of Arabia, the Waliyulh movement in India, the Sansusi movement in Libya, the Mahdi movement in the Sudan, and the Sarekat Islam in Indonesia. In Hinduism, there was Brahmo Samaj and Arya Samaj and later, Hindu Mahasahba.[11] In both Islam and Hinduism, these were movements founded to resist what they perceived as the *internal* deterioration of their faiths. The proto-fundamentalists in Islam were resisting the Shiite, the Sufi, and all others deemed unfaithful to their severe interpretation of the *sunna* (or custom) of the Prophet Muhammad. The proto-fundamentalists in Hinduism dissented against the pollution and degradations caused by the failure of Hindus to observe *dharma.* The view was that it was the degeneration of these faiths that had created conditions conducive to a foreign domination that only intensified the degradation of these faiths and their cultures.

It has really only been since the twentieth century (and more particu-

---

11. Robert L. Hargrave Jr. and Stanley A. Kochanek, *India: Government and Politics in a Developing Nation* (New York: Harcourt Brace Jovanovich, 2000).

larly, the mid-twentieth century) that the focus of animus, at least in Islamic revivalism, turned to the Western cultures. The critical figure in Islamic extremism was Sayyid Qutb, an Egyptian intellectual who, more than anyone else, theorized the rationale for contemporary Islamic radicalism. In his book *Milestones,* he wrote:

> Mankind today is on the brink of a precipice, not because of the danger of complete annihilation which is hanging over its head — this being just a symptom and not the real disease — but because humanity is devoid of those vital values which are necessary not only for its healthy development but also for its real progress. Even the Western world realizes that Western civilization is unable to present any healthy values for the guidance of mankind. It knows that it does not possess anything which will satisfy its own conscience and justify its existence. . . .
>
> If we look at the sources and foundations of modern ways of living, it becomes clear that the whole world is steeped in Jahiliyya [pagan ignorance of divine guidance], and all the marvelous material comforts and high-level inventions do not diminish this Ignorance. This Jahiliyya is based on rebellion against God's sovereignty on earth: It transfers to man one of the greatest attributes of God, namely sovereignty, and makes some men lords over others. It is now not in that simple and primitive form of the ancient Jahiliyya, but takes the form of *claiming that the right to create values, to legislate rules of collective behavior, and to choose any way of life rests with men, without regard to what God has prescribed.* The result of this rebellion against the authority of God is the oppression of His creatures. . . .
>
> The Islamic civilization can take various forms in its material and organizational structure, but the principles and values on which it is based are eternal and unchangeable. These are: the worship of God alone, the foundation of human relationships on the belief in the Unity of God, the supremacy of the humanity of man over material things, the development of human values and the control of animalistic desires, respect for the family, the assumption of the vice-regency of God on earth according to His guidance and instruction, and in all affairs of this vice-regency, the rule of God's law [al-Shari'a] and the way of life prescribed by Him. . . .[12]

12. Sayyid Qutb, *Milestones* (Beirut: The Holy Koran Publishing House, 1980), pp. 7-15, 286; emphasis added.

29

Here Qutb, as one would expect, identifies a constructionist and thus relativist view of knowledge, values, and law and the wide range of choices that a pluralistic culture creates as the central problems of our time. It represents a rebellion against the certainties provided by Islamic theology and law. The antidote, he writes, is Islam — "the only system which possesses [the] values and . . . way of life" capable of resisting this willful ignorance.[13]

* * *

Whether they emerge out of Western industrial and post-industrial societies or out of economically and technologically developing societies outside of the West, what all manifestations of fundamentalism share in common is a reassertion of certainties in meaning and moral order in a context in which those certainties are rendered implausible or denied altogether. Certainties are reasserted in all dimensions of cosmology. First, they are reasserted in *ontology* — the hard reality of the existence of God, of the bifurcation between the faithful and the unbeliever, and their respective places in the cosmos. Second, the truth about reality and the reality about truth are established *epistemologically* in creeds that are themselves grounded in sacred texts. This scripturalism, whether Torah for the Gush Emunim in Israel, the Koran for the Muslim Brotherhood in Egypt, the Vedas and Upanishads for the radical Hindu nationalists in Rashtriya Swayamsevak Sangh, the Mahavamsa (a post-canonical chronicle) for the Sinhalese Buddhists in Sri Lanka, or the Old and New Testament for the conservative Southern Baptists in Tupelo, Mississippi, all are trusted authorities within each respective tradition, which is why they are read and interpreted literally as the texts allow. Further, it is the texts and then the legal customs and traditions (such as the Talmud and *Halakha* in Judaism, the *hadith* and *madhhab* in Islam,[14] etc.) that provide the authoritative terms for sociality; from political authority and social ethics to family law and codes of personal morality.

Third, and not least, these certainties are reasserted in *teleology*. These are the creeds at the root of the literal messianism that informs many of these reactions in which all ambiguity, all tension, all impurity, and all

---

13. Sayyid Qutb, *Milestones*, pp. 7-15, 286.

14. The *hadith* are the traditions relating to the words and deeds of Muhammad. The *madhhab* are the various schools of thought in Islamic jurisprudence.

compromise and sin are overcome and the ideals of the faith are established for eternity. In Judaism, of course, it is the Messiah, the anointed one who will establish peace. In Islam, it is the Mahdi (and in Shia, the Imam Al-Mahdi or twelfth Imam) who will turn the world into a perfect and just Islamic society. In Christianity, it is the glorious return of Jesus Christ who will establish a reign of peace and justice. In Buddhism, it is the Maitreya Bodhisattva, the future Buddha who will not only bring an end to death, warfare, famine, and disease, but will rule the world with complete enlightenment and, thus, bring about a world of tolerance and love. And in Hinduism, it is Kalki, the tenth and final incarnation of Vishnu who is the destroyer of foulness, confusion, ignorance, and darkness.

There is another aspect of fundamentalist teleology that relates to "the time in-between" the founding of the faith and its golden age and the *eschaton*. This is the narrative of loss and recovery that fills all of human history, though especially sacred history, with meaning. All fundamentalisms tend to interpret history as having gone awry. (Though after the establishment of Israel at mid-century, for Jewish fundamentalists the worry is that history could go awry.) The burden of the fundamentalist, then, is to make history right again or to keep it on the right track in anticipation of the *eschaton*. This too they hold with certainty.[15]

Secular Fundamentalisms?

Underneath the vehemence of radical Islamicist movements in the Middle East and Indonesia, extreme Hindu nationalism, religious Zionism, and the tactics of intimidation by certain factions of the religious right in America is the propensity to reassert certainties in all of these areas of cosmology. But is this true for what some call secular or Enlightenment fundamentalists? This would seem to be a bit of a stretch and for this reason one should be careful not to overreach. Yet with that said, there are expressions of dogmatic secularism with undeniable family likeness to the religious expressions of fundamentalism. It is not just found in the recent assertions of an embittered and combative atheism (i.e., Dawkins, Hitchens, etc.) but the

---

15. J. D. Hunter, "Toward a General Theory of Fundamentalism," in *Religion and the Social Order: New Developments in Theory and Research*, ed. David Bromley (New York: JAI Press, 1991).

intolerance of the French government toward Muslim dress codes, the hysteria of scientific Darwinists in response to "Intelligent Design," and the condescension toward any manifestation of traditional faith in the faculty clubs of major universities. Here too, one finds a bewilderment about the resurgence of traditional religion in the modern world. For the secular fundamentalist, this turn can only represent history moving "off-track." Here too, there is a passion to make sure that history is set aright.

Fundamentalism and Relativism as Weak Cultures

On the face of it, relativism is the foundation for a weak culture. In the case of western Europe and North America where the structural dynamics that underwrite relativism are most pervasive, all aspects of the dominant normative order are fragmented and the plausibility structures that frame any particular subculture are fragile. It is no wonder that in these societies one finds little by way of strongly held beliefs, values, ideals, practices, and rituals shared in common. Relativism itself, whether a philosophy or a working set of assumptions for the average person, has no ethical coherence and it provides no language or vision for a common future and therefore it offers few if any resources for collective action.

By contrast, fundamentalism asserts itself as a strong culture. However implausible, unattractive, or impractical it is to most people, fundamentalism (in its variety) is rooted in a strong epistemology and therefore, in a limited way, it operates with a strong ontology, coherent ethics, and clear teleology. It is true that against the ubiquity and force of the global economy and its torrential flows of information, entertainment, and technology, fundamentalism is institutionally weak. Yet the culture of fundamentalism provides a strong normative framework for collective action.

But even as a normative order, the various fundamentalisms are far weaker than they appear. The weakness of fundamentalism is betrayed by its essentially negational character, a character that takes form in its highly cultivated resentments. What is also common to all fundamentalisms, in other words, is an identity rooted in a narrative of injury in which the faithful understand themselves to be victims. This narrative is reinforced by the very real external threats of secularism (and relativism) carried by globalization, by liberal parties within their own faith tradition, and by other hostile religions. In this light, resentment provides a distraction from the questions and doubts forced upon everyone to some degree by the modern world. For the fundamentalist, it is far easier to target enemies outside of the tradition than to seek answers within it. This is not to say that fundamentalism provides no answers to the important questions of life or that there is no genuine faith that animates the believers. Neither statement could be made categorically. What is true is that the narrative of injury and the hostility it generates increasingly become the dominant expression of the faith and the primary sources of collective identity for the most committed believers.

Another, perhaps more important, manifestation of the weakness of fundamentalism as a culture is the flip side of resentment. As a culture, fundamentalism in its variety is marked by an incapacity to make strong and constructive affirmations. As Josef Pieper has argued, healthy and sustainable cultures make space for leisure, philosophical reflection, scientific and intellectual mastery, and artistic and literary expression, among other things.[16] In a vital culture, individuals, families, and communities are animated by the idea of bettering themselves. The genius of all the great world religions has been their capacity to transcend the limitations of time, environment, and human circumstance by providing resources to imagine the horizons of progress and improvement. With fundamentalism, however, there is an inverse relationship between militancy and intellectual, spiritual, and aesthetic vitality. Fundamentalism can point to no creative achievements, it offers no constructive proposals for the everyday problems that trouble most people, and it provides no vital solutions to the problems of pluralism and change. Indeed, just the opposite.

What this means is that it is not just contemporary relativism that is nihilistic in character. In a different way and for different reasons, fundamentalism is every bit as nihilistic. The bitter irony for the fundamentalist is that in the name of resisting the internal deterioration of faith and the corruption of the world around them, fundamentalists unwittingly embrace one of the most corrosive aspects of this deterioration, namely, the will to power. This is one more way in which fundamentalism expresses its intrinsically postmodern character. It embraces a Nietzschean *Zeitgeist* that, in effect, reduces all social relations (especially with non-believers) to power relations.

16. Josef Pieper, *Leisure: The Basis of Culture* (South Bend, IN: St. Augustine's Press, 1998; original publication, 1948).

To listen carefully, one soon realizes that the stridency of fundamentalism — religious and, at times, secular — is itself inspired more by doubt than confidence, more by fear than by quiet faith and settled conviction. The loudness of their voices can be interpreted as an attempt to stop their ears from the annoying ring of uncertainty that drones incessantly. The brutality of their power plays and violence (when we see it) is not a demonstration of strength but a compensation for their own weak defenses against the terror that they might be wrong.

Concluding Thoughts

The central conundrum of our time is how and on what terms is a decent and just world possible. This is a difficult puzzle on its own terms, but making it even more difficult is the fact that the extremes almost always define the terms of reflection and debate. This is true with most issues of public discussion and it is certainly true of this important question as well. In this case, secular relativism offers no viable options or any constructive answers. Neither does religious fundamentalism — at least short of its achieving total power. Not only do fundamentalism and relativism both diminish our humanity, they also undermine the possibility of any kind of vital culture in between them. But there they are — inextricably linked and, as much as we can tell, together a permanent fixture of our social circumstances. The practical and immediate question before us is, how will we of various faiths and no faith who are neither fundamentalists nor relativists live in this place of pervasive plurality and enduring uncertainty with charity as we work to sustain the decency and justice we have attained, and by measure, to increase it as we are able?

An English Example: Exploring the Via Media in the Twenty-First Century

Grace Davie

I have been asked to contribute a piece on Europe to a collection of papers that seek a middle way between relativism and fundamentalism in the religious sphere. I have chosen to do this by looking in innovative ways at the Church of England. There are two ways into the argument. The first recognizes that the historic churches in Europe are very different from those in the United States in the sense that they are organized on a territorial basis (this is true at the local as well as the national level). As a result they serve, residually at least, all those that live in a particular area, or parish — a fact that in itself mitigates extreme or sectarian views. Some of these churches, however, resist the extremes more easily than others, a fact that is largely explained by the specificities of their history. I will argue that the Church of England is one such. Given the very nature of this church as a *via media* this is hardly surprising.

The second approach introduces a different way of working: rather than engaging the debate about whether or not the Church of England should remain aligned to the state, I will concentrate on the ways in which the historic link between church and state in this part of the United Kingdom can be made to work positively in the twenty-first century. The term "positively" is understood as the expression of religious convictions that are consonant with democratic values, in a society that is historically Christian but now contains many different religious constituencies and belief systems, including an increasingly self-conscious secular minority. The key to the argument lies in discerning the advantages of a "weak" state church — or more accurately a weak *established* church.

Bearing both approaches in mind, the chapter is structured as follows.

It considers first the characteristics of the historic churches in Europe, underlining both their links with political power and their hierarchical structure. It is at this point that their *territorial* nature is revealed. It then describes the different ways in which these links have unraveled, noting in particular the distinctive situation that has emerged in Britain, and England in particular. The following section frames the material in a different way, in the sense that it considers a whole range of factors that need to be taken into account if we are to understand the place of religion in Europe at the present moment. The crucial point to grasp is that these factors push and pull in different directions. The third section offers a more detailed analysis of the English case. The situation is by no means perfect, but I will argue that the current position of the Church of England (a powerless but nonetheless influential institution) can be used creatively to maximize both tolerance and inclusiveness. Both would be more difficult in France. The concluding paragraphs return once again to the wider scene (both inside and outside Europe), asking to what extent the experience of the Church of England can be generalized. In so doing, they re-pose the question that is central to this book as a whole: the search for a middle way between relativism and fundamentalism.

This introduction must end with a personal note. I am a member of the Church of England, and as a Lay Canon of its Diocese of Europe, I am one of the many hundreds, if not thousands, who hold office in the Church of England without receiving a salary. I am happy to nail my colors to the mast. Much more important, however, for the argument of this chapter is the fact that I am British — not only in terms of nationality, but in terms of my intellectual formation. As a result, I have a tendency to think pragmatically, and to look not so much for a principle as for a solution to the problem. The fact that this way of working fits relatively well with Anglican theology is not, of course, a coincidence, but given my training in the social sciences, it is the pragmatic thinking rather than the theology as such, that determines what follows.[1]

1. Much of this chapter draws on my own work — in particular Davie 1994, 2000, 2002, 2006a, 2006b, 2006c, 2007a, and 2007b.

The European Past: Commonality and Difference[2]

Three factors are crucial to an understanding of what has become known as "Europe" (O'Connell 1991). These are the Judeo-Christian tradition, Greek rationalism, and Roman organization. For nearly two millennia, these factors have combined in different ways to form and re-form our understanding of what it means to be European. This will continue to happen. Certain moments in this history are, however, crucial. One such can be found at the time of the industrial revolution, an upheaval that radically dislocated a pattern that had been in place for centuries.

The pattern itself reflects two features of the European past — first, that religious power was aligned with political power, and second, that the dominant mode of organization in both cases was territorial. The local resonance of this pattern is as important as the national. European populations, for example, lived in "parishes" (indeed they still do), which were civil as well as ecclesiastical units of administration. You were born in a parish, whether you liked it or not, and — very often — continued to live there for the rest of your life. The parish, moreover, structured the *everyday* lives of European people: what happened from Monday to Friday was as important as what happened on Sundays. A second point follows from this: the model fitted admirably within the relative stabilities of premodern Europe, a period in which the historic churches were dominant. Their power was considerable, with all the associated risks; such churches had the potential to be both excluding and exclusive, at all levels of society.

A model rooted in territory has advantages and disadvantages. Or to put the same point in a different way, permanence is more helpful in some situations than others. It is particularly unhelpful in times of rapid change. One such time occurred as Europe began bit by bit to industrialize, and — as the economic changes gathered pace — to urbanize. Populations moved extraordinarily fast to the cities associated with the new centers of industry

2. In addition to the references in Note 1, useful overviews of the place of religion in European societies can be found in Rémond (1999), Greeley (2003), Madeley and Enyedi (2003), McLeod and Ustorf (2003), Robbers (2005), and Byrnes and Katzenstein (2006). Attention should also be paid to the publications emerging from the European Values Study. These are listed on the frequently updated EVS website (http://www.europeanvalues.nl/index2.htm) and include both the analyses of Europe as a whole and publications pertaining to particular societies. The EVS is a useful source of statistics; so too the International Social Survey Programme (http://www.issp.org/data.htm).

that were powering Europe. The timing was different in different places, but a church embedded for centuries in the rural landscape was — almost by definition — unable to move fast enough to the cities where its "people" were now residing. Even now, in much of Europe, there are too many churches in the wrong places. The fact that many of them are architectural gems does not make their management any easier.

The particular nature of the European Enlightenment exacerbated these changes. Indeed it was part and parcel of them, in the sense that it was the new ways of thinking that emerged in and through the Enlightenment that enabled the technological innovations necessary for economic development. But the Enlightenment was more than this: it offered an entirely new conceptualization of the human person and his or her place in society. In some parts of Europe (most notably in France), this became an anti-religious movement: the *lumières* were seen more as a freedom from belief, than a freedom to believe (hence Voltaire's infamous cry: *écrasez l'infâme*). Enlightenment thinkers, moreover, frequently linked arms with the advocates of political change — a combination that exposed the churches to political as well as institutional attack. The result very quickly became a downward spiral: churches that were rooted in territory and supported the traditional order were harassed from all sides, a shock from which they have never fully recovered.

This process affected all European societies, but in somewhat different ways. At one extreme can be found the French case, in which a strict and ideologically motivated separation of church and state took place in 1905 following decades of acrimonious wrangling. France, however, industrialized relatively late, enabling the traditional model to endure well into the post-war period, at least in rural areas. From an institutional point of view, the collapse in France came late, but was all the more cataclysmic when it happened. Something rather similar is now taking place in Spain some thirty to forty years later. Elsewhere both process and outcome have been different — longer term and less confrontational. The British case is one such. In Britain, for example, new forms of religious life emerged alongside the historic model at a relatively early stage. Some of these grew as rapidly as the cities of which they were part, albeit for different reasons. Non-conformists, for instance, filled the spaces left by the historic church; the Catholic Church catered to new sources of labor coming in from Ireland. Either way, an incipient market was beginning to develop.

The transformations of a pre-industrial and primarily rural society are nonetheless pivotal; they reveal a critical disjunction in the evolution of religious life in Europe. Too quickly, however, the wrong inference was drawn: that there is a *necessary* incompatibility between religion per se and modern, primarily urban life. This is simply not the case. Something quite different happened in the United States, for example, where territorial embedding had never taken place and economic growth has stimulated rather than inhibited religious activity, not least in urban areas. Hence an upward rather than a downward spiral: in the United States, nation building, economic development, and a freedom *to believe* interacted positively with voluntarist forms of religion, which — unlike their European counterparts — were able to move rapidly and effectively into the growing cities of North America. The same has been true in many parts of the developing world; here some of the largest cities house some of the largest churches, not to mention tens of thousands of smaller ones.

The British Case

Bearing these points in mind, this chapter concentrates on the British situation and within this the Church of England. What, then, is its nature? Some hints have already been given: in Britain, the process of industrialization took place earlier and more gradually than it did elsewhere, and a greater degree of religious pluralism existed from an earlier stage than in many European societies. Enlightenment thinking was also distinctive: it was markedly less ferocious in its attacks on religion than was the case in France, a point made clear in recent scholarship.[3] Conversely both the Church of England and its Calvinist equivalent in Scotland were "parish" churches, organized on a territorial basis. They were, therefore, as unable to move fast into the growing cities of industrial Britain as their European counterparts and for the same reasons. What emerges in fact is a hybrid case: philosophically, there are evident links between Britain and the United States; institutionally, the ties are with Europe.

If Britain can be seen as a midway point between Europe and America, the nature of the Church of England reinforces this position. Its begin-

---

3. See in particular Porter (2000) and Himmelfarb (2004). Increasingly, in fact, the French Enlightenment becomes the *exceptional* case. In much of Europe, the Enlightenment was worked out as much *through* the dominant religious tradition as against it.

nings are quite rightly described as a "break from Rome," the moment when England (and its church) turned away from Europe and looked out across the world. Anglicanism, unlike most Christian traditions, has no "home" in continental Europe. It finds its inspiration elsewhere — in a Communion whose shape reflects the Empire. How could it be otherwise? Anglican ways of thinking, moreover, are distinctive, embodying *particular* advantages and disadvantages — a point that underpins much of the following discussion. What on the one hand enables both theological and pastoral generosity, leads on the other to a persistent, sometimes chronic, inability to make decisions. It is equally clear that growing and ever-more vibrant churches in the global South are exerting new pressures on the Communion — including a need to make decisions, very difficult ones. In a very real sense Anglicanism has become the victim of its own success.

The European Present: The Factors to Take into Account

The religious situation in modern Europe is complex. In order to understand both the opportunities and the limitations of the present context, it is necessary to take several factors into account. In two recently published articles (Davie 2006a and 2006b), I set out six such factors. They are:

1. the role of the historic churches in shaping European culture;
2. an awareness that these churches still have a place at particular moments in the lives of modern Europeans, even though they are no longer able to discipline the beliefs and behavior of the great majority of the population;
3. an observable change in the churchgoing constituencies of the continent, which operate increasingly on a model of choice, rather than a model of obligation or duty;
4. the arrival in Europe of groups of people from many different parts of the world, with very different religious aspirations from those seen in the host societies;
5. the reactions of Europe's secular elites to the increasing salience of religion in public as well as private life;
6. a growing realization that the patterns of religious life in modern Europe should be considered an "exceptional case" in global terms — they are not a global prototype.

Not all of these can be considered in detail in this chapter; used selectively, however, they provide a framework for the argument that follows.

One way of grasping the significance of the first three is to realize that there are effectively two religious economies running side by side in much of modern Europe, Britain included. The first is the one delivered by history: the parochial system outlined above, which embeds the churches of Europe in the physical and cultural landscape. This is Europe's cultural heritage. These churches, moreover, work as a "public utility": just like their parallels in health or welfare, they are there at the point of need for populations who will sooner or later require their services. The fact that these populations see no need to attend these churches on a regular basis does not mean that they are not appreciated.

In my own work, I have used the expression "vicarious religion" both to describe and explain this situation. By vicarious, I mean the notion of religion performed by an active minority but on behalf of a much larger number, who (implicitly at least) not only understand, but, quite clearly, approve of what the minority is doing. The first half of the definition is relatively straightforward and reflects the everyday meaning of the term — that is, to do something on behalf of someone else (hence the word "vicar"). The second half is more controversial and is best explored by means of examples. Religion, it seems, can operate vicariously in a wide variety of ways:[4]

- churches and church leaders perform ritual on behalf of others (notably the occasional offices) — if these services are denied, this causes offense;
- church leaders and churchgoers believe on behalf of others and incur criticism if they do not do this properly;
- church leaders and churchgoers embody moral codes on behalf of others, even when those codes have been abandoned by large sections of the populations that they serve;
- churches, finally, can offer space for the vicarious debate of unresolved issues in modern societies.

The last of these requires a little elaboration — quite apart from anything else, it offers one way into a specifically Anglican issue. Could it be

4. All of these ideas are explored more fully in Davie (2006c).

that churches offer space for debate regarding particular, and often controversial, topics that are difficult to address elsewhere in society? The current debate about homosexuality in the Church of England offers a possible example, an interpretation encouraged by the intense media attention directed at this issue — and not only in Britain. Is this simply an internal debate about senior clergy appointments in which different lobbies within the church are exerting pressure? Or is this one way in which society as a whole comes to terms with profound shifts in the moral climate? If the latter is *not* true, it is hard to understand why so much attention is being paid to the churches in this respect. If it *is* true, our thinking must take this factor into account.

With this in mind, I remain convinced that the notion of "vicarious religion" is helpful in understanding the current situation in both Europe and, more precisely, in Britain. It is not, however, the whole story. It is at this point that the second, somewhat newer, religious economy becomes significant — that which concerns Europe's diminishing but still significant churchgoers (i.e., those who maintain the tradition on behalf of the people described in the previous paragraphs). Here an observable change is quite clearly taking place, best summarized as a shift from a culture of obligation or duty to a culture of consumption or choice. What was once simply imposed (with all the negative connotations of this word), or inherited (a rather more positive spin), becomes instead a matter of personal choice: "I go to church (or to another religious organization) because I want to, maybe for a short period or maybe for longer, to fulfill a particular rather than a general need in my life and where I will continue my attachment so long as it provides what I want, but I have no *obligation* either to attend in the first place or to continue if I don't want to."

As such, this pattern is entirely compatible with vicariousness (this is important): "The churches need to be there in order that I may attend them if I so choose." The "chemistry," however, gradually alters, a shift that is discernible in both practice and belief, not to mention the connections between them. There is, for example, an observable change in the patterns of confirmation in the Church of England. The overall number of confirmations has dropped dramatically in the post-war period, evidence once again of institutional decline. In England, though not yet in the Nordic countries, confirmation is no longer a teenage rite of passage, but a relatively rare event undertaken as a matter of personal choice by people of all ages. Indeed, there is a very marked rise in the proportion of adults among the candidates overall, though not enough to offset the fall among teenagers. In short, membership in the historic churches is beginning to define itself in different ways, which — in this sense at least — become much more like their non-established counterparts. Voluntarism (a market) is beginning to assert itself, regardless of the constitutional position of the churches.

So much for points 1-3 above. The fourth factor is rather different and concerns the growing number of incomers in almost all European societies. There have been two stages in this process. The first was closely linked to the urgent need for labor in the expanding economies of post-war Europe — notably in Britain, France, Germany, and the Netherlands. The second wave of immigration occurred somewhat later (the 1990s). It included, in addition to the places listed above, both the Nordic countries and the countries of Mediterranean Europe (Greece, Italy, Spain, and Portugal), bearing in mind that the latter have traditionally been countries of emigration rather than immigration. The crucial point to grasp in both cases is that the motives for coming to Europe, both push and pull, were economic.

What, though, are the implications for the religious life of Europe? The short answer is that they vary from place to place, depending on both host society and new arrivals. Britain and France offer an instructive comparison. In Britain immigration has been much more varied than in France, both in terms of provenance and in terms of faith communities. Britain is also a country where ethnicity and religion crisscross each other in a bewildering variety of ways (only Sikhs and Jews claim ethno-religious identities). In this respect, the situation in France is quite different: here immigration has been largely from the Maghreb, as a result of which France has by far the largest Muslim community in Europe (between 5 and 6 million) — an almost entirely Arab population. Rightly or wrongly, Arab and Muslim have become interchangeable terms in popular parlance in France.

Beneath these differences lies however a common factor: the growing presence of other faith communities in general, and of the Muslim population in particular, is challenging some deeply held European assumptions.[5]

---

5. For understandable reasons, the material on Islam in Europe grows apace. The following offers a selection of titles: Maréchal et al. (2002), Esposito and Burgat (2003), Allievi and Nielsen (2003), Nielsen (2004), Cesari (2004), Cesari and McLoughlin (2005), Klausen (2005), and Al-Azmeh and Fokas (2007). Nielsen (2004) contains an extended bibliography of earlier work.

The notion that faith is a private matter and should, therefore, be pro-scribed from public life — notably from the state and from the education system — is widespread in Europe. Conversely, many of those who are cur-rently arriving in this part of the world have markedly different convic-tions, and offer — simply by their presence — a challenge to the European way of doing things. European societies have been obliged to re-open de-bates about the place of religion in public as well as private life — hence the heated controversies about the wearing of the veil in the school system, about the rights or wrongs of publishing material that one faith commu-nity in particular finds offensive, and about the location of "non-European" religious buildings. There have been moments, moreover, when a lack of mutual comprehension, together with an unwillingness to com-promise on many of these issues, have led alarmingly fast to dangerous confrontations, both in Europe and beyond.

Such episodes raise a further point: the extent to which the secular elites of Europe use these events in order to articulate alternatives — ideo-logical, constitutional, and institutional — to religion. It is important to remember, however, that such elites (just like their religious counterparts) vary markedly from place to place, a point at which we rejoin the empha-ses of the previous section — notably, an awareness that the *process* of reli-gious change has taken place differently in different places. What in Brit-ain, and indeed in most of Northern Europe, occurred gradually (starting with a de-clericalization of the churches from within at the time of Refor-mation), became in France a delayed and much more ideological clash be-tween a hegemonic, heavily clerical church and a much more militant sec-ular state. Hence "la guerre des deux Frances," which dominated French political life well into the twentieth century (Poulat 1987). The legacies still remain in the form of a self-consciously secular elite, and a lingering suspi-cion concerning religion of all kinds — the more so when this threatens the public sphere. The fact that these threats are no longer Catholic but Muslim does not alter the underlying reaction. In Britain, something rather different has occurred: *overlapping* elites (both religious and secu-lar) work together to encourage mutual respect between different world faiths, a policy admirably illustrated following the bombings in London in July 2005.

Underlying these differences lies a crucially important tension: the complex relationship between democracy and tolerance. This will be de-veloped at greater length in the following section, in a more detailed treatment of the British case. Before doing so, however, the sixth and final point listed above must be taken into account. It introduces a rather different idea: namely the growing realization that the patterns of religious life in modern Europe should be considered an "exceptional case" in global terms. In other words, the relative secularity of Europe is unlikely to be repeated elsewhere, however "modern" the rest of the world might become. Europe is not, therefore, a global prototype. This statement goes straight to the heart of an urgent and as-yet unresolved question: Is secularization intrinsic or extrinsic to the modernization process? Or to ask the same question in a different way: Is Europe secular because it is modern (or at least more modern than other parts of the world), or is it secular because it is European, and has developed along a distinctive pathway? I remain increasingly convinced that the latter is the case, in which case Europeans have somehow to remove from their consciousness the notion that what Europe does today, everybody else will do tomorrow. Everybody else, moreover, includes most of the Anglican Communion.

The Church of England:
The Advantages of a "Weak" State Church

What — within these parameters — is the role of the Church of England in English society at the start of the twenty-first century? The question will be approached in two ways. This first will develop the notion of two coexisting religious economies; the second will elaborate the tension between democracy and tolerance. Both have been chosen to explore the advantages of a "weak" state church and to reflect on the wider remit of this book — the need to negotiate a path between relativism and fundamentalism.

Two Religious Economies

The starting point for this discussion lies in the recognition that the two religious economies running side by side in modern Europe are sociologically as well as theologically explicable, and that both have a right to exist. It is not sensible to force a choice between them, however tempting this might be. Indeed looked at carefully, each "economy" corrects the more obvious faults of the other. A public utility based on territory can at times be too accepting; a model of choice runs the risk of excluding not only those who make different choices, but those who are unable, or disinclined, to choose at all. Much more effective, in this situation, are policies that support pastorally those (both priests and laity) who find themselves torn between two very different ways of working, a necessarily difficult situation. Any number of examples come to mind. The changing patterns of confirmation have already been described, a shift that has taken place relatively easily. Much more vexing is the evident confusion about baptism.

Historically, baptism in the Church of England has been as much a mark of Englishness as of Christian conviction, indeed for many people rather more so. There have been several phases in this history — ranging from obligation (more or less rigorously enforced), through encouragement (all are welcome), to a much more selective process in which only the children of the faithful are allowed the sacrament, at least in some parishes. Baptism, in other words, is changing in nature: it is becoming increasingly a sign of membership in a voluntary community, something that is chosen rather than ascribed. Theologies adapt accordingly.

So much is unsurprising: here is a church adjusting to new circumstances. Change, however, is painful and for everyone concerned — the more so when it occurs haphazardly and piecemeal. The consequences can be seen both inside and outside the church. Decisions about baptism, for example, divide parishes (sometimes very bitterly) when priest and people take different views, or when the congregation as a whole is split. Too often, moreover, the confusions of the church are projected onto an unwitting population: the blame is placed on those who ask, not on those who make the decisions. But looked at from the outside, the "logic" is very difficult to discern. Neighboring parishes do different things for no apparent reason, leading at best to confusion and at worst to an enduring sense of rejection. Without doubt, irreparable damage has been done, a fact evidenced by an endless stream of letters sent to diocesan bishops on precisely this issue.

How, then, can the debate move forward? One point is clear from the outset: a "weak" state church cannot enforce baptism, nor can it "make" recalcitrant parishes conform to one model or another. It can, however, learn to live with the tensions set out in the previous paragraph, recognizing that these derive from two very different models of church life, each of which is expressed in a different approach to Christian initiation. The debate, moreover, should be set in a broader context. The rite of baptism is but one of the occasional offices. And — so far at least — the Church of England has not placed similar conditions on those who require its services at the time of a death. Indeed it is at this point, if no other, that sizable sections of the English population (just like their European counterparts) continue to touch base with their churches, which respond accordingly. Of course there have been changes, notably the huge increase in the proportion of English funerals that now take place in a crematorium rather than the parish church, placing corresponding demands on clergy. But care at the point of need to those in a specified area, the essence of a public utility, is still very much intact. It is both expected and given, a situation that is unlikely to change in the foreseeable future. It follows that the two religious economies will endure for the time being. And if lessons can be learned, one surely must lie in the need to avoid the controversies surrounding baptism in the church's care to the dying and the bereaved — bearing in mind that at this moment in the life cycle, the stakes are higher still.

One further point concludes this section. It concerns statistics. It is important to recognize that comparisons across time and between countries in terms of the proportion of children baptized are very often misleading, for they do not compare like with like.[6] In England, for example, the figures for baptism have fallen dramatically in the post-war period, a drop that requires careful interpretation. At one level, this is — straightforwardly — an index of secularization. At another, it is the result of the confusions set out above. Parishioners are understandably reluctant to bring their children to an institution that appears to reject them.

Interestingly, in the Lutheran churches of the Nordic countries, no such fall has occurred. Here baptism (and indeed confirmation) figures stay very high indeed, reflecting not only a different understanding of the rite, but an entirely different notion of church membership, absent in the English case. That does not mean that the Nordic countries are either more or less secular than Britain; it does mean, however, that they are differently so. In the Lutheran countries of northern Europe, the public utility quite clearly remains the dominant model. It is supported by church tax, paid by the population as a whole, unless they "opt out" — which very few of them do. Why not becomes a very interesting question. Conversely, in terms of baptism, the situation in France is much more similar to that in

6. See Martin (2003).

England; in both countries the rite of Christian initiation is becoming increasingly a symbol of choice rather than obligation. The fact that this shift is occurring in churches with very different theologies, one Catholic and one Protestant, merits very careful consideration. It is not something that could be predicted from the outset.

Democracy and Tolerance: A Continuing Tension

In other respects, however, France and England (indeed Britain) are very different, a contrast that requires further exploration. The essence of the argument is easily summarized: both constitutionally and institutionally France is undoubtedly a more democratic society than Britain. But Britain is more tolerant than France if by tolerance is meant the acceptance of group as well as individual differences, and the right to display symbols of that group membership in public as well as private life. The following paragraphs pay particular attention to the role of a weak state church in this process that, once again, is in many respects counterintuitive.

Let us start with the French case. France is markedly more democratic than Britain on almost all institutional or constitutional measures. Here is a Republic, with a secular state, two elected chambers, and no privileged church (in the sense of connections to the state). There is a correspondingly strong stress on the equality of all citizens whatever their ethnic or religious identity. As a result, France follows a strongly assimilationist policy towards incomers, with the express intention of eradicating difference — individuals who arrive in France are welcome to maintain their religious belief and practices, provided these are relegated to the private sphere. They are actively discouraged from developing any kind of group identity. Exactly the same point can be put as follows: any loyalty (religious or otherwise) that comes between the citizen and the state is regarded in negative terms. In France, it follows, *communautarisme* is a pejorative word, implying a less-than-full commitment to the nation embodied in the French state.

Britain is very different. On a strict measure of democracy, Britain fares less well than France — with no written constitution, a monarchy, a half-reformed and so far unelected House of Lords, and an established church. More positively, Britain has a more developed tradition of accommodating group identities (including religious ones) within the framework of British society, a feature that owes a good deal to the relatively greater degree of religious pluralism that has existed in Britain for centuries rather than decades. Hence a markedly different policy towards newcomers: the goal becomes the accommodation of difference rather than its eradication. Rather more provocative, however, are the conclusions that emerge if you look carefully at who, precisely, in British society is advocating religious as opposed to ethnic toleration. Very frequently it turns out to be those in society who do *not* depend on an electoral mandate: the royal family and significant spokespersons in the House of Lords (where other faith communities are well represented by appointment, not by election).

They are both, of course, intimately connected to the established church, a significant player in its own right. Here the crucial point lies *precisely* in appreciating the difference between a historically strong state church and its modern, somewhat weaker equivalent. The former almost by definition becomes excluding and exclusive; the latter cannot. It can, however, use its still-considerable influence to include rather than exclude, to acknowledge rather than to ignore, and to welcome rather than despise. Even more positive are its capacities to create and to sustain a space within society in which faith is taken seriously — doing so *by means of* its connections with the state. If these things are done well, it would be hard to argue that an established church has no part to play in an increasingly plural society.

One trigger in the continuing controversies about establishment remains, however, the changing nature of society (the process of secularization) and the growth of religious minorities (pluralization). Given these changes, it is argued, an established church is becoming increasingly anomalous: it is less and less able to speak for the majority and it is, necessarily, hostile to minorities. Both issues draw the arguments of this chapter together. The first, for example, can be addressed in terms of "vicarious" religion. Implicitly, if not explicitly, the church can — it seems — both act and speak in the name of significant numbers of people who would not be pleased if such possibilities (the public utility) were suddenly withdrawn. In terms of the second, it is worth looking carefully at who exactly in British society is advocating what. One point becomes clear very quickly: very seldom do the religious minorities (more especially the other faith communities) demand disestablishment. It is not in their interests to do so. It is, conversely, very common for secular elites to argue the case "in the name" of other-faith communities — which is quite a different thing.

Their demands must be resisted. I would, in fact, go further still — and maintain that the debate about establishment is largely a side issue. Much more important is the recognition that faith communities (i.e., collectivities) of all kinds are and must remain an integral part of a tolerant and progressive society. The primary task, therefore, is to find ways of making this possible. Bearing in mind the difficulties experienced in France, it does not seem that a strictly secular state is likely to provide an immediate answer. Much more creative is a long hard look at what, precisely, history has delivered and then to use what is available as imaginatively as possible. The Church of England — in its current form — has clearly a role to play. At the very least, it can act as an umbrella of faith, ensuring that the debate about religion is both constructive in itself and heard by the powers that be. Increasingly, if not always consistently, this role is recognized, not only by the religious minorities but by significant sections of the political class. Religion is bit by bit regaining its place in the public sphere.[7]

Conversely, those who continue to question establishment fall into two camps. On the one hand can be found the secular elite for the reasons already described; on the other are significant sections of the evangelical community, currently in the ascendant in the Church of England — a group that advocates, with considerable conviction, the model of choice over and above the public utility. Politics, moreover, creates strange bedfellows. It was precisely these two constituencies that — for very different reasons — resisted the legislation regarding "the incitement to religious hatred."[8] The secularists feared anything that curtailed the freedom of speech; the evangelicals were apprehensive lest certain forms of evangelism were interpreted as derogatory to other faiths. The challenge for the established church is to mitigate both extremes and to demand courtesy in a debate that, at times, is necessarily robust.

Generalizing from the English Case

Is the relative success of the English case a matter of luck or of good judgment? It is probably a bit of both in the sense that policy decisions have in-

7. Paradoxically, it is the minorities, sometimes, who lead the way. A good example of such leading can be found in the debate that preceded the inclusion of a question about religion in the 2001 British census (Weller 2004).

8. The Racial and Religious Hatred Act 2006 creates an offense of inciting (or "stirring up") hatred against a person on the grounds of their religion.

deed been made, but within limiting parameters. Bit by bit, however (in a typically Anglican way) a virtue has been made out of necessity, leading to more positive understandings of the present situation. This leads to a second question: Is it possible to generalize from the English case? There are two ways of establishing an answer. The first is to look somewhat selectively at other European societies; the second considers Anglican examples outside Europe.

Regarding the former, for example, the Lutheran countries of northern Europe are clearly the close cousins of the Church of England, but not its siblings. For the reasons already noted, they have a much-better-funded public utility, which leads in turn to a greater capacity to dominate. The latter, interestingly, has been countered by constitutional change in Sweden. In the year 2000, the state church became a free folk church allowing, at least in theory, for greater religious pluralism. (Norway is likely to follow suit in a couple of decades.) Having said this, the Nordic societies have retained their relative homogeneity for longer — changes in this respect, though important, have come only in the last ten to fifteen years. Markedly different from this point of view is the Dutch case. In the Netherlands (as indeed in Belgium), what has become known as pillarization[9] reflects at least some aspects of British multiculturalism, and over a similar time span. The Dutch, however, have institutionalized these differences more deeply, leading in the present period to worrying cleavages in Dutch society — the inevitable consequence of pillars. The murders of Pim Fortuyn (2002) and Theo van Gogh (2004) have brought these unresolved and very emotive tensions into the open. Germany offers a different solution to bi-confessional identity. Here, the experience of World War II led those responsible for post-war rebuilding to disperse power systematically. The two largest churches (the German Catholic Church and the Evangelical Lutheran Church) are part and parcel of this process. For a start, they too are federalized. Rather differently, the churches have taken from the state considerable responsibilities — a good example can be found in their oversight of both the content and delivery of religious education in German schools.[10]

9. Pillarization describes the vertical division of Dutch and Belgian society, in which religion plays a central role. Traditionally this meant a separate life experience for Catholics and Protestants and so on. More recently this has mutated into something more harmful: policies that exclude from the mainstream the more recently arrived minorities, notably Muslims.

10. The extent to which these policies can be pursued in post-reunification Germany provokes interesting questions that lie beyond the scope of this paper.

Catholic Europe is somewhat different — a contrast stemming from resistance to reform from the inside. The comparison with France has exemplified this point in some detail, a process repeated in most of southern Europe, but with a less ideological focus. In Italy, Spain, and Portugal, moreover, the arrival of significant other faith populations is a relatively new experience. The Orthodox world, finally, displays yet another combination of inclusion and exclusion — showing, on the one hand, considerable tolerance to those "who belong," but on the other an edgy hostility to those who dare to encroach on Orthodox "space." Territory is particularly important in this instance. It is for this reason that Orthodoxy in diaspora is not only different, but significant for the argument of this book, a situation explored more fully in Michael Plekon's essay in this volume. Incidentally, Anglicans get on reasonably well with the Orthodox: seen from an Orthodox perspective Anglicanism has a recognizable ecclesiology, but has none of the historic antagonisms associated with Catholicism.

The crucial point is the following: all European societies have to find a way forward in a rapidly changing situation, which combines declining levels of religiousness overall with the growing presence of religious minorities — within which group identities are as important as individual ones. Each of these societies engages this process within a distinctive, historically determined framework of church-state relations. Some European nations are clearly more advanced in this process than others, and some appear to be more successful than others, though none have found it easy. All, moreover, have to take account of the global situation in which religion is asserting itself as an ever-more significant factor. For the Church of England, this takes the form of increasing tensions within the Anglican Communion, not least between its mother church and its constituent provinces, which are themselves very diverse. Some are in dominant positions and some are not; some are wealthy and some not; and some, quite clearly, are exposed to harassment, leading at times to outright persecution. These are situations in which a *via media* is much less easy to sustain.

What unites these provinces, especially in the global South, is the sheer weight of numbers, capable of challenging the tradition, precedent, knowledge, and power that reside in the North (Jenkins 2002). This is a new situation that has found a focus in the heated, and very divisive, controversy relating to homosexuality, already a touchy subject even in Britain (see above). The outcome of these complex and painful debates is far from clear despite the evident flexibilities of Anglicanism if these are compared with the Catholic Church. One thing, however, is certain. The Church of England can no longer ignore what is happening elsewhere; nor can the churches in the North dominate the agenda. Interestingly, the secular press is beginning to grasp this point. It is as ready to pay attention to these discussions as its religious equivalents. One reason for this lies in the issue itself: homosexuality attracts attention both inside and outside the churches. Another can be found in a growing, if gradual, awareness of the religious factor in the modern world order and its capacity to influence the global agenda.

The modern world, however, is arriving in Europe in ever-greater numbers. With this in mind, the situation outlined in this chapter could, in a generation or two, look very different. It becomes much more important, therefore, to create a space in European societies in which a serious discussion of religious issues is able to take place in a constructive and forward-looking way. Finding a middle way between relativism and fundamentalism will be a central feature of this process, in which the historic churches have an important part to play.

Bibliography

Al-Azmeh, A., and E. Fokas, eds. 2007. *Islam in Europe: Diversity, Identity and Influence.* Cambridge: Cambridge University Press.

Byrnes, T., and P. Katzenstein, eds. 2006. *Religion in an Expanding Europe.* Cambridge: Cambridge University Press.

Cesari, J. 2004. *Islam in the West.* Basingstoke: Palgrave/Macmillan.

Cesari, J., and S. McLoughlin, eds. 2005. *European Muslims and the Secular State.* Aldershot: Ashgate.

Davie, G. 1994. *Religion in Britain Since 1945: Believing Without Belonging.* Oxford: Blackwell.

Davie, G. 2000. *Religion in Modern Europe: A Memory Mutates.* Oxford: Oxford University Press.

Davie, G. 2002. *Europe: The Exceptional Case.* London: Darton, Longman & Todd.

Davie, G. 2006a. "Is Europe an Exceptional Case?" *The Hedgehog Review,* 8/1-2: 23-35.

Davie, G. 2006b. "Religion in Europe in the 21st Century: The Factors to

Take into Account," *Archives européennes de sociologie/European Journal of Sociology/Europaeisches Archiv für Soziologie*, XLVII/2, 2006: 271-96.

Davie, G. 2006c. "Vicarious Religion: A Methodological Challenge," in N. Ammerman, ed., *Everyday Religion: Observing Modern Religious Lives*, pp. 21-36. New York: Oxford University Press.

Davie, G. 2007a. *The Sociology of Religion*. London: Sage.

Davie, G. 2007b. "Pluralism, Tolerance and Democracy: Theory and Practice in Europe," in T. Banchoff, ed., *The New Religious Pluralism and Democracy*, pp. 223-42. New York: Oxford University Press.

Fetzer, J., and J. C. Soper. 2004. *Muslims and the State in Britain, France and Germany*. Cambridge: Cambridge University Press.

Greeley, A. 2003. *Religion in Europe at the End of the Second Millennium: A Sociological Profile*. London: Transaction.

Himmelfarb, G. 2004. *The Roads to Modernity: The British, French and American Enlightenments*. New York: Knopf.

Jenkins, P. 2002. *The Next Christendom: The Coming of Global Christianity*. New York: Oxford University Press.

Klausen, J. 2005. *The Islamic Challenge: Politics and Religion in Western Europe*. Oxford: Oxford University Press.

Madeley, J., and Z. Enyedi, eds. 2003. *Church and State in Contemporary Europe: The Chimera of Neutrality*. London. Frank Cass.

McLeod, H., and W. Ustorf, eds. 2003. *The Decline of Christendom in Western Europe*. Cambridge: Cambridge University Press.

Martin, B. 2003. "Beyond Measurement: The Non-quantifiable Religious Dimension in Social Life," in P. Avis, ed., *Public Faith: The State of Religious Belief and Practice in Britain*, pp. 1-18. London: SPCK.

Nielsen, J. 2004. *Muslims in Western Europe*. Edinburgh: University of Edinburgh Press.

O'Connell, J. 1991. *The Making of Modern Europe: Strengths, Constraints and Resolutions*, University of Bradford Peace Research Report no. 26. Bradford: University of Bradford.

Porter, R. 2001. *Enlightenment: Britain and the Creation of the Modern World*. Harmondsworth: Penguin.

Poulat, E. 1987. *Liberté, laïcité: La guerre des deux Frances et le principe de la modernité*. Paris: Le Cerf.

Rémond, R. 1999. *Religion and Society in Modern Europe*. Oxford: Oxford University Press.

Robbers, G., ed. 2005. *State and Church in the European Union.* Baden-Baden: Nomos Verlagsgesellschaft.

Weller, P. 2004. "Identity Politics and the Future(s) of Religion in the UK: The Case of the Religion Questions in the 2001 Decennial Census," *Journal of Contemporary Religion* 19: 3-21.

Evangelicals in Search of a Political Theology

Craig M. Gay

Resentment is easy. Theology is hard.

John Bowlin[1]

At least since the middle of the last century, American evangelicals have deliberately positioned themselves between "fundamentalism" and "relativism" both theologically and culturally, though in a slightly different sense than we are using these terms. For evangelicals "fundamentalism" initially denoted disengagement from the larger culture — i.e., Professor Berger's "less ambitious" fundamentalist project — and it has come to mean intellectual obscurantism combined with a militant and obdurate public presence — i.e., Professor Berger's "more ambitious" fundamentalist project. American evangelicals have been concerned to distance themselves from both "projects." At the same time evangelicals have understood themselves to stand over and against "mainline" Protestant liberalism, modernism, and "secular humanism." Liberal Protestants, from an evangelical point-of-view, have tragically lost sight of the cosmic and transcendental significance of the resurrection of Jesus Christ and have abridged the Gospel (the *evangelion*) to a moral system, a therapeutic vehicle, and/or a legitimation of a variety of "this-worldly" socio-political agendas. Modernists and "secular humanists," for their part, assume that the resurrection story is simply a primitive myth, that "this world" is all there is, and

---

1. Bowlin cited in Jeffrey Stout, *Democracy and Tradition* (Princeton: Princeton University Press, 2004), p. 92.

that human progress will be better served by the frank confession of atheism, naturalism, evolution, and ethical relativism. The key to American evangelical self-understanding, then, has been the combination of traditional (conservative) Protestant theology and engagement with the larger culture — intellectually, socially, and politically — for the sake of personal transformation (religious conversion) and cultural renewal. As Carl F. H. Henry contended in 1947 in *The Uneasy Conscience of American Fundamentalism:*

> If historic Christianity is again to compete as a vital world ideology, evangelicalism must project a solution for the most pressing world problems. It must offer a formula for a new world mind with spiritual ends, involving evangelical affirmations in political, economic, sociological, and educational realms, local and international. The redemptive message has implications for all of life.[2]

Henry's use of the terms "compete," "project," "offer," and "affirm," indicates an implicit, if perhaps begrudging, recognition of pluralism, and while he was perhaps overly confident that evangelicals *could* suggest solutions to the world's most pressing problems, he clearly recognized the need for evangelicals to contend for these solutions in a civil and engaging manner. And evangelicals have by and large continued to believe — in spite of media portrayals to the contrary — that theological insights into the problems of the day must be voiced with civility and sensitivity. Of course, to say this is not to gainsay that American evangelicals are a very diverse and contentious lot comprised of many dozens of conservative Protestant denominations and representing a wide variety of cultures and viewpoints. In the 2004 election, for example, while 51 percent of weekly evangelical church-attenders may well have voted Republican, 48 percent voted Democrat; and although abortion and traditional family values are well known to be "evangelical issues" so, it turns out, are AIDS, human rights, and the environment. Still, the hallmark of American evangelicalism — in all of its variety — has been and continues to be the combination of evangelical theology and cultural engagement.

In view of their commitment to engage contemporary culture, American evangelicals can boast success on a number of fronts over the last fifty

---

2. Carl F. H. Henry, *The Uneasy Conscience of Modern Fundamentalism* (Grand Rapids: Eerdmans, 1947), p. 68.

years, particularly in the area of education.[3] Yet in the sense of "competing as a vital ideology," evangelicals have not enjoyed as much success as their sheer numbers might suggest that they should have, with the survival of *Roe v. Wade* perhaps best symbolizing the movement's political impotence. Hence there have been and continue to be a number of pressures tempting American evangelicals to disengage from the larger culture and, either to retreat back into a fundamentalist enclave, or to adopt an overtly fundamentalist posture over and against what they believe to be deepening cultural decadence. Some of these temptations are theological, stemming from pre-millennial eschatology and/or traditional notions of piety, perhaps even from the traditional Anabaptist rejection of political involvement, but most of the temptations to disengage from the larger culture or to adopt an overtly fundamentalist stance over and against it are socio-cultural. The process of privatization continues to deter religious believers from trying to bring their beliefs into the public sphere. The viciousness of the contemporary "culture wars," furthermore, combined with the increasingly negative portrayals of conservative Christianity in the media, have discouraged many evangelicals from getting involved in public life, not to mention tempting them to become cynical and/or apathetic. Fear and resentment, on the other hand, have tempted many others to resort to fundamentalist militancy. The critical question, then, is not whether American evangelicalism is capable of a "constructive middle" position between fundamentalism and relativism, but whether or not American evangelicals can manage, under contemporary conditions, to *stay* in the constructive middle; as well as whether they can continue to contribute, and perhaps contribute more fruitfully, to contemporary public policy discourse. The thesis I want to advance in the following essay is simply that for evangelicals to stay in the constructive middle and for them to contribute fruitfully to contemporary public policy discourse they will need, above all, to *remember* a theological context within which gracious, well-mannered, and *patient* political participation makes sense. That evangelicals have themselves recognized the importance of this remembering was clearly reflected in a position paper issued in 2005 by the National Association of Evangelicals entitled "For the Health of the Nation: An Evangelical Call to Civic Responsibility" (Appendix A). A careful reading of this statement can, I think, give us a sense both

---

3. See Alan Wolfe, "The Opening of the Evangelical Mind," *The Atlantic Monthly* 286, no. 4 (October 2000): 55ff.

of where evangelicals currently are with respect to civic participation as well as how well or poorly they are situated to *stay* in the constructive middle between fundamentalism and relativism:

"For the Health of the Nation"

Founded in 1942, the National Association of Evangelicals (NAE) represents sixty denominations (fifty-one at the time the statement was issued), 45,000 churches, and well over 30 million people. Recognizing the need for a consistent "political theology," the NAE launched a process several years ago to begin to articulate a specifically evangelical framework for public policy engagement. To this end a steering committee was formed that requested a number of prominent evangelical scholars to contribute relevant essays to a book that would "nurture a widely embraced evangelical framework for public engagement."[4] The resulting book, edited by Ronald J. Sider and Diane Knippers, was published in 2005 and titled *Toward an Evangelical Public Policy: Political Strategies for the Health of the Nation.* The NAE statement "For the Health of the Nation" was subsequently prepared by a drafting committee working from an early draft of this book.

Nearly ninety evangelical leaders have signed off on "For the Health of the Nation," including Richard Land, president of the Southern Baptist Ethics & Religious Liberty Commission (ERLC); James Dobson, founder of Focus on the Family; Charles Colson, founder of Prison Fellowship; and Rick Warren, pastor of Saddleback Church in Southern California and author of best-selling *The Purpose-Driven Life.* Other signers include Barrett Duke, the ERLC's vice president for public policy; NAE President (since resigned) Ted Haggard; Jack Hayford, president of the International Church of the Foursquare Gospel; Walter Kaiser, president of Gordon-Conwell Theological Seminary; Diane Knippers, president of the Institute on Religion and Democracy; David Neff, editor of *Christianity Today;* John Perkins, founder of Voice of Calvary Ministries; Ronald Sider, president of Evangelicals for Social Action; and author and apologist Ravi Zacharias.[5]

---

4. Ronald J. Sider and Diane Knippers, eds., *Toward an Evangelical Public Policy: Political Strategies for the Health of the Nation* (Grand Rapids: Baker, 2005), p. 10.

5. Tom Strode, "Evangelical Leaders Call for Broader Approach to Public Policy; Land, Dobson Lend Support," BPNEWS.NET.

The statement begins with a Preamble reminiscent of Carl Henry's original call to evangelical social responsibility: "Evangelical Christians in America face a historic opportunity," the document states. "We make up fully one quarter of all voters in the most powerful nation in history. Never before has God given American evangelicals such an awesome opportunity to shape public policy in ways that could contribute to the well-being of the entire world." The Preamble goes on to suggest that, while evangelicals may not agree about specific policy initiatives, there are a number of overarching concerns upon which they can agree, such as concern for the well-being of families and children, care for the poor, the protection of the unborn, sick, and disabled, and the defense of those persecuted and/or oppressed by reason of their religious beliefs. While these issues in no way exhaust the concerns of good government, the statement concedes, "they provide the platform for evangelicals to engage in common action." The Preamble then goes on to recognize the temptation to "opt out" of public policy discourse and confesses that evangelicals have failed "to engage with the breadth, depth, and consistency to which we are called," but recalls the reformist legacy of William Wilberforce, William Booth, Charles Finney, and other early evangelicals in an attempt to spur contemporary evangelicals to creative political and social engagement. "Disengagement," the authors write, "is not an option."

The statement goes on to outline a theological basis for evangelical civic engagement by briefly considering a number of disparate biblical themes, the first being that of the divine command (Gen. 1:27-28) to "steward" or to "have dominion" over the earth. Their confession of the "Lordship of Christ" over all of life, furthermore, ought to prevent evangelicals from restricting their understanding of this stewardship to the "private sphere." While recognizing that Christians must wait for the consummation of God's kingdom, nevertheless the statement asserts that the church must speak "prophetically" at present in the interests of justice and peace and that it must seek to model wholeness and integrity. Following a reiteration of the Golden Rule, the theological section of "For the Health of the Nation" concludes that the goal of evangelical civic engagement is "to bless our neighbors" by making good laws, fostering a free press, participating in open debate, voting, and holding public office.

Under the heading of "The Method of Christian Civic Engagement," the statement recognizes the need for thorough factual as well as normative analysis. "The more carefully and precisely we Christians think about the complex details of both," the document states, "the more clearly we will be able to explain our views to others and understand — and perhaps overcome — disagreements with others." Of course, the document recognizes that evangelicals will differ with other Christians as well as with non-Christians on matters of public policy, but urges humility and civility in evangelical civic involvement. The statement also seeks to temper expectations. Sin, entrenched interests, the complexity of contemporary society, and ignorance, the document suggests, will all impede "solutions" to political and social problems. For this reason evangelical sights ought to be set simply on "modest and attainable goals for the good of society." Attaining these goals, furthermore, will require patience, persuasiveness, and magnanimity.

The NAE's statement recognizes the historical diversity of social and political structures, but contends that all governing structures are divinely authorized to maintain order, restrain human evil, and promote the common good. Constitutional democracy is singled out as a form of government for which evangelicals ought to be particularly grateful, however. Yet the document is at some pains to relativize evangelical allegiance to the United States over and against their allegiance to "Christ, his kingdom, and Christ's worldwide body of believers." In fact, readers are urged to keep their eyes open "to the potentially self-destructive tendencies of [U.S.] society and government." Evangelicals are also urged to resist government "when it exercises its power in an unjust manner (Acts 5:27-32) or tries to dominate other institutions [i.e., families, churches, schools, labor unions, and businesses] in society."

The document then goes on at some length, under the heading of "Principles of Christian Political Engagement," to detail those matters upon which evangelicals are especially encouraged to focus: First Amendment issues; the family; the sanctity of life (abortion and biotechnology); justice for the poor; the defense of human rights; peace and the judicious use of military force; and care of the environment. The document concludes with a call to evangelicals to become better informed on matters of public policy, to cultivate an ethos of civic responsibility, and to renew their commitment to engage socially and politically in the interests of life, justice, freedom, and peace.

Craig M. Gay

Discussion

"For the Health of the Nation" is clearly an in-house document. It is not so much a manifesto as it is an appeal to the NAE's constituency to take civic responsibility more seriously than they have perhaps been in the habit of doing. The gist of the statement might be summarized simply as follows: Get involved! Do your homework! Watch your tongue! Don't stoop to unethical or underhanded tactics! Be realistic and patient! In addition, the statement has more or less obviously been written by a committee. It is a kind of assemblage of observations and ideas that are not arranged in a strictly linear fashion and are not developed at any great length. Still, the statement is useful for our purposes both because it reflects the historical makeup of the evangelical family — denominationally as well as in terms of traditional social and ethical concerns — and also because it serves as a fairly accurate indication of the depth of the average evangelical believer's reflection on social and political issues.

Perhaps surprisingly, "For the Health of the Nation" is less traditionally "conservative" than one might have expected. Early press reports, for example, were quick to note the "leftward drift" of the document because of its inclusion of social justice and environmental responsibility alongside the traditional evangelical issue of abortion and its pro-family agenda.[6] Yet in addition to being somewhat more diverse in its concerns, the NAE's statement is surprising for more interesting reasons. In the first instance, the document says very little about Christ and/or the church. Not only is it not triumphalistic, but it is only very minimally theological. And neither is the document particularly patriotic, either in the sense of stressing America as a "Christian Nation" or in the sense of "America: Love It or Leave It." While the statement clearly aims to thwart the allure of privatized/individualized piety and/or fundamentalism, its protest is not especially robust. What if, for example, American evangelicals did *not* make up "one fourth of the electorate of the most powerful nation on earth" and hence did *not* face "a historic opportunity" to "shape public policy in ways that could contribute to the well-being of the entire world"? What if, in other words,

6. See, for example, Mark Totten, "A New Agenda for US Evangelicals," *Christian Science Monitor* (December 18, 2006); Susan Page, "Christian Right's Alliances Bend Political Spectrum," *USA Today* (June 14, 2005); Darryl Hart, "Leftward Christian Soldiers," *The American Conservative* (January 29, 2007).

evangelical prospects for having an impact on the political process were not so bright? Would the evangelical call to civic responsibility be any less valid? While the authors of the statement would almost certainly answer such a question in the negative, the statement itself leaves room for doubt. It would seem that consistent evangelical civic involvement would require a much more carefully developed theological rationale than the statement provides. Indeed, it would and *will* require, as Oliver O'Donovan recently put it, the rediscovery of a "full political conceptuality."[7] Short of such a rediscovery, evangelical civic engagement would seem fated, if not to outright futility, then at least to limited effect. The frustration born of limited effectiveness, in turn, could render evangelicals all the more vulnerable to the temptations of fundamentalism, on the one hand, and to those of cynicism and apathy, on the other. In what follows, then, I want to consider some of the possibilities currently open to evangelicals for the rediscovery of a full political conceptuality.

Evangelicals in Search of a Political Theology

When it comes to fitting civic engagement within a larger theological context, Christianity's long tradition offers a wealth of material. Yet longstanding conflicts within the tradition as well as the fact that not much of this material is immediately applicable to the (post)modern situation makes the job of theologizing contemporary social and political engagement difficult. Of the proposals for political theology currently on offer in evangelical seminaries, some would appear to be more helpful than others in promoting civic engagement. On the less-than-helpful side, in my opinion, is the work of Duke ethicist Stanley Hauerwas on the one hand and on the other the theological movement sometimes termed "Radical Orthodoxy." Both are currently influencing the coming generation of evangelical leaders in their search for a political theology but not necessarily in ways that would seem to encourage constructive political engagement.

---

7. Oliver O'Donovan, *The Desire of the Nations: Rediscovering the Roots of Political Theology* (Cambridge: Cambridge University Press, 1996), p. 2.

Craig M. Gay

Stanley Hauerwas

Borrowing the term from Anabaptist theologian John Howard Yoder, Hauerwas labels both liberal and conservative American Protestants "Constantinian" (read: "accommodationist") because, however much liberals and conservatives may differ theologically, both camps are, as Hauerwas puts it, concerned "to underwrite American democracy."[8] Because liberal democracy exists primarily to assist the assertion of *individuality*, however, Christian support for democracy unwittingly undermines the *communal* essence of the gospel message. Both liberals and conservatives, in Hauerwas's view, have thus been badly compromised by the demands and priorities of American politics. Indeed, even attempting to translate theological convictions into "secular" reasons for the sake of civility and in the interest of participating with non-Christians in public policy discourse gives evidence, Hauerwas believes, of this unfortunate compromise.

By contrast to the "secular activism" of the liberals and the individualistic "conversionism" of the conservatives, Hauerwas and William H. Willimon advocate a "confessing church." "The confessing church," they write in *Resident Aliens: Life in the Christian Colony,*

> is not a synthesis of the other two approaches, a helpful middle ground. Rather, it is a radical alternative. Rejecting both the individualism of the conversionists and the secularism of the activists and their common equation of what works with what is faithful, the confessing church finds its main political task to lie, not in the personal transformation of individual hearts or the modification of society, but rather in the congregation's determination to worship Christ in all things.[9]

Worshiping Christ in all things from this perspective means "being the Church" *over and against* the priorities and demands of national politics and speaking out "prophetically" against the liberal emphasis upon individual freedom as well as against the collective effort to create space for the individual pursuit of happiness under the banners of "national interest" and/or "national security."

---

8. Stanley Hauerwas and William H. Willimon, *Resident Aliens: Life in the Christian Colony* (Nashville: Abingdon, 1989), p. 32.
9. Hauerwas and Willimon, *Resident Aliens*, p. 45.

"Radical Orthodoxy"

"Radical Orthodoxy" is a movement of young Cambridge-trained theologians following the lead of University of Virginia (formerly of Cambridge University) theologian John Milbank. The movement was recently introduced on the American evangelical scene by James K. A. Smith of Calvin College.[10] In short, Radical Orthodoxy attempts to apply post-structuralist criticism to modern institutions and habits of thought for the sake of recovering an authentically (read: pre-modern) Christian faith and practice. As Smith puts it, Radical Orthodoxy is "orthodox insofar as it seeks to be unapologetically confessional and Christian; it is radical insofar as it seeks to critically retrieve premodern roots *(radix)*."

The chief target of Radical Orthodoxy's criticism is the modern notion of "the secular," that is, the notion that there is a religiously neutral zone open to value-neutral inquiry and deliberation. As Milbank puts it: "Either the entire Christian narrative tells us how things truly are, or it does not. If it does, we have no other access to how things truly are, nor any additional means of determining the question."[11] Building on Alasdair MacIntyre's contention that ethical discourse must always be embedded in a larger, essentially religious narrative, Radical Orthodoxy sees little value in encouraging Christians to find common ground with non-Christians or even to seek a common cause on social and political issues. As Smith, citing Milbank, puts it: "There is not a tidy continuity between what the Christian narrative describes as 'good' and what modern liberals consider 'good' practices; rather, there is a deep antithesis that brokers no overlapping consensus."[12] Even engaging others in conversations about social and political matters cannot be expected to yield, for Christians, genuinely new insights. Smith writes: "Radical Orthodoxy defers to no experts and engages in no dialogues because it does not recognize other valid points of view outside the theological."[13] Needless to say, Radical Orthodoxy is deeply suspicious of liberal democracy and, not coincidentally, deeply hostile to modern capitalism.

10. James K. A. Smith, *Introducing Radical Orthodoxy: Mapping a Post-secular Theology* (Grand Rapids: Baker Academic, 2004).

11. John Milbank, *The Word Made Strange: Theology, Language, Culture* (Oxford: Blackwell, 1997), p. 250.

12. Smith, *Introducing*, p. 241; Smith cites Milbank, "Can Morality Be Christian?" in *Word Made Strange*, pp. 219-32.

13. Smith, *Introducing*, p. 70.

Discussion

Radical Orthodoxy is nothing if not an interesting, if somewhat bracing, theological development. The goal of recovering and reconstituting a comprehensive Christian vision is surely refreshing after a century and a half of "apologetic" (read: accommodationist) modern theology in which, as R. R. Reno notes, "[t]he deep end of 'truth' has been ceded to science, while theology swims in the shallow end of 'meaning.'"[14] And the same can be said of Hauerwas's "confessing church" theology. While both may be said to make a kind of "communitarian" contribution to contemporary public policy discourse, there are obviously any number of reasons to believe that the impact these theologies will have upon evangelical civic engagement — to the extent that they have any impact at all — will be largely enervating.[15] True, while no one taking either position seriously would be likely to become either a fundamentalist or a relativist, neither could they be expected to become vital contributors to a common and reasoned quest for moral and philosophical agreement. For Hauerwas, following Yoder, political life is simply an evil. Radical Orthodoxy, in its turn, holds out no hope whatsoever for any kind of "overlapping consensus" between Christians and non-Christians. Politics, from these two perspectives, is not so much fitted *within* a larger theological context as it is simply removed *from within* it.

Is such an assessment too harsh? Perhaps so. After all, as G. K. Chesterton once observed, the critics are almost always right about what is wrong. The problem is that they are almost always wrong about what is right. In this case, Hauerwas, Milbank, and other critics appear to get so carried away with all of the things that are wrong with liberal modernity, that they can neither appreciate its obvious *practical* strengths nor recognize the more or less obvious fact that the liberal tradition — for all of its problems — still bears witness to a number of profoundly Christian *theological* ideas. Exposing the religious (read: idolatrous) character of "the

---

14. R. R. Reno, "The Radical Orthodoxy Project," *First Things* (February 2000): 37ff.

15. Radical Orthodoxy's ambivalence with respect to Scripture and biblical theology combined with its contention that evangelicalism is simply a modern (read: illegitimate) development — not to mention its criticism of democracy and capitalism — make it unlikely that the movement will have much of an impact upon American evangelicalism at large. The same could be said of Hauerwas. The impact of these theologies in the seminaries, however, may be more pronounced, further complicating the evangelical search for a political theology.

secular," in other words, is one thing, but repudiating Christian participation in secular life is quite another. The latter does not seem to me to follow necessarily from the former.

Neo-Calvinism

Interestingly in his introduction of Radical Orthodoxy, Smith is at pains to point out the similarities between Radical Orthodoxy and an older tradition of Christian social and political engagement sometimes termed "neo-Calvinism." Originating in the work of Dutch theologian and statesman Abraham Kuyper (d. 1920) and in the philosophical theology of Herman Dooyeweerd (d. 1977), neo-Calvinism has represented an interesting approach to the modern theological task. As Christian Reformed intellectuals working within this tradition have played and continue to play a particularly influential role in shaping contemporary evangelical social and political-economic thought, it is well worth revisiting the neo-Calvinist tradition.

Calvinism, Kuyper insisted, was a logically consistent "life-and-world-view"[16] that represented the "completed evolution of Protestantism, resulting in a both higher and richer stage of human development."[17] While the support Kuyper offered for this bold claim need not be pursued here, he appears to have envisioned Calvinism as the only theological system capable of reconciling the characteristically modern understanding of historical development with classical theological notions of ontology. Insofar as theological ontology was concerned, Kuyper stressed the permanence, or fixity, of the creation. The diversity given in our experience of the creation, then, as Albert Wolters has noted describing the Kuyperian position, is not "merely [a] product of evolution or the historical process in the sense that any kind of thing might turn into any other kind of thing in the course of time, but [it is] rooted in creation."[18] Every existing thing, including the "things" people have ostensibly created such as forms of social organization, Kuyper understood to have been created ultimately by God.

---

16. Abraham Kuyper, *Lectures on Calvinism* (Grand Rapids: Eerdmans, 1931), p. 190.

17. Kuyper, *Lectures on Calvinism*, p. 41.

18. Albert M. Wolters, "The Intellectual Milieu of Hermann Dooyeweerd," in *The Legacy of Hermann Dooyeweerd: Reflections on Critical Philosophy in the Christian Tradition*, ed. C. T. McIntire (New York: University Press of America, 1985), p. 6.

As God's creation, then, they bore within themselves laws, or "creational ordinances"[19] for their continued existence and development.

Specifically with reference to human culture, Kuyper identified a series of creational "spheres," principally the state, the society, and the church,[20] each having its own set of creational ordinances and each understood to require a measure of sovereignty relative to the others. Kuyper proposed this system in opposition to the notion of "popular sovereignty" (as given, for example, in the French and American Revolutions), and also in opposition to the Hegelian notion of "state sovereignty."[21] Whereas "popular sovereignty" located social authority solely within human nature conceived autonomously and so ignored the authority of God over social life, "state sovereignty" conceded too much power to the government, thus making it possible for the state to infringe upon, and to damage, areas of social life not within its jurisdiction. Commenting on the relation of the societal spheres to the state, for example, Kuyper noted:

> In a Calvinistic sense we understand . . . that the family, the business, science, art, and so forth are all social spheres, which do not owe their existence to the state and which do not derive the law of their life from the superiority of the state, but obey a high authority within their own bosom; an authority which rules, by the grace of God, just as the sovereignty of the state does.[22]

Further describing Kuyper's position, Wolters has noted:

> [T]he sociological principle that distinct kinds of societal institutions (e.g. state, family, school, church) or cultural sectors (e.g. commerce, scholarship, art) have their proper jurisdictions limited and defined by the specific nature of the "sphere" concerned . . . became the guiding principle for the Christian political party which Kuyper led and provided a rationale for limiting the authority of the state and protecting the distinct rights and responsibilities of institutions like church and family.[23]

19. Kuyper, *Lectures on Calvinism*, p. 70.
20. Kuyper, *Lectures on Calvinism*, p. 79.
21. Kuyper, *Lectures on Calvinism*, p. 85.
22. Kuyper, *Lectures on Calvinism*, p. 90.
23. Wolters, "The Intellectual Milieu," p. 6.

On the question of history, Kuyper emphasized that the creation had been ordained by God in such a way as to allow for historical development, development called forth from the potentialities that had been created within the various spheres. Indeed, Kuyper's understanding of human stewardship over creation, often termed humanity's "cultural mandate,"[24] suggested the conscious human direction of this ongoing historical development in such a way that it brought glory to God by enabling each created thing, whether it was natural or social, to conform to the ordinances inhering within it. Wolters has commented:

> If salvation is really re-creation and if recreation means a restoration of everything to its proper creational place and function, then, Kuyper thought, there must be a norm, or standard, for each kind of thing to which it must be restored and by which it is distinguished from every other kind of thing. . . . God is sovereign, therefore his word is law for all creatures. That law-word constitutes the normative nature and distinctive identity of every kind of created thing, whether they be oak trees, human rationality, or the body politic . . . everything has its own "law of life," the standard to which it must conform if it is to live or function fully and authentically.[25]

Just how created things, both natural and social, actually developed according to their divinely ordained potentialities was the problem Herman Dooyeweerd, a student of Kuyper's at the Free University of Amsterdam, attempted to work out philosophically. An important theme Dooyeweerd added to the Kuyperian system in this regard was that of "disclosure," which has been described by Wolters as follows:

> Creation . . . in the neo-Calvinistic world-view was eschatological in an encompassing cultural sense and had implications for a complete philosophy of history. It is this idea which Dooyeweerd worked out in his conception of the "opening process" [or disclosure] of creation and his theory of historical development. . . . This process means that history involves the differentiation and progressive unfolding of the unique creational nature of each social institution and cultural sector.[26]

24. Wolters, "The Intellectual Milieu," p. 8.
25. Wolters, "The Intellectual Milieu," p. 5.
26. Wolters, "The Intellectual Milieu," p. 8.

Dooyeweerd stressed that the chief barrier to the progressive unfolding or disclosure of creation was well summarized in the theological notion of idolatry, or the refusal of fallen humanity to worship its Creator and its choice instead to worship isolated aspects, or spheres of creation, to the detriment of creation as a whole. Indeed, Dooyeweerd felt that the resistance idolatry posed to the stewardly disclosure of creation was what chiefly characterized the human condition.

Evidence of the impact that the neo-Calvinist tradition has had upon American evangelical thought is given in the emphasis the NAE's "For the Health of the Nation" places upon exercising self-consciously Christian "stewardship" over all aspects of social and political life. It is also given in the statement's concern that the "dominion mandate" not be interpreted simply in terms of government, but rather that it also be extended to other spheres of life, including families, churches, labor unions, businesses, etc. The concern, voiced under the heading of "Just Government and Fundamental Liberty," that government not be allowed to impinge upon these other spheres of human activity also very clearly bears the neo-Calvinist stamp.

Yet just what the "creational spheres" are, what the relations between them ought to look like, and how the "norms" governing development in each sphere ought to be understood have been hard to work out, and this difficulty has plagued the neo-Calvinist tradition both intellectually and practically. While the tradition has offered a promising theologically developed *theory* of social and political life, in other words, this theory has proven almost impossible to work out *in practice*. In his Foreword to Smith's book John Milbank, for example, criticizes the Kuyperian tradition for its "ahistoricist" and "static" division of human life into distinct spheres.[27] The particular features of social and political life, Milbank continues, are too historically contingent for set boundaries to be drawn around them and the Kuyperian tradition too readily cordons off certain domains — e.g., the economic — and insulates them from substantive religious criticism. Others have criticized the Kuyperian tradition for its abstraction and have suggested that, however the principles for evangelical civic engagement are understood, they must be grounded in and developed primarily out of scriptural exegesis and not out of a philosophical system. One influential neo-Calvinist scholar who has attempted to do just

27. John Milbank, "Foreword," in Smith, *Introducing*, p. 13.

this is Nicholas Wolterstorff in his excellent contribution to *Toward an Evangelical Public Policy.*[28]

Nicholas Wolterstorff

Wolterstorff observes that the question of what kind of relationship the church ought to have with the surrounding culture presented itself almost immediately to first-century Christians. The apostolic answer to this question, then, was that the church must remain "in but not of" the world.

> Nowhere are Christians urged to go off by themselves to set up their own social institutions. With the exception, of course, of religious institutions, they are to participate side by side with non-Christians in the institutions of their society: marriage, family, economy, and polity. They are to do so with a difference, however, a difference both in how they understand the significance of those institutions and in how they conduct themselves within them.[29]

Christian participation in the institutions of civil society, furthermore, was not to be understood as a necessary evil, but as part and parcel of God's providential rule of humankind. Human government was thus not understood simply in remedial terms — i.e., as necessary to restrain evil — but as a critical aspect of God's ongoing and providential care for his creation *qua creation.*[30]

The primary responsibility of government in apostolic teaching is to enact *justice,* i.e., to vindicate those who have been wronged and to convict and carry out retributive punishment on those who have done the wrongdoing.[31]

This performance of justice requires government to undertake legislative and executive as well as judicial functions. For if those who do right are to be affirmed and those who do wrong punished, the laws on the basis of which judges render their decisions must themselves be just, and judicial decisions must be executed fairly and properly.

---

28. Nicholas Wolterstorff, "Theological Foundations for an Evangelical Political Philosophy," in Sider and Knippers, eds., *Toward an Evangelical Public Policy,* pp. 140-62.
29. Wolterstorff, "Theological Foundations," p. 142.
30. Wolterstorff, "Theological Foundations," p. 149.
31. Wolterstorff, "Theological Foundations," p. 148.

Yet the responsibility of government, Christianly understood, extends beyond justice to the coordination of social life in the interests of the common good.[32] Here Wolterstorff cites Calvin and Calvin's contention that the "appointed end" of civil government is to promote "general peace and tranquility" as well as to preserve justice *per se* (*Institutes* IV.20.2).[33]

> The idea is that it belongs to the task of government to serve the common good — the *shalom*, the flourishing of the people. Of course, in promoting justice, government is already serving the flourishing of the people. And let us not forget the lesson of history, that when governments go beyond promoting justice and aim at serving what they regard as the common good, they all too often wreak appalling injustice. Nonetheless, I think it is impossible to deny that, in addition to promoting justice, government serves an indispensable coordinating function; and that this coordinating function, when properly exercised, aims at the common good, the general welfare.[34]

Wolterstorff does note what he calls the "perplexity" so often caused by the tension in the New Testament between the apostle Paul's exhortation to *obey* those in authority and Jesus' command to *love* one's enemies. "What sense does it make," he writes, "to approve the punishment of the criminal at the hands of the authorities while at the same time bringing him love-baskets?"[35] This only makes sense, Wolterstorff contends, in terms of the traditional distinction of the "two rules."

> [T]he majority of Christian thinkers have held, sometimes explicitly, usually tacitly, that the clue to the solution of the perplexity lies in distinguishing between acting in one's capacity as the holder of some office or position, and acting in one's own person. . . . It is because the main tradition of the church has operated with this distinction that it has seen nothing contradictory in one and the same person faithfully mediating Christ's rule as head of the state by sentencing the criminal to retributive punishment and faithfully following Christ's rule as head of the church by visiting the criminal in prison.[36]

32. Wolterstorff, "Theological Foundations," p. 150.
33. Wolterstorff, "Theological Foundations," p. 149.
34. Wolterstorff, "Theological Foundations," p. 150.
35. Wolterstorff, "Theological Foundations," p. 151.
36. Wolterstorff, "Theological Foundations," p. 152.

Wolterstorff does consider Yoder's alternative Anabaptist resolution of this tension, but concludes that there simply isn't any textual evidence in the New Testament for Yoder's assertion that government *per se* is evil and hence that Christians must remain aloof from the tasks of governing.

Wolterstorff further observes that rumination on the biblical texts has given rise to a number of important political ideas in Western Christian history. The most important idea, he suggests, and the idea to have emerged first, was the "rule of law."[37] Following on from the rule of law were the ideas of "constitutionalism"[38] and the "separation of powers."[39] Wolterstorff also notes how the biblical affirmation that human beings are created "after the image and likeness of God" gradually gave rise to the emergence of the idea of "right" and eventually to the assertion of "human rights" vis-à-vis human governments.[40] Lastly Wolterstorff comments on the development, within Dutch Calvinism and Roman Catholicism, of the idea that not only must governments be prevented from violating individuals, but they must also be prevented from violating and/or absorbing the manifold institutions of civil society, i.e., churches, families, businesses, labor unions, voluntary associations, etc.[41] Wolterstorff concludes his article with a list of thirteen "theses" concerning government that he believes most evangelicals can agree on.[42] Here are a few of them:

1. Government is not merely a human creation, nor is it the work of the devil. Government is instituted by God as a part of God's providential care for his human creatures.

2. The task assigned by God to government is twofold: to promote justice, both primary and corrective, and in its coordinating activities to enhance the common good.

4. When government acts as it ought to act, it acts with genuine authority. That authority is to be understood as not merely human but as mediating Christ's authority.

---

37. Wolterstorff, "Theological Foundations," pp. 157-58.
38. Wolterstorff, "Theological Foundations," p. 158.
39. Wolterstorff, "Theological Foundations," p. 158.
40. Wolterstorff, "Theological Foundations," p. 158.
41. Wolterstorff, "Theological Foundations," p. 159.
42. Wolterstorff, "Theological Foundations," p. 160.

5. The corollary of the exercise by government of genuine authority is that its subjects are obligated to obey that authority.

9. The Christian may serve in the offices of government; in doing so, he is mediating the rule over the state of that very same Christ who is the ruler of the church.

13. Christians will honor and respect government; they will not talk and act as if government has no right to exist. And they will support government by paying taxes. . . .[43]

While Wolterstorff does not say anything particularly new in attempting to lay the theological foundations for an evangelical political philosophy, his succinct reiteration of the position of the Magisterial Reformers is very helpful. For these are exactly the kind of theologically reasoned ideas that evangelicals must now remember if they are to remain constructively engaged in American public life. The biblical vision does not expect government to be Christian, to enact specifically Christian legislation, or to be staffed exclusively by Christians. It does expect Christians to interact positively and honorably with government, both for the sake of their love of God and for the sake of their neighbors.

Oliver O'Donovan

The problem with Wolterstorff's overview is that it remains very general. For American evangelicals to develop an effectual "political theology," Wolterstorff's theses will need to be refined and perhaps expanded to speak specifically into the context of contemporary liberal democracy. Very few evangelicals have attempted to do this to date.[44] Practically all of the theoretical work on democracy since the mid-nineteenth century has been undertaken by "secular" scholars. There are indications that evangelical scholars are waking up to the importance of this task, however. With his publication of *The Desire of the Nations* (1996), for example, Oliver O'Donovan has done much to revive the discussion of political theology in

43. Wolterstorff, "Theological Foundations," pp. 160-61.
44. Glenn Tinder's *The Political Meaning of Christianity: The Prophetic Stance, An Interpretation* (San Francisco: HarperSanFrancisco, 1989) is a notable exception to this rule.

evangelical circles, and he has revived the discussion in such a way as to be more or less immediately relevant to democratic practice.

Evangelical theology, O'Donovan contends, needs more than an assemblage of political images. Rather it needs a "full political conceptuality."[45] Central within this conceptuality, he believes, is the notion of *legitimate authority,* for he insists that genuine political freedom is only possible when circumscribed by legitimate authority. Along this line, O'Donovan recognizes that the relation between freedom and authority is paradoxical in the sense that political authority would appear to stand only as an impediment to human freedom, but he argues that while appearing to impede freedom legitimate political authority actually mediates those boundaries within which true freedom becomes possible.

> Political authority . . . mediates good to us, but it is a distinct form of mediation which can have the immediate character of a limitation. [Hence] [T]he task of any theory of authority is to explain how the good can and must present itself to us in this alienated and alienating form, and yet without ceasing to be our good, that to which our action is oriented.[46]

Political authority, O'Donovan continues, can only do this if it is understood as a function and extension of "the kingly rule of God."[47] God has determined what is good for his creation, and it is only within the limits that God has set for his creatures that they can truly prosper and experience the kind of freedom for which he has created them. Political authority, then, is understood as an aspect of God's providential governance of his creation.

O'Donovan goes on to insist that such a notion of legitimate authority cannot be established by reason alone, but must be determined in the light of "revealed history" and, in particular, in light of the history of Israel.[48] He thus spends a great deal of time in *The Desire of the Nations* distilling the following political "theorems" from Israel's history in the Old Testament:

45. O'Donovan, *The Desire of the Nations,* p. 2.
46. O'Donovan, *The Desire of the Nations,* p. 31.
47. O'Donovan, *The Desire of the Nations,* pp. 30ff.
48. O'Donovan, *The Desire of the Nations,* p. 21.

Political authority arises where power, the execution of right and the per-petuation of tradition are assumed together in one coordinated agency.

That any regime should actually come to hold authority, and should con-tinue to hold it, is a work of divine providence in history, not a mere ac-complishment of the human task of political service.

In acknowledging political authority, society proves its political identity. [i.e., that political life is basic, not a devolution from an original pre-political state of some kind].[49]

The authority of a human regime mediates divine authority in a unitary structure, but is subject to the authority of law within the community, which bears independent witness to the divine command.[50]

Hence the only appropriate unifying element in political order, as well as the sole source of legitimate political authority, is not government *per se,* but *law,* law derived ultimately from the law of God.[51]

The New Testament, O'Donovan suggests, adds little to this under-standing of political authority, but it does universalize it. Such an under-standing is not simply applicable to the nation of Israel, but to all nations and governments and at all times. The church also reinterprets the role that political authority plays in the "perpetuation of tradition" to mean simply that it is the task of government to preserve whatever social "space" is necessary for the Christian message to be preached freely and in a peace-ful and orderly fashion.[52] The primary way governments provide and en-sure this space is by way of their exercise of "judgment," i.e., punishing wickedness. In the apostle Paul's teaching, for example, the articulation and execution of judgment alone justifies secular government.[53]

Yet O'Donovan observes that the New Testament also understands secular government to pose a threat to the church in the form of a kind of idolatrous alternative to the kingdom of Christ, thus interpreting the long-standing tension in the church's understanding of its relation to the state.

---

49. O'Donovan, *The Desire of the Nations,* pp. 46-47.
50. O'Donovan, *The Desire of the Nations,* p. 65 (italics in the original).
51. O'Donovan, *The Desire of the Nations,* p. 72.
52. O'Donovan, *The Desire of the Nations,* p. 146.
53. O'Donovan, *The Desire of the Nations,* p. 148.

[I]t was possible for the apostolic church to look at the relation of church and secular government from one of two angles. On the one hand, government could be seen as thrust back by Christ's victory to the margins, there to be reauthorised to perform a single function of which the church outside the world stood in need for the time being. On the other hand, it could be seen as goaded by Christ's victory to a last desperate assertion of itself, momentarily overwhelming the church's solidarity in an alternative, massively smothering solidarity of refusal. Either way the victory of Christ was the key to the relation.[54]

The church's stance vis-à-vis the state, then, might be described as one of "loyal opposition." On the one hand, the church fully supports the state's ministry of justice and its preservation of civil order. Indeed, the church seeks to model and exemplify the ideals of civility in its own life and organization. O'Donovan calls this modeling political theology in its "ecclesiastical mode."[55] On the other hand, in its "liberal mode" the church prophetically denounces false ideas and ideologies, particularly those that would elevate the state above its proper and relatively limited place.[56] While the church's political theology in both "modes" evolved in a variety of ways over successive centuries, the idea that the authority of human regimes derives ultimately *from* and is accountable *to* divine authority was always preserved. Indeed, O'Donovan insists that the final and greatest legal accomplishment of Christendom "was the conception that there exists, not merely as an ideal but in fact, an international law, dependent on no regime and no statute, but on the Natural Law implanted in human minds by God, and given effect by international custom and convention."[57]

Turning his attention to modern democracy, O'Donovan first stresses that democracy must have pride of place in contemporary Christian consideration of political systems. "There is no other model available to us," he writes, "of a political order derived from a millennium of close engagement between state and church. [Democracy] ought, therefore, to have the first word in any discussion of what Christians can approve, even if it ought not to have the last word."[58] Not only does democracy bear witness

54. O'Donovan, *The Desire of the Nations*, pp. 156-57.
55. O'Donovan, *The Desire of the Nations*, p. 123.
56. O'Donovan, *The Desire of the Nations*, p. 123.
57. O'Donovan, *The Desire of the Nations*, p. 236.
58. O'Donovan, *The Desire of the Nations*, p. 228.

to the high value Christianity places upon human freedom before God, but it also bears witness to how carefully political authorities must, before God, treat individual persons. In addition, democracy bears witness to the importance of *speech* within Christian understanding for, as O'Donovan notes, anyone within the public realm who can address the community about the common good must be allowed to speak, lest the voice of prophecy, echoing the divine law, should go unheard.[59]

Yet O'Donovan observes that under the influence of seventeenth-century "contract theory," modern democracy has become increasingly detached from the theological convictions that originally gave rise to it. Rather than understanding the state's responsibility primarily in terms of adherence to divine law, the state's responsibility has increasingly come to be understood as being simply to "the people" by whose act the state was supposedly constituted. The act of "popular will" has thus come to be understood as the sole source of all law and constituted order.[60] Among other things, this unfortunate shift has resulted in the disconnection of freedom from authority in the name of liberty, in the devolution of the notion of Natural Right into merely individual "rights," and in the emergence of such a Babel of "free speech" that true prophecy can no longer be heard.[61] Modern democracy thus stands, no less than an evangelical church seeking to ground civic engagement, in need of a recovery of the roots of political theology.

The full conceptuality for political theology that O'Donovan offers evangelicals in *The Desire of the Nations* is excellent and important. Like Wolterstorff, O'Donovan grounds political life in basic theological affirmations and makes it abundantly clear that participation in civic affairs is an evangelical duty fully authorized by the gospel of Jesus Christ. The emphasis O'Donovan places upon human freedom, furthermore, makes it very clear that Christian participation in political life must be such as to respect the freedom — and particularly the freedom of speech — of others. The prospects for "this-worldly" political and social change within O'Donovan's system, finally, are plainly circumscribed by Christian hope for the "world to come." Indeed, O'Donovan concludes: "The church will frame its political witness with authenticity, avoiding the characteristic

---

59. O'Donovan, *The Desire of the Nations*, p. 269.
60. O'Donovan, *The Desire of the Nations*, p. 241.
61. O'Donovan, *The Desire of the Nations*, pp. 275ff.

evils of abstract idealism [might we say "fundamentalism"?] and colourless assimilation [might we say "relativism"?], when it stands self-consciously before [the eschatological] horizon and confesses that it looks for the resurrection of the dead and the life of the world to come."[62]

Jeffrey Stout

Admittedly, O'Donovan's diagnosis of the decomposition of democracy under "late modern" conditions is disquieting, and one wonders if in spite of having privileged democracy in his discussion of political theology O'Donovan's criticism of it may not actually have the effect — similar perhaps to that of Radical Orthodoxy — of discouraging evangelical participation in contemporary public policy discourse. Could it not be that contemporary democracy, for all of its failings and in spite of the avowedly secular explanations that are most often offered for it, still gives evidence of a deep goodness that Christian theologians must find some way to affirm? And could it not be that this deep goodness is more than simply a reflection of what remains of Christian cultural capital in the post-Christian context? What if democratic *practice* has — by the grace of God — simply evolved in such a way as to be recognizably good and right? These are the sorts of questions that Princeton religion professor Jeffrey Stout has recently raised in another important assay into the relation of church and state entitled *Democracy and Tradition*.[63]

Stout's central argument is that, however modern democracy is understood in theory, *in practice* it is not and never has been hostile to substantive religious commitments and neither does it exclude from the public square those whose convictions and values are decisively shaped by religious beliefs. Modern democracy, on Stout's account, is itself a "tradition" within which certain goods and virtues are valued and cultivated and within which the notions of "good" and "virtue" are themselves constantly evolving.

Modern democracy inculcates certain habits of reasoning, certain attitudes toward deference and authority in political discussion, and love for

---

62. O'Donovan, *The Desire of the Nations*, p. 288.
63. Stout, *Democracy and Tradition*.

certain goods and virtues, as well as a disposition to respond to certain types of actions, events, or persons with admiration, pity, or horror. This tradition is anything but empty. Its ethical substance, however, is more a matter of enduring attitudes, concerns, dispositions, and patterns of conduct than it is a matter of agreement on a conception of justice. . . .[64]

What modern democracy does ask of all of its participants, Stout continues, is the willingness to give and to explain *ethical* reasons for policy positions and proposals as well as the willingness to respectfully *listen* to those explanations offered by others. It is the democratic practice of giving and asking for ethical reasons, Stout argues, "where the life of democracy principally resides."[65] The life of democracy does not, in other words, reside in procedural neutrality, and neither does it reside in any single comprehensive conception of the good. Rather modern democracy exists in a particular kind of conversation, a conversation ordered and disciplined by civility, humility, reciprocity, and pragmatism.

Democracy involves substantive normative commitments, but does not presume to settle in advance the ranking of our highest values. Nor does it claim to save humanity from sin and death. It takes for granted that reasonable people will differ on their conceptions of piety, in their grounds for hope, in their ultimate concerns, and in their speculations about salvation. Yet it holds that people who differ on such matters can still exchange reasons with one another intelligibly, cooperate in crafting political arrangements that promote justice and decency in their relations with one another, and do both of these things without compromising their integrity. Cooperating democratic citizens tend also to be individuals who care about matters higher than politics, and expect not to get their way on each issue that comes before the public for deliberation.[66]

Stout labels this principled exchanging of reasons and this pragmatic cooperation for the sake the common good a "*modus vivendi* pluralism."[67]

Stout's adversaries in *Democracy and Tradition* are, on the one hand, those who with the late John Rawls have insisted that the only reasons

---

64. Stout, *Democracy and Tradition,* p. 3.
65. Stout, *Democracy and Tradition,* p. 6.
66. Stout, *Democracy and Tradition,* p. 298.
67. Stout, *Democracy and Tradition,* p. 297.

modern democracy can, in effect, process are those that no reasonable person can reasonably deny. Yet such a standard, Stout suggests, unreasonably rules religious reasoning out-of-bounds for public policy purposes. Stout is also critical of those who with Hauerwas and Milbank have denied that purely "secular" reasons can ever be given by anyone and hence that what purports to be religiously neutral political discourse always simply masks an underlying modernist metanarrative. Both positions, Stout contends, misunderstand the peculiar genius of the democratic tradition.

Yet while Stout's criticism of Hauerwas and Milbank would seem to be on target, his criticism of Rawls's notion of "public reason" veers perhaps a bit wide of the mark. For as K. Roberts Skerrett notes in a thoughtful review of Stout's book, while Stout's proposal is attractive as a vision of the public square, it does not provide an adequate account of legitimate lawmaking.[68] The reason for this inadequacy, Skerrett reasons, has to do with the problem of *legitimacy* in a pluralistic democracy. Legitimacy is a problem in a pluralistic democracy because eventually after ethical reasons have been exchanged among citizens, laws must still be passed and these laws will be enforced by the coercive power of the state. If these laws are seen to compromise or even contradict the expressive norms of particular — say, religious — communities, what will keep the political system from seeming illegitimate to those "losing" communities?[69] Pluralism thus makes legitimacy "both difficult and crucial to achieve":

> difficult, because there are indeed reasonable but irreconcilable comprehensive doctrines that guide citizens' norms of what is good; crucial, because it is easy for such rival doctrines to become enemies and to seek to dominate each other through the coercive power of the state. Liberty and legitimacy thus entail each other: liberty makes pluralism an inevitable reality; pluralism makes legitimacy inevitably difficult; legitimacy is necessary to stabilize the basic structures on which liberty depends.[70]

Legitimacy, then, was the thorny problem Rawls sought to resolve with the notion of "public reason," i.e., that when it comes to lawmaking the only

---

68. K. Roberts Skerrett, "Political Liberalism and the Idea of Public Reason: A Response to Jeffrey Stout's Democracy and Tradition," *Social Theory and Practice* 31:2, 173+ (http://www.questia.com/PM.qst?a=o&d=5012080523).

69. Skerrett, "Political Liberalism."

70. Skerrett, "Political Liberalism."

"reasons" that may be deemed admissible are those that can be shown to be undeniable by all reasonable persons.

Now, whether or not the notion of "public reason" actually solves the problem of legitimacy in a pluralistic democracy is debatable, but it is a problem that surely begs for some sort of solution, and Stout's "*modus vivendi* pluralism" does not, in and of itself, appear to solve it. Legitimacy would seem to require, beyond the commitment to give and listen to ethical reasons, the *belief* on the part of democracy's participants that some "common ground" — or "overlapping consensus" to use Rawls's term — exists within which genuine reciprocity is possible. Although this belief is perhaps implicit in Stout's understanding of the democratic "tradition," legitimacy would seem to require this belief to be affirmed more explicitly.[71] Affirming such a belief more explicitly, however, means that Stout's "democratic tradition" consists in more than "enduring attitudes" and "patterns of conduct." It obviously also consists in the common affirmation of an intelligible moral order.

The reason for raising the issue of legitimacy here is simply because, in addition to remembering why and how civic responsibility has been "authorized" within the Christian tradition, fruitful evangelical participation in a *modus vivendi* pluralistic democracy will hinge, it seems to me, upon their being able to think carefully and *theologically* about the possibility of an "overlapping consensus" within which real sense can be made of the notion of *reciprocity*. Put differently, evangelicals must find some way to balance their strong convictions about truth and authority with an equally strong sense of "fairness" and "fair play" in the hurly burly of modern pluralistic democracy. There are plentiful resources within the larger Christian tradition to help evangelicals to do this, i.e., the Natural Law tradition, Luther's and Calvin's emphasis on the Decalogue as the summation of universal moral order, the Golden Rule, etc. Yet unfortunately, because the peculiar problems of multicultural pluralism were not problems with which Christendom had to deal, the tradition does not provide answers ready-at-hand. Evangelicals will have to work them out. Along this line, Stout com-

---

71. It is at just this point that Stout's "*modus vivendi* pluralism" parts company with Chantal Mouffe's "agonistic pluralism" as well as the "postmodern democracy" of Richard Rorty and Stanley Fish, *et al.* For the assumption — made either implicitly or explicitly — that there will always be "common ground" within which sense can be made of "fairness" and "decency" is ultimately metaphysical. It necessarily implies a moral order to which human practical reason has more-or-less immediate intuitive access.

mends Barth's reflections on the relation of "the Truth" to "human truths." Christians who openly affirm Christ as the Truth speak truly, Stout writes, describing Barth's position:

> They utter a truth. The difference between the definite and indefinite articles matters greatly in this context. The church is one place where truths are spoken. It is also, however, a place where many falsehoods are spoken. And it is not the only place where truths are spoken. It does not follow from affirmation of Christ as the one Word of God "that every word spoken outside the circle of the Bible and the Church is a word of false prophecy and therefore valueless, empty and corrupt" (CD IV/3, 97). . . . Thus, when Christians are considering the question of where truths — in the plural — are to be found, they must be prepared to look both inside the church and outside of it. Wherever they look, they must be suspicious and critical, as well as open to the possibility of needing to change their minds. Wherever they find important truths being spoken by other human beings, they must take themselves to have been addressed by Christ himself, by the Truth, the Light, the Word.[72]

Taking a slightly different tack, Glenn Tinder contended in *The Political Meaning of Christianity* (1989) that for Christians to become defensive in the defense of Christian truth signals that something is fundamentally amiss with their grasp of the Christian faith:

> Christians who are very anxious about the fate of God's truth must have forgotten the doctrine of the Holy Spirit, which implies that God does not send his truth into history like a ship that is launched and then forgotten. He is the source at once of the truth human beings face and of the inspiration that enables them to recognize it as the truth and, in a measure, to understand it. If God were not the Holy Spirit, who provides understanding, his Word would be inaudible and the life of Christ without significance. . . . Need Christians, then, fear that God's voice will be drowned out by human error? When they succumb to the temptation of intolerance, do they not betray an assumption that God is incapable of caring for his own concerns?[73]

---

72. Stout, *Democracy and Tradition,* p. 110.
73. Tinder, *The Political Meaning of Christianity,* p. 131.

Tinder's and Barth's comments suggest that there is something fundamentally less-than-Christian about Christian fundamentalism and also that the temptation to fundamentalism is a symptom of a kind of theological amnesia. This amnesia, it seems to me, is the single most significant quandary confronting evangelicals in their search for a constructive political theology. If evangelicals can manage to *stay* in the "vital center" of the modern political discourse it will be because they have somehow managed to remember crucial elements of their own tradition.

Prospect

Remembering their own theological tradition will not come easily for evangelicals, and for any number of reasons. As Daniele Hervieu-Léger argues in *Religion as a Chain of Memory,* the processes of differentiation and modernization have been such as to have cut *all* religious communities off from their memories and traditions. The style of "religiosity" that results from this disconnection with tradition, Hervieu-Léger contends, tends to be individualistic, resistant to the notion of authority and therefore much more susceptible to the vicissitudes of the surrounding culture including, we might add, the mass mediation of "cultural warfare." In addition to this, modern and postmodern "liberalisms" continue to be openly contemptuous of traditional notions of religious authority, particularly in the ambit of higher education where evangelicals might otherwise be expected to have to work their political theology out. Add to this American evangelicalism's own peculiar history of anti-traditionalism and anti-intellectualism, and the obstacles confronting evangelicals in their search for a genuinely Christian political theology would seem to be daunting indeed.[74] As O'Donovan laments in the Prologue to *The Desire of the Nations,* "[T]he relation of the contemporary political theology to the tradition can be summed up in a single bleak word: ignorance . . . for the most part the tradition, with its wealth of suggestive theopolitical debate and analysis, has been occluded by the shadow of the modern period."[75] Yet short of remembering the political-theological resources

---

74. See Mark Noll, *The Scandal of the Evangelical Mind* (Grand Rapids: Eerdmans, 1994); also Noll, "The Evangelical Mind Today," *First Things* 146 (October 2004): 34ff.

75. O'Donovan, *The Desire of the Nations,* p. 4.

within their own tradition it would seem that American evangelicals must remain, by and large, "single-issue" oriented and subject to the polarizing and decidedly uncivil dynamics of the ongoing culture war.

On the other hand, it is also worth remembering the very significant contributions evangelical Christians have made, and continue to make, to the civility and decency of what Stout has called the "democratic tradition." If democratic citizens are those who "care about matters higher than politics, and do not expect to get their way on each issue that comes before the public for deliberation,"[76] then historically many of these citizens have been — and many continue to be — evangelical Christians. In addition, as Wolterstorff observes in prefacing his "theses on government" cited above, there are a number of points on which contemporary evangelicals do, in fact, *already* agree, i.e., that government is divinely authorized, that it is an evangelical duty to support government, that the gospel requires evangelicals to cooperate graciously and in a principled manner with non-Christians, that evangelical expectations of government must be tempered by their understanding of original sin, etc. None of Wolterstorff's theses, with the exception of those with which the Anabaptist tradition would disagree, are particularly controversial within contemporary American evangelicalism, and taken together they provide quite a solid foundation for constructive evangelical engagement with the larger culture both socially and politically. So there is reason for hope.

And speaking of hope, perhaps the single most important thing that bears constant reiteration in the context of a forgetful, anxious, and impatient American culture is that constructive public policy discourse must *always* be informed by hope. Insofar as evangelicals are concerned, hope has always been what has enabled them to act in the world, tackling visible injustices without needing to be assured that their skill and their effort would somehow rid the world of injustice altogether.[77] Christian hope, after all, does not need to *see* what it hopes for (Heb. 11:1); and neither does it require believers to *comprehend* the end of history. Rather it simply requires believers to trust that even the most outwardly insignificant of faithful actions — the cup of cold water given to the child, the widow's mite offered at the temple, the act of hospitality shown to the stranger, none of which have any overall strategic socio-political significance so far

---

76. Stout, *Democracy and Tradition*, p. 298.
77. Tinder, *The Political Meaning of Christianity*, p. 66.

as they can tell — will nevertheless be made to contribute in some signifi-cant way to the construction of God's kingdom by the action of God's cre-ative and sovereign grace. As Oliver O'Donovan comments at the end of his study of evangelical ethics, *Resurrection and Moral Order* (1986), "How-ever much our moral decisions strive for clarity, they are never unambigu-ous or translucent, even to ourselves. But — and is this not the gospel at the heart of evangelical ethics? — it is given to them by God's grace in Christ to add up to a final and unambiguous Yes, a work of love which will abide for eternity."[78]

When it comes to remembering their own theological tradition, then, evangelicals would do well to begin by remembering the hope to which they have been called in Christ. Hope is what will free them to act magnan-imously in whatever social and political circumstances they may happen to find themselves, and it provides the basis for confidence that things will — by the grace of God — turn out well in the end. As Emil Brunner once commented,

> [T]he New Testament says we are living in a wicked world. Therefore to live as a Christian in the State means above all to hope for the new world which lies beyond history — beyond history which always was and will be the history of States — for that world where death and killing, force, coercion, and even law will cease, where the only "power" which will then be valid is the power of love. It is the *meditatio vitae futurae* which makes it possible for the Christian to do his difficult duty in this politi-cal world without becoming hard; and it is this which prevents him from lapsing into irresponsibility out of the fear of becoming hard. Both his joyful readiness for service and his sanity in service spring from this hope.[79]

Needless to say, Brunner's is a profoundly evangelical point of view, and if American evangelicals can be encouraged to remember this they will un-doubtedly make constructive and fruitful contributions to American pub-lic life.

---

78. Oliver O'Donovan, *Resurrection and Moral Order: An Outline for Evangelical Ethics* (Grand Rapids: Eerdmans, 1986), p. 264.

79. Emil Brunner, *The Divine Imperative: A Study in Christian Ethics*, trans. Olive Wyon (Philadelphia: Westminster, 1957), p. 482.

APPENDIX A

For the Health of the Nation:
An Evangelical Call to Civic Responsibility

Preamble

Evangelical Christians in America face a historic opportunity. We make up fully one quarter of all voters in the most powerful nation in history. Never before has God given American evangelicals such an awesome opportunity to shape public policy in ways that could contribute to the well-being of the entire world. Disengagement is not an option.

We must seek God's face for biblical faithfulness and abundant wisdom to rise to this unique challenge.

The special circumstances of this historic moment underline both the opportunity and the challenge.

- Although we have the privilege to help shape the actions of the world's lone superpower, only half of all evangelical Christians bother to vote.
- The presence and role of religion in public life is attacked more fiercely now than ever, making the bias of aggressive secularism the last acceptable prejudice in America.
- Since the atrocities of September 11, 2001, the spiritual and religious dimensions of global conflict have been sharpened.
- Secular media outlets have long acknowledged evangelical involvement in pro-life and family issues, but are taking belated notice of evangelicals' global involvement in activities such as disaster relief, refugee resettlement, and the fights against AIDS/HIV, human rights abuses, slavery, sexual trafficking, and prison rape.
- Some key American political leaders now conceive of their roles in

moral terms. And they see themselves as stewards of the blessings of representative democracy, religious freedom, and human rights in a world where many nations are endangered by the forces of authoritarianism or radical secularism.

Evangelicals may not always agree about policy, but we realize that we have many callings and commitments in common: commitments to the protection and well-being of families and children, of the poor, the sick, the disabled, and the unborn, of the persecuted and oppressed, and of the rest of the created order. While these issues do not exhaust the concerns of good government, they provide the platform for evangelicals to engage in common action.

Despite our common commitments and this moment of opportunity, American evangelicals continue to be ambivalent about civic engagement.

In 1947, Carl F. H. Henry pricked our uneasy consciences and spurred us toward responsible social and political engagement. In the years since, the National Association of Evangelicals has routinely engaged our political leaders through its Office of Governmental Affairs and worked to educate member churches on current issues. In recent decades, a variety of evangelical political voices have emerged. Yet evangelicals have failed to engage with the breadth, depth, and consistency to which we are called.

Scholars and leaders have inspired us by drawing attention to historical exemplars of evangelical public responsibility from Wilberforce and the Booths in England to Edwards, Backus, Garnet, Finney, and Palmer in America. Our spiritual ancestors did not always agree on the specifics of governance and the best roads to social reform. Yet their passion and sacrifice inspire us to creative engagement, even when we cannot fully agree on policy prescriptions.

Against this historical background and in view of these common commitments, we offer the following principled framework for evangelical public engagement.

The Basis for Christian Civic Engagement

We engage in public life because God created our first parents in his image and gave them dominion over the earth (Gen. 1:27-28). The responsibilities that emerge from that mandate are many, and in a modern society those responsibilities rightly flow to many different institutions, including governments, families, churches, schools, businesses, and labor unions. Just governance is part of our calling in creation.

We also engage in public life because Jesus is Lord over every area of life. Through him all things were created (Col. 1:16-17), and by him all things will be brought to fullness (Rom. 8:19-21). To restrict our stewardship to the private sphere would be to deny an important part of his dominion and to functionally abandon it to the Evil One. To restrict our political concerns to matters that touch only on the private and the domestic spheres is to deny the all-encompassing Lordship of Jesus (Rev. 19:16).

Following in the tradition of the Hebrew prophets, Jesus announced the arrival of God's kingdom (God's "reign" or "rule") (Matt. 4:17; Mark 1:15). This kingdom would be marked by justice, peace, forgiveness, restoration, and healing for all. Jesus' followers have come to understand the time between his first and second comings as a period of "already, but not yet," in which we experience many of the blessings of God's reign and see initial signs of restoration, while we continue to suffer many of the results of the Fall. We know that we must wait for God to bring about the fullness of the kingdom at Christ's return. But in this interim, the Lord calls the church to speak prophetically to society and work for the renewal and reform of its structures. The Lord also calls the church to practice the righteous deeds of the kingdom and point to the kingdom by the wholeness and integrity of the church's common life. This example will require us to demonstrate God's love for all, by crossing racial, ethnic, economic, and national boundaries. It will also often involve following Jesus' example by suffering and living sacrificially for others.

As Christian citizens, we believe it is our calling to help government live up to its divine mandate to render justice (Rom. 13:1-7; 1 Pet. 2:13-17). From the teachings of the Bible and our experience of salvation, we Christians bring a unique vision to our participation in the political order and a conviction that changed people and transformed communities are possible. In the power of the Holy Spirit, we are compelled outward in service to God and neighbor.

Jesus calls us as his followers to love our neighbors as ourselves. Our goal in civic engagement is to bless our neighbors by making good laws. Because we have been called to do justice to our neighbors, we foster a free press, participate in open debate, vote, and hold public office. When Christians do justice, it speaks loudly about God. And it can show those who are

not believers how the Christian vision can contribute to the common good
and help alleviate the ills of society.

The Method of Christian Civic Engagement

Every political judgment requires both a normative vision and factual
analysis. The more carefully and precisely we Christians think about the
complex details of both, the more clearly we will be able to explain our
views to others and understand — and perhaps overcome — disagreements with others.

Every normative vision has some understanding of persons, creation,
history, justice, life, family, and peace. As Christians committed to the full
authority of Scripture, our normative vision must flow from the Bible and
from the moral order that God has embedded in his creation.

Evangelical Christians seek in every area of life to submit to the authority of Scripture (2 Tim. 3:16-17; Rom. 15:4; 1 Cor. 10:11). Nevertheless,
many contemporary political decisions — whether about environmental
science, HIV/AIDS, or international trade — deal with complex sociological or technological issues not discussed explicitly in the Bible. As Christians engaged in public policy, we must do detailed social, economic, historical, jurisprudential, and political analysis if we are to understand our
society and wisely apply our normative vision to political questions. Only
if we deepen our Christian vision and also study our contemporary world
can we engage in politics faithfully and wisely.

From the Bible, experience, and social analysis, we learn that social
problems arise and can be substantially corrected by both personal decisions and structural changes. On the one hand, personal sinful choices
contribute significantly to destructive social problems (Prov. 6:9-11), and
personal conversion through faith in Christ can transform broken persons
into wholesome, productive citizens. On the other hand, unjust systems
also help create social problems (Amos 5:10-15; Isa. 10:1-2) and wise structural change (for example legislation to strengthen marriage or increase
economic opportunity for all) can improve society. Thus Christian civic
engagement must seek to transform both individuals and institutions.
While individuals transformed by the gospel change surrounding society,
social institutions also shape individuals. While good laws encourage good
behavior, bad laws and systems foster destructive action. Lasting social

change requires both personal conversion and institutional renewal and reform.

The Bible makes it clear that God cares a great deal about the well-being of marriage, the family, the sanctity of human life, justice for the poor, care for creation, peace, freedom, and racial justice. While individual persons and organizations are at times called by God to concentrate on one or two issues, faithful evangelical civic engagement must champion a biblically balanced agenda.

Humility and Civility

As sinners who are thankful for God's grace, we know that we do not always live up to our civic responsibility. Christians must approach political engagement with humility and with earnest prayer for divine guidance and wisdom. Because power structures are often entrenched, perfect solutions are unobtainable. Because cultural changes produce problems that are often not amenable to legislative solutions, we must not expect political activity to achieve more than it can. Because social systems are complex and our knowledge is incomplete, we cannot predict all the effects of laws, policies, and regulations. As a result, we must match our high ideals with careful social analysis and critical reflection on our experience in order to avoid supporting policies that produce unintended and unfortunate consequences.

We will differ with other Christians and with non-Christians over the best policies. Thus we must practice humility and cooperation to achieve modest and attainable goals for the good of society. We must take care to employ the language of civility and to avoid denigrating those with whom we disagree. Because political work requires persuasion and cooperation with those who do not share our Christian commitment, we must offer a reasoned and easy-to-grasp defense of our goals.

When we as Christians engage in political activity, we must maintain our integrity and keep our biblical values intact. While we may frequently settle for "half-a-loaf," we must never compromise principle by engaging in unethical behavior or endorsing or fostering sin. As we rightly engage in supporting legislation, candidates, and political parties, we must be clear that biblical faith is vastly larger and richer than every limited, inevitably imperfect political agenda and that commitment to the Lordship of Christ and his one body far transcends all political commitments.

Craig M. Gay

The Structures of Public Life

In the beginning, God called human beings to govern and to care for the creation.

Faithfulness to this call has taken different forms as human beings have lived in family groups, in tribes and clans, in kingdoms and empires, and now in modern nation-states in an increasingly interconnected global community. Today we live in a complex society in which few people are directly involved in governing and in which complicated problems do not readily yield straightforward solutions.

God has ordered human society with various institutions and set in place forms of government to maintain public order, to restrain human evil, and to promote the common good. God has called all people to share responsibility for creating a healthy society. Human beings work out their different ways of obeying God's call as spouses, parents, workers, and participants in the wide variety of human networks. Some, however, are called to particular roles of governance. We must support and pray for all those who shoulder the burdens of government (1 Tim. 2:1-2).

Representative Democracy

We thank God for the blessings of representative democracy, which allow all citizens to participate in government by electing their representatives, helping to set the priorities for government, and by sharing publicly the insights derived from their experience. We are grateful that we live in a society in which citizens can hold government responsible for fulfilling its responsibilities to God and abiding by the norms of justice.

We support the democratic process in part because people continue to be sufficiently blessed by God's common grace that they can seek not only their own betterment, but also the welfare of others. We also support democracy because we know that since the Fall, people often abuse power for selfish purposes. As Lord Acton noted, power tends to corrupt and absolute power corrupts absolutely. Thus we thank God for a constitutional system that decentralizes power through the separation of powers, fair elections, limited terms of office, and division among national, state, and local authorities.

As Christians we confess that our primary allegiance is to Christ, his kingdom, and Christ's worldwide body of believers, not to any nation. God has blessed America with bounty and with strength, but unless these blessings are used for the good of all, they will turn to our destruction. As Christian citizens of the United States, we must keep our eyes open to the potentially self-destructive tendencies of our society and our government. We must also balance our natural affection for our country with a love for people of all nations and an active desire to see them prosper. We invite Christians outside the United States to aid us in broadening our perspectives on American life and action.

Just Government and Fundamental Liberty

God is the source of all true law and genuine liberty. He both legitimates and limits the state's authority. Thus, while we owe Caesar his due (Matt. 22:15-22; Mark 12:13-17; Luke 20:20-26), we regard only Jesus as Lord. As King of Kings, Jesus' authority extends over Caesar. As followers of Jesus, we obey government authorities when they act in accord with God's justice and his laws (Titus 3:1). But we also resist government when it exercises its power in an unjust manner (Acts 5:27-32) or tries to dominate other institutions in society. A good government preserves the God-ordained responsibilities of society's other institutions, such as churches, other faith-centered organizations, schools, families, labor unions, and businesses.

Principles of Christian Political Engagement

We work to protect religious freedom and liberty of conscience.
God has ordained the two co-existing institutions of church and state as distinct and independent of each other with each having its own areas of responsibility (Rom. 13:1-7; Mark 12:13-17; Eph. 4:15-16, 5:23-32). We affirm the principles of religious freedom and liberty of conscience, which are both historically and logically at the foundation of the American experiment. They are properly called the First Freedom and are now vested in the First Amendment. The First Amendment's guarantees of freedom of speech, association, and religion provide the political space in which we can carry out our differing responsibilities. Because human beings are responsible to God, these guarantees are crucial to the exercise of their God-

given freedom. As God allows the wheat and tares to grow together until the harvest, and as God sends the rain on the just and on the unjust, so those who obey and those who disobey God coexist in society and share in its blessings (Matt. 5:45, 13:24-30). This "gospel pluralism" is foundational to the religious liberty of all.

Participating in the public square does not require people to put aside their beliefs or suspend the practice of their religion. All persons should have equal access to public forums, regardless of the religious content or viewpoint of their speech. Likewise, judicial standards should protect and respect not only religiously compelled practices, but also religiously motivated behavior.

The First Amendment's Establishment Clause is directed only at government and restrains its power. Thus, for example, the clause was never intended to shield individuals from exposure to the religious views of nongovernmental speakers. Exemptions from regulations or tax burdens do not violate the Establishment Clause, for government does not establish religion by leaving it alone. When government assists nongovernmental organizations as part of an evenhanded educational, social service, or health care program, religious organizations receiving such aid do not become "state actors" with constitutional duties. Courts should respect church autonomy in matters relating to doctrine, polity, the application of its governing documents, church discipline, clergy and staff employment practices, and other matters within the province of the church (Acts 18:12-17).

Religion is not just an individual matter, but also refers to rich communal traditions of ultimate belief and practice. We resist the definition of religion becoming either radically individualized or flattened out to mean anything that passes for a serious conviction. Thus, while the First Amendment protects religiously informed conscience, it does not protect all matters of sincere concern.

We work to nurture family life and protect children.

From Genesis onward, the Bible tells us that the family is central to God's vision for human society. God has revealed himself to us in the language of family, adopting us as his children (Rom. 8:23; Gal. 4:5) and teaching us by the Holy Spirit to call him *Abba Father* (Rom. 8:15; Gal. 4:6). Marriage, which is a lifetime relationship between one man and one woman, is the predominant biblical icon of God's relationship with his people (Isa. 54:5; Jer. 3:20, 31:32; Ezek. 16:32; Eph. 5:23, 31-32). In turn, family life reveals something to us about God, as human families mirror, however faintly, the inner life of the Trinity. The mutuality and service of family life contrast strongly with the hypermodern emphasis on individual freedom and rights. Marriage, sexuality, and family life are fundamental to society. Whether we are married or single, it is in the family that we learn mutual responsibility, we learn to live in an ordered society with complementary and distinct roles, we learn to submit and to obey, we learn to love and to trust, we learn both justice and mercy, and we learn to deny ourselves for the well-being of others. Thus the family is at the heart of the organic functioning of society.

Government does not have the primary responsibility for guaranteeing wholesome family life. That is the job of families themselves and of other institutions, especially churches. But governments should understand that people are more than autonomous individuals; they live in families and many are married. While providing individuals with ways to remedy or escape abusive relationships, governments should promote laws and policies that strengthen the well-being of families.

Many social evils — such as alcohol, drug, gambling, or credit-card abuse, pornography, sexual libertinism, spousal or child sexual abuse, easy divorce, abortion on demand — represent the abandonment of responsibility or the violation of trust by family members, and they seriously impair the ability of family members to function in society. These evils must be viewed not only as matters of individual sin and dysfunction, but also as violations of family integrity. Because the family is so important to society, violations of its integrity threaten public order. Similarly, employment, labor, housing, health care, and educational policies concern not only individuals but seriously affect families. In order to strengthen the family, we must promote biblical moral principles, responsible personal choices, and good public policies on marriage and divorce law, shelter, food, health care, education, and a family wage (James 5:1-6).

Good family life is so important to healthy human functioning that we oppose government efforts to trespass on its territory: whether by encroaching on parental responsibilities to educate their children, by treating other kinds of households as the family's social and legal equivalent, or by creating economic disincentives to marriage.

We commit ourselves to work for laws that protect and foster family life, and against government attempts to interfere with the integrity of the family. We also oppose innovations such as same-sex "marriage." We will work for measures that strengthen the economic viability of marriages and families, especially among the poor. We likewise commit ourselves to work within the church and society to strengthen marriages, to reduce the rate of divorce, and to prepare young adults for healthy family life.

We work to protect the sanctity of human life and to safeguard its nature. Because God created human beings in his image, all people share in the divine dignity. And because the Bible reveals God's calling and care of persons before they are born, the preborn share in this dignity (Ps. 139:13).

We believe that abortion, euthanasia, and unethical human experimentation violate the God-given dignity of human beings. As these practices gain social approval and become legitimized in law, they undermine the legal and cultural protections that our society has provided for vulnerable persons. Human dignity is indivisible. A threat to the aged, to the very young, to the unborn, to those with disabilities, or to those with genetic diseases is a threat to all.

The book of Genesis portrays human attempts to transcend creaturely humility before God as rebellion against God. Christians must witness in the political sphere to the limits of our creatureliness and warn against the dangers of dissatisfaction with human limits.

As many others in the West, we have had such faith in science and its doctrine of progress that we are unprepared for the choices biotechnology now brings us. We urge evangelicals with specialized scientific knowledge to help Christians and policymakers to think through these issues. As technologies related to cloning and creating inheritable genetic modifications are being refined, society is less able to create a consensus on what is good and what limits we should place on human modification. The uniqueness of human nature is at stake.

Where the negative implications of biotechnology are unknown, government ought to err on the side of caution. Christians must welcome and support medical research that uses stem cells from adult donors and other ethical avenues of research. But we must work toward complete bans on human cloning and embryonic stem-cell research, as well as for laws against discrimination based on genetic information.

We seek justice and compassion for the poor and vulnerable.
Jesus summed up God's law by commanding us to love God with all that we are and to love our neighbors as ourselves (Matt. 22:35-40). By deed and

parable, he taught us that anyone in need is our neighbor (Luke 10:29-37). Because all people are created in the image of God, we owe each other help in time of need.

God identifies with the poor (Ps. 146:5-9), and says that those who "are kind to the poor lend to the Lord" (Prov. 19:17), while those who oppress the poor "show contempt for their Maker" (Prov. 14:31). Jesus said that those who do not care for the needy and the imprisoned will depart eternally from the living God (Matt. 25:31-46). The vulnerable may include not only the poor, but women, children, the aged, persons with disabilities, immigrants, refugees, minorities, the persecuted, and prisoners. God measures societies by how they treat the people at the bottom.

God's prophets call his people to create just and righteous societies (Isa. 10:1-4, 58:3-12; Jer. 5:26-29, 22:13-19; Amos 2:6-7, 4:1-3, 5:10-15). The prophetic teaching insists on both a fair legal system (which does not favor either the rich or the poor) and a fair economic system (which does not tolerate perpetual poverty). Though the Bible does not call for economic equality, it condemns gross disparities in opportunity and outcome that cause suffering and perpetuate poverty, and it calls us to work toward equality of opportunity. God wants every person and family to have access to productive resources so that if they act responsibly they can care for their economic needs and be dignified members of their community. Christians reach out to help others in various ways: through personal charity, effective faith-based ministries, and other nongovernmental associations, and by advocating for effective government programs and structural changes.

Economic justice includes both the mitigation of suffering and also the restoration of wholeness. Wholeness includes full participation in the life of the community. Health care, nutrition, and education are important ingredients in helping people transcend the stigma and agony of poverty and re-enter community. Since healthy family systems are important for nurturing healthy individuals and overcoming poverty, public policy should encourage marriage and sexual abstinence outside marriage, while discouraging early onset of sexual activity, out-of-wedlock births, and easy divorce. Government should also hold fathers and mothers responsible for the maintenance of their families, enforcing where necessary the collection of child-support payments.

Restoring people to wholeness means that governmental social welfare must aim to provide opportunity and restore people to self-sufficiency.

While basic standards of support must be put in place to provide for those who cannot care for their families and themselves, incentives and training in marketable skills must be part of any well-rounded program. We urge Christians who work in the political realm to shape wise laws pertaining to the creation of wealth, wages, education, taxation, immigration, health care, and social welfare that will protect those trapped in poverty and empower the poor to improve their circumstances.

We further believe that care for the vulnerable should extend beyond our national borders. American foreign policy and trade policies often have an impact on the poor. We should try to persuade our leaders to change patterns of trade that harm the poor and to make the reduction of global poverty a central concern of American foreign policy. We must support policies that encourage honesty in government, correct unfair socioeconomic structures, generously support effective programs that empower the poor, and foster economic development and prosperity. Christians should also encourage continued government support of international aid agencies, including those that are faith based.

Especially in the developing world, extreme poverty, lack of health care, the spread of HIV/AIDS, inadequate nutrition, unjust and unstable economies, slavery and sexual trafficking, the use of rape as a tool of terror and oppression, civil war, and government cronyism and graft create the conditions in which large populations become vulnerable. We support Christian agencies and American foreign policy that effectively correct these political problems and promote just, democratic structures.

We work to protect human rights.
Because God created human beings in his image, we are endowed with rights and responsibilities. In order to carry out these responsibilities, human beings need the freedom to form associations, formulate and express beliefs, and act on conscientiously held commitments.

As recipients of God's gift of embodied life, people need food, nurture, shelter, and care. In order to fulfill their God-given tasks, all people have a right to private property. God's design for human existence also implies a right to marry, enjoy family life, and raise and educate children. While it is not the primary role of government to provide everything that humans need for their well-being, governments are obligated to ensure that people are not unjustly deprived of them and to strengthen families, schools, businesses, hospitals, social-service organizations, and other institutions so they can contribute to human welfare. At the same time, government must fulfill its responsibilities to provide for the general welfare and promote the common good.

Governments should be constitutionally obligated to protect basic human rights. Documents like the UN's Universal Declaration of Human Rights are attempts to articulate the kind of treatment that every person deserves from the government under which they live. Insofar as a person has a human right, that person should be able to appeal to an executive, legislative, or judicial authority to enforce or adjudicate that right.

We believe that American foreign policy should reward those countries that respect human rights and should not reward (and prudently employ certain sanctions against) those countries that abuse or deny such rights. We urge the United States to increase its commitments to developing democracy and civil society in former colonial lands, Muslim nations, and countries emerging from Communism. Because the Creator gave human beings liberty, we believe that religious liberty, including the right to change one's religion, is a foundational right that must be respected by governments (Article 18, Universal Declaration of Human Rights). Freedom of expression and freedom of assembly are closely related to religious liberty, and people must be free to express their vision for a just social order without fear of torture or other reprisal.

We also oppose the expansion of "rights talk" to encompass so-called rights such as "same-sex marriage" or "the right to die." Inappropriately expanded rights language has begun to function as a trump card in American discourse that unfairly shuts down needed discussion.

America has a tragic history of mistreating Native Americans, the cruel practice of slavery, and the subsequent segregation and exploitation of the descendants of slaves. While the United States has achieved legal and social equality in principle, the legacy of racism still makes many African Americans, Hispanics, and other ethnic minorities particularly vulnerable to a variety of social ills. Our churches have a special responsibility to model good race relations (Rom. 10:12). To correct the lingering effects of our racist history, Christians should support well-conceived efforts that foster dignity and responsibility.

We seek peace and work to restrain violence.
Jesus and the prophets looked forward to the time when God's reign would bring about just and peaceful societies in which people would enjoy the

fruits of their labor without interference from foreign oppressors or unjust rulers. But from the beginning, Christians have recognized that God did not call them to bring in God's kingdom by force. While all Christians have agreed that governments should protect and restore just and peaceful social orders, we have long differed on when governments may use force and whether we may participate in government-authorized force to defend our homelands, rescue others from attack, or liberate other people from oppression.

The peaceful settling of disputes is a gift of common grace. We urge governments to pursue thoroughly nonviolent paths to peace before resorting to military force. We believe that if governments are going to use military force, they must use it in the service of peace and not merely in their national interest. Military force must be guided by the classical just-war principles, which are designed to restrain violence by establishing the right conditions for and right conduct in fighting a war. In an age of nuclear and biological terrorism, such principles are more important than ever.

We urge followers of Jesus to engage in practical peacemaking locally, nationally, and internationally. As followers of Jesus, we should, in our civic capacity, work to reduce conflict by promoting international understanding and engaging in non-violent conflict resolution.

We labor to protect God's creation.

As we embrace our responsibility to care for God's earth, we reaffirm the important truth that we worship only the Creator and not the creation. God gave the care of his earth and its species to our first parents. That responsibility has passed into our hands. We affirm that God-given dominion is a sacred responsibility to steward the earth and not a license to abuse the creation of which we are a part. We are not the owners of creation, but its stewards, summoned by God to "watch over and care for it" (Gen. 2:15). This implies the principle of sustainability: our uses of the Earth must be designed to conserve and renew the Earth rather than to deplete or destroy it.

The Bible teaches us that God is not only redeeming his people, but is also restoring the whole creation (Rom. 8:18-23). Just as we show our love for the Savior by reaching out to the lost, we believe that we show our love for the Creator by caring for his creation.

Because clean air, pure water, and adequate resources are crucial to public health and civic order, government has an obligation to protect its citizens from the effects of environmental degradation. This involves the urgent need to relieve human suffering caused by bad environmental practice. Because natural systems are extremely complex, human actions can have unexpected side effects. We must therefore approach our stewardship of creation with humility and caution.

Human beings have responsibility for creation in a variety of ways. We urge Christians to shape their personal lives in creation-friendly ways: practicing effective recycling, conserving resources, and experiencing the joy of contact with nature. We urge government to encourage fuel efficiency, reduce pollution, encourage sustainable use of natural resources, and provide for the proper care of wildlife and their natural habitats.

Our Commitment

We commit ourselves to support Christians who engage in political and social action in a manner consistent with biblical teachings. We call on Christian leaders in public office or with expertise in public policy and political life, to help us deepen our perspective on public policy and political life so that we might better fulfill our civic responsibility.

We call on all Christians to become informed and then to vote, as well as to regularly communicate biblical values to their government representatives. We urge all Christians to take their civic responsibility seriously even when they are not full-time political activists so that they might more adequately call those in government to their task. We also encourage our children to consider vocations in public service.

We call churches and trans-denominational agencies to cultivate an understanding of civic responsibility and public justice among their members. Seminaries and Christian colleges have a special responsibility to imbue future leaders with a sense of civic responsibility.

We call all Christians to a renewed political engagement that aims to protect the vulnerable and poor, to guard the sanctity of human life, to further racial reconciliation and justice, to renew the family, to care for creation, and to promote justice, freedom, and peace for all.

Above all, we commit ourselves to regular prayer for those who govern, that God may prosper their efforts to nurture life, justice, freedom, and peace.

THEOLOGICAL DIRECTIONS

Religious Conviction in a Diverse World: A Jewish Perspective on Fundamentalism and Relativism

David M. Gordis

From the perspective of the early years of the twenty-first century, the widespread expectations of a few decades ago that religion would decline in its influence on world affairs or even disappear completely, tax credibility. Religious voices are more audible in the public square than perhaps at any time in recent history. The nexus of religion and political power has been strengthened across the globe and religiously motivated conflict continues to erupt in widely separated arenas. Defying earlier expectations, religion is a force to be reckoned with in world affairs, and no informed and competent observers are suggesting that this religious voice will diminish in audibility or impact in the foreseeable future. This observation provides the backdrop for this inquiry.

Having said this, neither "fundamentalism" nor "relativism" is a term that finds a comfortable place in Jewish discourse. In fact, though I will attempt to clarify my focus in the present inquiry, I should state that I find the "fundamentalism-relativism" dipole somewhat problematic. "Fundamentalism" is, of course, a term that arose in a specific Protestant context and gradually came to more generally describe the belief in the literal truth of scripture, as opposed to a more liberal approach to the canon and to classical religious formulations. "Relativism" is meant to imply the assertion that all values are "relative" and therefore to deny the ultimate truth claims of any value set. Relativism as commonly understood denies the claims to absolute authority, allegiance, and commitment of any value system, religious or otherwise. It follows that the inquiry into a middle ground between fundamentalism and relativism might best be recast as an inquiry into the question: Can religiously rooted values generate commitment and allegiance though they are based on something other than a literal interpretation of scripture and canon?

At first glance, the answer to the question so stated seems self-evident: Of course, non-literal religious approaches can and do generate commitments to values. A simple perusal of the broad range of adherents of non-literalist religious positions who affirm both in theory and practice a passionate commitment to religious values should set the matter to rest. But the question remains: How does a non-literalist religious position ground its value commitment?

The timeliness, and even urgency, of this inquiry does not, however, rest on the epistemological question, as interesting as it may be. What is of particular and immediate significance is not the *process* through which non-literalists ground their value systems but rather the content of those value systems, and their articulation in the public square. Whether derived from a literalist or a liberal reading of scripture, a commitment to protect the poor and underprivileged or to protect human life, for example, creates no societal problem in the abstract, even if some applications of these values to specific situations may raise issues. Specifically, the contemporary challenge raised by the renewed presence of religiously generated attitudes, beliefs, and behaviors relates to the treatment of the "other" in religious formulations. No religious formulations are immune to the dangers of triumphalism inherent in positions that claim exclusive access to truth and virtue, a claim that characterizes all of our Abrahamic religious traditions in one form or another. But fundamentalist/literalist religious positions have historically been most prone to translating these claims of exclusive access to truth and virtue into hostility to "others."

The mechanism of this translation is readily understood. If my position represents the truth, then yours does not. Your rejection of the truth constitutes a challenge. My response to that challenge is to attempt to transform you into a copy of myself, i.e., bring you into my group and compel you to accept my truth claims, or rid your presence from whatever environment I control through expulsion or annihilation. Clearly, commitment to this position makes coexistence in a diverse society or world difficult if not impossible.

The problem generated by religious claims to exclusive access to truth is compounded by the role of the religious narrative in shaping identity. Clearly, the development of identity is linked to membership in a variety of groups including family, nation, and religious community and the establishment of borders between those who are in the group and those who are outside it. To the extent that this process invokes invidious comparison with the other, the problem of dealing with the "other" is compounded. If the process of identity formation is accomplished through explicit or implicit contrasting by the "insider" of the in-group with those who are outside it, the nexus of this process with religious truth claims becomes particularly problematical.

I write as a modern religious person, which is worth noting here because of my understanding of the two key insights provided by modernity related to the human condition: the universality of the human odyssey despite the range of cultural expressions and narratives adopted to describe this odyssey; and the critical need to ask not only "religious" questions, i.e., "What are my beliefs and how are they grounded?" but also "metareligious questions," i.e., "What is the impact of my beliefs on the world?"

All this leads me to formulate the current inquiry in the following terms: Given the prominent role of religion in addressing the human condition and providing instruments for traversing the experience of human life, how can one best respond to the reality that religion has historically contributed to generating or aggravating the pathological pattern of human interrelationships and continues to contribute to that pathology in the contemporary world? This may be a particularly acute issue for literalist/fundamentalist positions, but all religious positions have contributed to the problem. Is the appropriate response to abandon religion entirely as irredeemable? Is the only alternative to absolutism and literalism the abandonment of commitment to values entirely? Can religion be recast in such ways that it does not contribute to the pathology of dealing with otherness? And further, can we uncover in religious traditions resources to not only not compound the problem but also to contribute to healing and repair of the tattered fabric of human relationships in the contemporary world?

What I shall attempt to offer here is a Jewish response to these questions. My intention is twofold: first, to offer Jews a reading of their tradition that allows them to see the other in a non-problematical way, not as a challenge but as a resource for the enhancement of their own human experience; second, to offer a religious approach to all religious communities that can suggest ways of constructive attitudes towards others, without abandonment of the religious commitments of their respective traditions. The latter will require me to find a way to transcend particularist lines and propose a mode of thinking that can be helpful irrespective of one's confessional community. I will set out on this task in three steps: first, I will briefly describe the parameters of Jewish tradition and culture; second, I will cite specific references to dealing with the other in Jewish traditional sources and formulations; third, I will attempt to draw some generally applicable lessons for contemporary religion from the character of Jewish discourse.

It is important to offer a disclaimer at the outset: the Jewish community has no religious hierarchy, and there is no "formal" or "official" Jewish view on virtually any subject. I am certainly not proposing to offer *the* definitive Jewish view of the matter at hand. Rather, I am offering *a* Jewish view, which I hope will be read as true to the tradition and culture from which I speak but which will certainly be viewed as idiosyncratic or even inconsistent with Jewish tradition by some, not all of whom should be characterized as literalists or fundamentalists.

Let me begin my conspectus of Jewish tradition and culture by suggesting that it is both an essentially literary tradition and a complex one. It embraces Biblical canon, apocryphal literature, an interpretive tradition that proceeds along two interrelated but discrete tracks, legal or *halakhic* and ethical or *aggadic,* a history of legal codification, a philosophical tradition, a rich and evolving liturgical history, and an extensive belletristic corpus as well. Judaism is best understood as a "religious civilization" to use the term created by the creator of the Reconstructionist branch of Judaism, Mordecai M. Kaplan, in the last century.[1] Religion is a core component of Jewish civilization but Jews have related to the complex of this civilization in diverse ways throughout Jewish history, and much of this diversity is related to how Jews viewed the other, both individually and corporately. There were Jews from earliest times who reached across particularist lines to embrace the cultures and traditions of others and to form significant and synergistic relationships with members of other communities. And so, a recurrent theme in the broad range of Jewish literature, from canon to commentary, philosophy to poetry, in law and liturgy, is the nature of the boundary separating the Jew and Judaism from others and other traditions, describing and prescribing the limits of relationships and finding multiple modes of characterizing the other. It is tempting to

---

1. Mordecai M. Kaplan, *Judaism as a Civilization* (New York: Reconstructionist Press, 1934).

read the sources tendentiously, i.e., to find in them just what one is seeking. For an understanding of what characterizes Jewish views of the other, it is essential to reference both the sources of inclusiveness and tolerance of the other on the one hand, and also sources that are insular and even xenophobic. But if one's objective is to uncover resources in the tradition to enhance our attitudes toward the other, I would argue that a selective reading is appropriate as long as one bears in mind that one is perusing the sources for that purpose. In other words, it's necessary both to underline the former constructive sources but also to stipulate the existence of and develop an approach to dealing with the uncomfortable or difficult sources. I would suggest that while I am engaging here in a Jewish exploration, this comment and caveat apply to other confessional communities as well.

I have suggested that the crux of the fundamentalism-relativism tension lies in the treatment of the other in our respective traditions, and having stipulated further that our traditions contain resources for constructive navigation of these poles and also problematic passages that require an approach to dealing with them, it may now be useful to explore some of the resources within the Jewish tradition for constructive attitudes toward otherness and the other. A comprehensive review of the literature falls beyond the scope of this paper, but reference to a number of sources can be helpful: I have intentionally chosen a range of references, including Biblical, Rabbinic, legal, ethical, and liturgical, and sources that cover a rather broad time span.

It can be misleading to suggest a monochromatic "Biblical" approach to any topic in view of the composite nature of the text. If one is willing to put issues of textual history aside, however, it can be useful to suggest fundamental themes and directions in the canonical text that may, in fact, be the end product of a complex textual history but gained canonical status in their final and synthesized form. This is true of the core text of Hebrew Scripture, namely, the Pentateuch. The prevalence of references to the *ger* or stranger suggests an awareness both of the borders of demarcation between "us" and "them" and a degree of interaction requiring guidelines in attitudes towards "others" and "otherness." The historical background and the status implied in a range of references to "outsiders" of whom the community was aware and with which the community was in contact is very much in doubt. But bearing that in mind, it can still be useful to construct a composite of Pentateuchal resources on dealing with the outsider. This follows from my view that dealing with "otherness" is the central challenge to religious positions generally and to those who seek to identify a position between fundamentalism and relativism specifically.

I would suggest that the reading of the composite Pentateuchal sources suggests four discrete but related themes in dealing with the stranger: first, non-discrimination; second, favorable and even preferential treatment of the stranger in view of the stranger's existentially disadvantaged position; third, participation of the non-Jew in Jewish religious ritual; and fourth, the requirement to love the stranger both out of the fulfillment of the religious requirement of *imitatio dei*, emulation of God, who is described as loving the stranger. On most of these themes multiple sources could be adduced. I have generally chosen one or two sources that clearly articulate the theme rather than presented a comprehensive collection of sources that would be beyond the scope of this paper.

We begin with a classical text requiring non-discrimination:

> You shall not subvert the rights of the stranger or the fatherless; you shall not take a widow's garment in pawn. Remember that you were a slave in Egypt and that the Lord God redeemed you from there; therefore do I enjoin you to observe this commandment.[2]

The admonition against subverting the rights of strangers is repeatedly related in scripture to the capacity for empathy and the need to empathize, a natural corollary of the Jews' own experience.

Another clear articulation of the requirement of non-discrimination and the requirement of equal treatment is the following:

> There shall be one law for you and for the resident stranger; it shall be a law for all time throughout the ages. You and the stranger shall be alike before the Lord; the same ritual and the same rule shall apply to you and to the stranger who resides among you.[3]

Note that there is a degree of ambiguity here: the source clearly stipulates that there are both "insiders" and "outsiders"; at the same time it requires equal treatment, this time without grounding the requirement in any specific rationale.

---

2. Deuteronomy 24:17-18. Translations of Hebrew Scripture are based on the *JPS Hebrew-English Tanakh* (Philadelphia: Jewish Publication Society, 1999).

3. Numbers 15:15-16.

More concisely, the admonition is stated as follows:

> You shall not oppress the stranger, for you know the feelings of the stranger, having yourselves been strangers in the land of Egypt.[4]

The second theme, that of preferential treatment, can be seen in the following source:

> When you reap the harvest in your field and overlook a sheaf in the field, do not turn back to get it; it shall go to the stranger, the fatherless, and the widow — in order that the Lord your God may bless you in all your undertakings. When you beat down the fruit of your olive trees, do not go over them again; that shall go to the stranger, the fatherless, and the widow. When you gather the grapes of your vineyard, do not pick it over again; that shall go to the stranger, the fatherless, and the widow. Always remember that you were a slave in the land of Egypt; therefore do I enjoin you to observe this commandment.[5]

Once again, the preferential treatment of the disadvantaged, including the stranger, is rooted in the national memory of slavery and the implied capacity for and admonition to empathize with the plight of the less fortunate, including the stranger.

Finally, required behaviors toward the stranger are not sufficient. Even in the context of what appears a strongly particularist formulation, there emerges a striking characterization of the stranger:

> And now, O Israel, what does the Lord your God demand of you? Only this: to revere the Lord your God, to walk only in his paths, to love him, and to serve the Lord your God with all your heart and soul, keeping the Lord's commandments and laws, which I enjoin upon you today, for your good. Mark, the heavens to their uttermost reaches belong to the Lord your God, the earth and all that is on it! Yet it was to your fathers that the Lord was drawn in his love for them, so that he chose you, their lineal descendants, from among all peoples — as is now the case. Cut away, therefore, the thickening about your hearts and stiffen your necks no more. For the Lord your God is God supreme and Lord supreme, the great, the mighty, and the awesome God who shows no favor and takes

4. Exodus 23:9.
5. Deuteronomy 24:19-22.

no bribe, but upholds the cause of the fatherless and the widow, and befriends the stranger, providing him with food and clothing. You too must befriend the stranger, for you were strangers in the Land of Egypt.[6]

In sum, the Biblical sources adduced suggest that while stipulating a distinction between "insiders" and "outsiders," and alluding to the complex and challenging notion of chosenness, the border between insider and outsider is permeable, in terms of societal protection, ritual participation, and an honored place in the divine scheme which respects difference and does not require transformation from outsider to insider. The presence of the outsider and interaction with him/her do not in and of themselves constitute a challenge or a problem. The claims to special position of the insider are both stipulated and tempered by the status of the outsider; the biblical worldview relating to claims of exclusive access to truth and virtue, it necessarily follows, postulates that it is not a zero sum game.

Moving next to a remarkable source that found its way into Muslim tradition later, a Mishnaic text from the tractate Sanhedrin embeds an *aggadic* or ethical motif into the context of the *halakhic* or legal description of the process of admonishing prosecution witnesses in capital cases prior to their testimony:

How did they admonish the witnesses in capital cases? They brought them in and admonished them, saying: "Perhaps you will say what is but supposition or hearsay or second-hand, or you may report that you heard it from a trustworthy person. You may not realize that we will subject you to examination and inquiry! You must know, moreover, that capital cases are not like non-capital cases: in non-capital cases a man may pay money and so make atonement, but in capital cases the witness is answerable for the blood of the person (wrongly condemned) and the blood of his posterity (who remain unborn because of his conviction) to the end of the world. For so have we found it with Cain who slew his brother, for it is written: *the* bloods *of your brother cry* (Genesis 4,10). It is not the 'the blood of your brother' but 'the bloods of your brother,' his blood and the blood of his posterity. . . . Therefore but a single man was created in the world, to teach that if any man has caused a single soul to perish (from Israel) Scripture imputes it to him as though he had caused a whole world to perish; and if any man saves a single soul (from Israel)

6. Deuteronomy 10:12-19.

Scripture imputes it to him as if he had saved an entire world. In addition, (human beings were created as a single person) for the sake of peace among mankind, that none should say to another: 'My father was greater than your father.' . . . In addition, (human beings were created as a single person) to proclaim the greatness of the Holy One Blessed be He; for man stamps many coins with a single stamp and they are all identical; but the King of Kings, the Holy One Blessed be He, has stamped every man with the seal of the first man, yet no two are alike. . . ."[7]

The words "from Israel" appear in most printed texts of this citation from the second-century CE text, but they make no sense since what is being described is the creation of Adam, clearly precedent to the birth of Israel or any other nation. The source celebrates the uniqueness of each individual, and proclaims that differences are testimony to the greatness of God. It speaks eloquently against assertions of superiority or exclusive access to truth or virtue, viewing such assertions as undermining "peace among nations." This citation affirms a divine order in which, though differences may be stipulated and even celebrated, assertiveness of ultimate superiority by any group is counter to the divine will and scheme.

This "universalist" perspective, or perhaps, more accurately, this mode of navigating particularism and universalism that I have argued is the key concern implicit in the fundamentalism/relativism dipole, finds expression in a range of classical Jewish sources beginning in the rabbinic period that deal with the doctrine of the Noachide laws, and recurring in the literature of many centuries and many genres, including the legal and philosophical literature. The earliest formulation of the Noachide laws occurs in the Talmudic tractate Sanhedrin.[8] The fundamental assumption of the doctrine of the Noachide laws is that the Bible enjoins obligations on all people, Jews and Gentiles alike, distinguishing between Jews who are obligated to observe the entire Torah while Gentiles are referred to as "Children of the Covenant of Noah" and are obligated to observe seven fundamental, primarily moral, laws. While there are some variations in formulation, the traditional formulation includes prohibitions against idolatry, blasphemy, murder, sexual sins, theft, and eating the flesh from a live animal, as well as the positive requirement to establish a legal system. The last item on the list

---

7. Mishnah, *Sanhedrin* 4:5. The translation is based on Herbert Danby, *The Mishnah* (London: Oxford University Press, 1933), with some stylistic modifications by the author.

8. Babylonian Talmud, *Sanhedrin*, pp. 55-60. Translations are the author's.

in this formulation is clearly different from the first six: the first six are pro-scribed behaviors affecting the individual; the last is a societal obligation; individuals do not create legal systems. Notably absent from the list is any reference to belief or requirement of creedal affirmation. The Noachide laws, at least in this traditional formulation, are concerned with "works" not "faith," and may be described as representing in that sense a Jewish formulation.

The Noachide Laws represent a complex subject attended by a variety of issues. Were these laws ever considered enforceable and if so, under what Jewish legal jurisdiction? Were they meant to represent requirements for the non-Jew to attain some formal status in the Jewish community, such as *"ger toshav"* or resident alien? If so, when? Beyond these questions lies the fundamental question of the source of authority adduced for these laws. Were they part of revealed law which non-Jews were required to ac-cept? Or, were they a kind of Natural Law to which all principled people would consent, whatever their national or religious context? Jewish sources are equivocal on these issues.

Maimonides, writing in the twelfth century, appears to opt unequivo-cally in his Code of Jewish Law[9] for authority as opposed to consent as the only acceptable basis for adoption of the Noachide obligations on the part of non-Jews. The key sentence in Maimonides states that a non-Jew who accepts the Noachide laws out of intellectual conviction (as opposed to re-vealed commandment) does not attain the status of resident alien, is not considered one of the righteous of the nations of the world, nor of their wise men. Maimonides does not provide a description of what such a per-son is considered, and seems to be focusing on specific status designations that the non-Jew who does not affirm the authority of revelation cannot attain. The Maimonidean formulation is interesting particularly because he represents an extraordinary but still characteristic embodiment of the medieval Jewish philosophical preoccupation with bridging the divide be-tween reason and revelation, arguing that they represent two parallel paths to reach the same ultimate goal. This would suggest the legitimacy of rea-son as a path to attaining right behavior. The natural corollary would be that non-Jews who come to adopt the Noachide obligations out of intellec-tual conviction, even if not considered righteous, should be ranked among the "wise men" of the nations of the world. If an alternate reading of the

---

9. Maimonides, *Mishneh Torah, Hilkhot Melakhim*, 8:11.

Maimonidean formulation is correct, which is not at all certain, the problem would be eased: According to this reading Maimonides wrote that the non-Jew who accepted the Noachide commandments out of intellectual conviction is not considered one of the righteous of the nations of the world but *rather* one of their wise men.

What is the relevance of the Noachide laws to our consideration of the fundamentalism/relativism dipole? To reprise, I have argued that the challenge to define a middle ground between the poles is not primarily epistemological. There is no reason to be troubled by those who choose to read scripture literally, unless that reading generates attitudes and behaviors that are destructive and offensive. Similarly, relativism is not a problem if it simply contextualizes ethical imperatives and suggests the human predicament of not having access to absolute truth, even in the areas of moral and ethical concern. The challenge to find a "between" position in navigating the dipole is a concern with the content of the values and behaviors generated by either pole, and specifically, the place of the other in one's narrative. A literalist or fundamentalist reading of scripture leading to a rejection of the legitimacy of the other, a position for which scriptural bases have so often been adduced, often by literalists, leads to behaviors that are pernicious in a world of diversity. No less objectionable are arguments for the denial of rights to others on the basis of the argument that no values at all can be supported or affirmed. Our inquiry has begun with the attempt to uncover within Jewish sources a way of both affirming the authority of these sources for Jews, including their stipulation of Jewish particularism, as well as a way of validating the privileging of those outside the Jewish religious and national community. We have stipulated that there are sources within the Jewish corpus that focus on particularism and are exclusionary; we need to develop techniques for dealing with those sources. But we are here focusing on modes of navigating particularism and universalism within this religious tradition, effectively precluding the pathological implications that some would uncover in their reading of their sacred texts. Though read selectively, the Biblical and post-Biblical sources adduced here provide a foundation for this kind of narrative, which includes the "stranger" and the Noachide in the divine scheme, and abjures claims to exclusive status in God's world.

I have referred to the fact that I am suggesting a selective reading of texts from the Jewish corpus. It is appropriate to put forward explicitly my implicit criteria for selection. Quite simply, there must be a way of reading this tradition that enhances relationships and provides for repair and healing of a world torn by hatred and bloodshed. My understanding is that this is the function of religious traditions including my own. To suggest a God who wishes to see his word used as an instrument for oppression and cruelty is simply not an option. Sadly, the pages of history are riddled with just such abuse of religious scripture and misinterpretation of the divine voice. The contemporary world continues that pattern. It is not only literalists/fundamentalists who are responsible for this abuse; other modes of reading religious texts are not immune. But a fundamental tenet of contemporary literary theory is relevant here: meaning is formed in the encounter between the text and the reader. In my view, the reading of religious texts must represent a conversation between the reader and the tradition. The process of reading even sacred and privileged texts must invoke both imperatives and expectations imposed by the tradition on the reader, but also demands and expectations of the reader on the text. The text cannot require that which is destructive and pernicious, whether or not formulated in God's name. While this is certainly not a literalist approach to reading sacred texts, I would suggest that the conversation with the text I describe is an accurate description of the fundamentalist's reading mode as well. We bring to these texts what we are looking for, and we find it. The critical issue: What is it that we are seeking in these texts? I state unequivocally that I am seeking formulations and articulations that will enhance my experience as a human being and help me navigate the challenge of being human in a world of diversity. This is what I seek to uncover in my conversation with the sources, and I believe that I have been strengthened by the resources I have uncovered in my reading of Jewish tradition.

As a Jew, I am helped by this mode of reading to develop an inclusive narrative while at the same time affirming my particularism as a member of a religious/cultural community. I would like now to reflect on a corollary question: Are there insights from my experience and approach to reading Jewish traditional sources that may be of interest and use to those outside the community? I have suggested a mode of reading of Jewish sources that may be (and, of course, is commonly) appropriated by readers of other traditions. I am asking the further question: Are there characteristics of Jewish discourse that in and of themselves define it, and might these characteristics be relevant to other traditions as well?

Once again, I am attempting in this formulation to straddle both subjective and objective perspectives. I would hope that my approach to reading sacred texts might be suggestive for those outside the Jewish community and for texts beyond the Jewish corpus. In my view, our religious cultures embrace parallel narratives and contexts for confronting fundamental questions about the meaning of human experience and for structuring the resources of time and energy we are given to navigate this journey of being alive. While I am at home in my own culture and community, I view religious cultures as part of an anthology of resources for enhancement of human experience. As a visitor in other cultures, I can be assisted on my own journey and enhanced by my visit. What might a visitor to the world of Jewish culture find of use and potential enhancement?

I would suggest that objectively, in the nature of Jewish discourse, and subjectively in the way I choose to read it, there exists a resource that attunes the reader to the ability to hear alternative narratives. This description applies to the Biblical narrative as well as to post-Biblical literature including even liturgical texts, as I shall attempt to demonstrate.

The narratives of the Hebrew Bible contain no unflawed ideal types. A scholar of the Hebrew Bible once commented that the Bible does not describe a single personality that you would want a child of yours to grow up resembling! Rather, the personalities in the Biblical narrative struggle, sometimes with success and sometimes failing, to apply values *in vivo*, in real-life situations. In so doing, they invite reaction and response from the reader of the narrative. They do not elicit unalloyed admiration and expectation of emulation. Put another way, the narrative invites the reader to enter into conversation with the text. This is part of a characteristic "ambivalence" toward texts that characterizes the Jewish exegetical tradition. On the one hand, the text is "at the center"; on the other, the text is challenged, even subverted. Allow me just one illustration:

The Book of Genesis recounts the unsettling account of the Patriarch Abraham's encounter with his wife Sarah over her concern for the influence of Ishmael, Abraham's son from his concubine Hagar, on her son Isaac.[10] Sarah demands that Ishmael and his mother be banished. Abraham complies and Hagar and Ishmael are sent off to the desert. In the *dénouement* of the story Abraham is reassured by God, who promises that all will work out well, and that Ishmael will be the ancestor of a great na-

10. Genesis 21:9-21.

tion. The reader of this narrative, I would assert, is not meant to be reassured. Abraham's capitulation is an embarrassment. In real-life experience this kind of *deus ex machina* does not emerge to save the day. For this reader the narrative's resounding line is: *Vayera hadavar me'od beeinei avraham*. This was very evil in Abraham's eyes.[11] Nevertheless, Abraham capitulated. From this weakness the reader learns the vulnerability of even heroic figures and of the struggles to deal with conflicting demands. This narrative invites the reader to enter a conversation with the text, to hear Sarah's demands along with Abraham, to recoil at them and to shudder at Abraham's compliance. The reader is an active partner in shaping the meaning of this story; absent the reader's participation the story simply does not work!

While other examples from Hebrew Biblical narratives can be adduced, I now move to what might be described as the most characteristic genre of classical Jewish discourse, the Talmudic pericope. A brief and of necessity highly schematic overview of Jewish literary development in the post-Biblical period may be helpful. Following the canonization of Hebrew scripture probably in the fourth to third century BCE, there developed the two exegetical directions to which I have referred earlier, the legal or *halakhic* and the ethical or *aggadic*. In time, the accumulating oral traditions were redacted into literary texts, initially in an exegetical or *midrashic* style. The legal tradition developed substantially during the latter part of the first century CE and especially during the second century CE by scholarly authorities known as *Tannaim*. The capstone of their work was a legal compilation known as the Mishnah, already cited, redacted by Rabbi Judah the Nassi at about the turn of the second century. Along with other Tannaitic material that continued to circulate, including a collection structured similarly to the Mishnah, known as the *Tosefta*, the Mishnah became the principal text studied in Rabbinical academies in Palestine and Babylonia and served as the primary legal reference as well. The text was central both in Palestinian and Babylonian academies for several hundred years, and the end products of the circulating oral traditions were transformed into literary texts first in Palestine in a somewhat laconic and disjointed text, the Palestinian Talmud, or Talmud of Jerusalem (actually produced in Galilean centers and not in Jerusalem) redacted about 400 CE, and some fifty years later in a much larger and more highly structured lit-

---

11. Genesis 21:11.

erary text, the Babylonian Talmud. Common references to the Talmud are to the Babylonian Talmud, and it is principally to its discourse that I refer here.

The Babylonian Talmud is an idiosyncratic text, and can be described without exaggeration as *sui generis*. While it is replete with discussions of legal matters and these materials are subsumed under relevant paragraphs of the Mishnah, the Talmud contains extensive theological, folkloristic, exegetical, historical, and other types of material as well. Moreover, its legal discussions are of an unusual nature. By and large, Talmudic legal discourse is inconclusive; it is not preoccupied with resolving legal issues, often, in fact, shying away from formulating conclusions at all. Redactors who were responsible for transforming what they received of the circulating oral tradition into a literary text were guided by a number of principles: first, they sought as much as possible to preserve traditions they had received rather than to select from among them; second, they inclined to embed these traditions in dialogical form, resorting even to creating anachronistic dialogues and transforming free-standing apodictic statements into components of dialogue, even when this required distorting the original meaning of the apodictic statement and creating an entirely new context for it. Though sometimes referred to as a legal code, and certainly relevant to later legal codifiers, the Talmud itself is certainly not a legal code. Further, it should be noted significantly that the Talmud consistently preserves minority views, even those that have been refuted in the discourse. The text is composed in an admixture of Hebrew and Aramaic, is laconic in style and often obtuse in argumentation. Maimonides, in his introduction to his own elegant literary code, the Mishneh Torah, which we have cited earlier, comments that he is writing his code to save the student the tedium of entering the world of Talmudic discourse and argumentation. But in this effort Maimonides failed. The Talmudic text above any other defines the status of the literate Jew. The knowledgeable Jew is one who can find his or her way in a page of Talmudic discourse, who can successfully "swim in the sea of the Talmud."

How then does this most characteristic of Jewish literary genres address the reader? It invites him, in fact it requires him, to enter into conversation with the text. The student/reader enters into the process of argumentation, considers conflicting views, weighs relative strengths and weaknesses of alternative positions, and along with the redactors themselves comes to appreciate the centrality of the process of *shakla vetarya*, of give and take, as even more significant than the bottom line. I might add that in addition to periodic consolidation of the legal materials in legal codes, the genre that followed upon the completion of Talmud and continues into contemporary Jewish life is the form of Responsum, or the continuing exchange of questions and answers, in which the importance of the question is never underestimated. I remember being told by the late Nobel-Prize-winning physicist Isador Rabi what he considered a "very Jewish" recollection. When he was growing up, Rabi recounted, his friends reported that when they came home from school their parents would ask them: "Did you behave well in school? What did you learn?" In his home it was different, said Rabi. His mother would say to him: "Did you ask any good questions today?"

These selected citations from Biblical, Rabbinic, and post-Rabbinic literature are meant to suggest the flavor of Jewish discourse as dialogical in nature and contributing to an enhanced ability to hear alternative narratives. A few additional comments might be usefully appended. Some questions that would appear to be amenable to straightforward and "linear" answers turn out to be far more complex than they might seem. If, for example, one were to attempt to convey the Hebrew Bible's conception of God, one would face an insurmountable problem: There is simply no single conception of God in the anthology of works that constitute Hebrew Scripture. The anthology embraces the Creator of the early chapters of Genesis, the conversational partner of Abraham who receives a reminder re Sodom and Gomorrah that the "judge of all the earth" needs to behave justly. God is the lawgiver in the Exodus codes, the remote source of the Theophany, also in Exodus, the magisterial figure on an angel-surrounded throne in the sixth chapter of Isaiah, the warrior God of the early prophets, the communicator of the message of social justice to the classical prophets, the sensuous lover and beloved, at least in the allegorical interpretation of the Song of Songs, the object of Ecclesiastes' gentle cynicism, and Job's interlocutor in the book that bears his name. Rather than a unified characterization of God, Hebrew Scripture embraces an anthology of human encounters with the experience of divinity, and so invites its readers to be instructed by the record of past encounters and add to that anthology by joining the living conversation.

Even classical Jewish liturgy must be understood as part of this anthology, rather than as a textbook of Jewish theology. There is a glaring absence of an authoritative catechistic formulation. Every attempt to formulate one in the Jewish context was met with alternative formulations. The prayer book is replete with competing and even conflicting metaphors and juxtapositions that are strikingly destabilizing. One example: In the early morning daily prayers in a section that is often given short shrift in its recitation as it precedes the core of the morning service, the liturgy states:

> What are we? What is our life? What is our strength? . . . Behold, all the mighty are as non-existent before you and the famous as if they never were, the wise as if ignorant and the understanding as if without sense. . . . And the superiority of human beings over (other) animals is nothing, for everything is vanity.[12]

What immediately follows, introduced by the word *aval,* however, is a diametrically antipodal characterization:

> We are the children of Abraham, how fortunate we are, how exalted our lot, how pleasant our fortune, for we are able to proclaim both early in the morning and in the evening: Hear O Israel, the Lord our God, the Lord is One.

This is a striking, and intentionally dissonant juxtaposing of ideas, each of them reflecting a dimension of human experience and suggesting a needed corrective to the other, tempering both presumptuousness and capitulation to lethargy. It anticipates a later Hassidic custom: A person should carry a stone in his right pocket and another in his left pocket. On one should be inscribed the words: "I am but dust and ashes." On the other should be inscribed: "The world was created for my sake." Other intentionally striking juxtapositions are present, such as the combining of two essentially incompatible metaphors for God in the single oft-repeated refrain: Our Father, Our King. It was clear to the author of the refrain and to the compiler of the liturgy as it must be to the reader that a king is not a father and a father not a king. Each is an attempt to describe and articulate the experience of the divine as conceived, and the very juxtaposition is meant to destabilize rather than invoke assent and facile pronouncements of "amen."

---

12. *The Authorized Daily Prayer Book,* ed. Joseph H. Hertz (New York: Bloch Publishing Co., 1955), pp. 26-28. Translations are the author's.

David M. Gordis

Let me then recapitulate the path we have traveled and summarize the argument. In my view the challenge we face here is not primarily to develop an epistemology that 1) is rooted in religious text/tradition read in a non-literalist way, and 2) at the same time affirms commitment to values. One can just as easily affirm commitment to values as affirm the literal truth of revealed scripture! The source of concern for me is the content of value systems rooted in religious tradition, read literally or otherwise, that leads to pernicious consequences for the world. This content relates especially to the place of the other in one's religious narrative. This inquiry is directed to the question: For a world in which religious beliefs and behaviors so frequently contribute to the pathology of intergroup relations, is it possible to uncover resources within religious traditions that can generate beliefs and behavior that enhance healing relationships and attitudes toward the other? Moreover, can one do so in a way that is faithful to one's religious tradition and not do violence to it? Stipulating that I have adopted an approach to textual meaning that locates it in the intersection of text and reader, and also that one most often can and will find in the text what one seeks, I attempt to provide a set of resources for respectful and loving attitudes toward the other out of Jewish tradition. I have proposed a selection from the anthology; there are constructive and helpful texts and others that are problematical. Problematical texts need to be deprivileged and dealt with in some way. My approach is rooted in the assertion (perhaps even a fundamentalist/literalist position!) that destructive texts that contribute to the pathology of interrelationships must not be considered authoritative. Through some process of historical contextualization, creative exegesis, or even radical emendation, their claims must be rejected.

If pressed to ground and rationalize the boldness of this approach, I would offer two responses: First, I have no alternative, since I am heir and custodian of this tradition, accept it as central in my life, and at the same time consider as a central imperative for me to engage in the process of repair of the world. Having said that, my mode of selective reading is internally derived. By that I mean that I am conditioned to apply these criteria to my reading in the anthology by my having been conditioned to do so by my very immersion in this tradition and culture. My nurturing in this tradition has conditioned me to read the tradition this way, and I do so as an insider rather than as an outsider looking in.

After citing from Biblical, post-Biblical, Rabbinic, philosophical, medieval, and liturgical sources to convey what I find in these sources and how I read them, again claiming not that my reading is the only way they can be read but arguing for the legitimacy of my reading, I reach the conclusion that a member of the Jewish community who, as I do, seeks resources for a respectful and tolerant stance toward the other and towards alternative narratives, can find them within this tradition. I argue for an intersection of the subjective and objective dimensions of my argument. In other words, I attempt to make the case that there are characteristics of Jewish discourse objectively studied, which condition the reader and participant to the ability to hear and value alternative narratives, and to respect those who bring with them alternative narratives and formulations. I finally suggest that these characteristics might have some usefulness across particularistic lines, in two ways. First, some of these texts that are shared by our Abrahamic religions can contribute to shaping not only Jewish attitudes and behaviors but those of Christians and Muslims as well. Moreover, this inquiry suggests a way of navigating particularism and universalism, the affirmation of the values of distinctive religious and cultural diversity, while at the same time nurturing a sense of appreciation of the other as a resource for enhancement of one's self rather than as a challenge and a problem.

The valence of religion in world affairs is powerful and palpable. If the torn and broken world in which we live is to be repaired and healed, religious traditions need to contribute their resources for that healing. It is to that end and in that spirit that these thoughts and suggestions are proffered.

Christianity in an Age of Uncertainty: A Catholic Perspective

Ingeborg Gabriel

Roman Catholicism and the Challenge of Liberal Modernity

"All that is solid melts into air."[1] This title of a book published nearly a quarter of a century ago describes a prevalent mood, particularly in Western societies. The pace, complexity, and the sheer extent of the changes that have taken place in the past decades and affected all areas of life have created substantive feelings of insecurity. There are several reasons for the growing unease in liberal modernity: the rapid erosion of religious and moral traditions, an increase in pluralism and individualism, the high-risk potential of technical inventions, growing material inequality, and environmental devastation. In Europe, and perhaps also elsewhere, this has been aggravated by the still unforeseeable psychological consequences of the totalitarian regimes — which were the political expression of the other side of modernity.[2] The fears are enhanced by the interdependence and globalization of these trends. All of this nourishes the suspicion that we are losing control and that in the long run the harmful effects of liberal modernity may outweigh the beneficial ones, thus making the overall balance negative.

This may lead to two responses. One may with a sort of defiant determination continue as before, clinging to the belief that everything will turn

---

1. Marshall Berman, *All That Is Solid Melts into Air: The Experience of Modernity* (London: Verso, 1983).

2. Cf. Samuel N. Eisenstadt, *Die Antinomien der Moderne* (Frankfurt: Suhrkamp, 1998); Gertrude Himmelfarb, *The Roads to Modernity: The British, French and American Enlightenments* (New York: Knopf, 2005).

out well. This attitude is often underpinned by an evolutionist worldview that takes progress as the natural course of things. Or, one may look for certainties elsewhere. The best "candidates" for this, after the "end of [secular] ideologies," are religions, which may be tempted, therefore, to present themselves as the only viable alternatives to a liberal way of life considered to be in decay. Giving oneself a clear profile and offering firm and definite certainties is, moreover, a rational strategy in a pluralist world, in which trademarks and distinctions draw further attention and lead to public success. Thus black-and-white views are gaining support, in the Roman Catholic Church and elsewhere, with a great potential for polarization.

There are three positions religions can take towards modernity: a fairly unconditional acceptance, a more or less outright rejection, or a middle way that attempts to distinguish between modernity's positive and negative sides. I will argue in this paper that only the last approach is in agreement with the theological self-understanding of Roman Catholicism. It was a great achievement of the Second Vatican Council (1962-1965) that it formulated theological positions showing a middle way between a downright rejection of modernity and tendencies towards its too-uncritical acceptance. Thus, the Council was able to overcome Catholic anti-modernism, which for a variety of reasons, historic and otherwise, was strong in the nineteenth and the first half of the twentieth century.[3] Because of this, and since the Council repositioned the Catholic Church with regard to the main issues relevant for this book, I will take its positions as the point of departure for the following reflections.

The date of its announcement, January 25, 1959, symbolically shows its major aims: it was the feast of the conversion of St. Paul, who initiated what may be called the first *aggiornamento* in Christian history — and the last day of the week of prayer for Christian unity. Just as the apostle left behind the Jewish law in order to inculturate Christianity into Hellenistic culture, the Council was to leave behind the Constantinian era with unity of Church and State, the Tridentine epoch with its strong anti-Protestant apologetics, and a period of opposition to modernity on principle. This was to make the

---

3. According to the Canadian philosopher Charles Taylor, anti-modernism, both religious and secular, has accompanied modernity from its beginnings. Its central features are the priority given to the collective over the individual, skepticism towards freedom, and the replacement of the modern concept of linear progress by one of linear (moral) decay. Cf. Charles Taylor, *A Catholic Modernity? Charles Taylor's Marianist Award Lecture* (New York: Oxford University Press, 1999).

Church fit for the transition into the global era and for facing its public tasks as a world Church. An important step on this way was the redefinition of the relationship of Roman Catholicism to the modern world (particularly its political institutions), to the other churches, and to the other religions. In order to accomplish this, it was to assess "those values which are most highly prized today and to relate them to their divine source" (*Gaudium et spes* 11). Its agenda thus had two focal points, which are interlinked and of equal importance: *aggiornamento* and *ressourcement*. The idea was not simply to bring Catholicism *à jour,* but to interpret its theological, spiritual, and ethical traditions, so as to relate them to the aspirations and questions of the present age. The continuous reinterpretation of religious texts is actually a normal process that, however, was artificially interrupted by neo-traditionalism, attempting to immunize traditions against change at the expense of their viability and relevance. This was particularly problematic, as the dynamic character of modernity as well as its social pluralism require more rather than fewer interpretative efforts. In this regard our age resembles that of the church fathers, and will require a similar degree of theological creativity. It was the merit of a number of eminent theologians, mainly of French and German origin, who had worked for decades — frequently under difficult circumstances — to reinterpret the Catholic heritage within the context of liberal modernity.[4] Incidentally, this refutes the argument of authors of different backgrounds that Vatican II was a capitulation to the overly optimistic *Zeitgeist* of the 1960s. Such a view is far too superficial. The *kairos* of the Council was such that the insights of these theologians accorded with those of Pope John XXIII, who was a pastor deeply anchored in traditional Roman Catholic piety, and by no means a progressive intellectual. His personal experiences during his long life had convinced him of the necessity of theological and ecclesiastical reforms.[5]

---

4. On the German side it was particularly Karl Rahner whose transcendental theology influenced the Council's documents. His theology proceeds from the reflection on the everyday experiences of the individual and interprets God's revelation in the light of these experiences. French theology, represented for instance by the Dominicans Marie-Dominique Chenu and Yves Congar, starts with the social and historical reality of time as the place of God's revelation in history. Although both follow an inductive approach, the theological differences between them led to intense discussions at Vatican II due to their different points of departure.

5. As nuncio in Bulgaria he became acquainted with Orthodox Christianity, his years in Istanbul brought him into contact with the Muslim world, and in Paris he encountered laicist French modernism.

The basis of the *aggiornamento* of Vatican II was the definition of the Church as "a sacrament or a sign and instrument" for unity with God and mankind.[6] That points to the fact that the Church does not exist for itself: its *raison d'être* is to unite man and God and to serve humankind by contributing to its spiritual and material good. The religious and ethical, that is humane, dimensions are thus inextricably intertwined in its mission.[7] Therefore the concept of the "signs of the time," central to Vatican II, is not only of sociological (as is often falsely assumed), but also of ethical and — even more — theological relevance. Sociological analysis, which is necessary in view of the complexity of the modern world, is to help "decipher the authentic signs of God's presence and purpose" in the present age (*Gaudium et spes* 4:11). The question is: Which of these social trends can serve God's purpose because they have the potential to make the world a better and more humane place? For this reason they are to be supported by the Church and its faithful. I would like to call this hermeneutical approach *the principle of good eyes*. It has deep roots in Roman Catholic theology with its strong emphasis on creation (and incarnation), affirming its goodness despite human sin and corruption (Gen. 1:31). The promise of faith is that this universe will be completed at the end of time in "a new heaven and a new earth, in which justice reigns" (1 Peter 3:13), thus realizing God's original aim with his creation. In this historical process, Jesus Christ is the ultimate word of God, his "Yes" to everything that exists in his Son, in whom he renews his creation (2 Cor. 1:19). Acknowledging the positive potential of a time (as of a person), therefore, is a spiritual attitude rooted in faith, which is able to discern the seeds of the world to come in the present reality. In addition to these theological reasons, there are also good ethical and pastoral ones for taking a positive view of present social realities.

Ethically, the main change brought about by Vatican II was that it recognized liberal modernity's central normative ideas, "liberty, equality, and fraternity," as *common ground* between Roman Catholicism and the modern world. Because of these humanistic elements, which have Christian roots, secular and Christian humanism are natural allies and may even

---

6. Cf. The Dogmatic Constitution on the Church (*Lumen gentium* 1).

7. Cf. *Gaudium et spes* 11: "The People of God and the human race in whose midst it lives render service to each other. Thus the mission of the Church will show its religious, and by that very fact, its supremely human character."

learn from each other.[8] As much as this has been obscured by polarization in the so-called culture wars, one must not be oblivious to the high degree of consensus that exists between Christian and secular ethics in most areas. To mention but one example: any look at history shows that non-violent ways of conflict resolution are the great exception. It is a major achievement that this has become possible in democratic societies to an astonishing degree, and should encourage joint efforts to extend this accomplishment to the international sphere. *Pastorally,* a rejection of liberal modernity may support trends towards resignation and ultimately nihilism, which lurk in the background as negative possibilities and weaken the resources for responsible and far-sighted action. It is precisely in view of haunting questions regarding the future that Roman Catholicism should guard the humanistic impulses of modernity and oppose tendencies to its self-destruction. Moreover, a Catholic hermeneutics of suspicion that debunks the world as evil can easily become ideological. Even if there may be good reasons for cultural pessimism, Abraham's pleading to God for the salvation of the city for the sake of the few just people living there (Gen. 18:20-33) is a better model for Christians than the self-righteous pharisee in the temple (Luke 18:9-14).

It is on this basis that the urgently needed criticism of modernity's life-threatening tendencies gains credibility. The Roman Catholic Church shares this prophetic mission with the other monotheistic religions. What makes for the singularity of Christian faith is the sense of urgency in this prophetic ministry. Violence, injustice, and the disregard for life of any form, as well as the irresponsible use of power, wealth, and natural resources, stand in sharp contrast to God's vision of the world as a place of goodness and justice for all human beings. Trying to steer a middle course through the turbulent waters of late modernity, avoiding the Scylla of relativism that threatens social dissolution, as well as the Charybdis of fundamentalism that breeds rigidity and violence, demands a struggle on two fronts. The first has to be directed against a moral "anything goes" attitude, and the second, against the temptation to isolation or opposition on principle that leaves little room for civil interaction and compromise.

The precondition for intellectual and practical cooperation with others, be they Christians of other denominations, non-believers, or members

---

8. This position was first developed by the French Catholic philosopher Jacques Maritain. Cf. also *Gaudium et spes* 11.

of other religious communities, is their acceptance as equals. I will, therefore, show in the first part why and on which theological grounds the Roman Catholic Church accepts religious liberty and pluralism. In the second part, I will examine the specific nature of religious claims to truth, which is at the heart of the argument against fundamentalism. Finally, in the third part I will discuss some areas in which Roman Catholicism can contribute to civility today by taking moral positions against relativist tendencies, both nationally and globally. The following reflections cover a wide territory, which inevitably makes them fragmentary at best. However, I hope this overview can demonstrate that Roman Catholicism has a considerable potential to help find a middle ground in a situation increasingly characterized by polarizations, the question being whether and in what ways this potential is being brought into play by Catholic Christians and the Church as a whole.

The Roman Catholic Church and Pluralism: The Theological Affirmation of Religious Freedom and the Dignity of Conscience

The main challenge for the Roman Catholic Church in coming to terms with modernity was the acceptance of religious pluralism. Giving up the position of a state Church, which it had held in many European countries since the fourth century, demanded major changes in its self-understanding and outlook. The loss of its social monopoly in faith and morals after one and a half millennia was a trauma, the after-effects of which have not been overcome in Europe even today. The experience of the French Revolution and its violent anti-religious excesses led to the attempt to build a Catholic subculture, an attempt that ultimately was doomed to failure. This shows that an institution even as large and potent as the Roman Catholic Church could not sustain an isolationist course in the long run.[9] The period of integralism instead left a backlog that Catholicism has not yet been able to overcome completely.[10] But it also had grave consequences for society: al-

---

9. One actually has to distinguish between two phases: the period of outright rejection of modern ideas in the nineteenth century and the period that began with Pope Leo XIII (1878-1905), who tried to take a more differentiated position towards liberal modern culture.

10. The relationship between integralism and fundamentalism requires further reflection. Both share an anti-modernist approach, albeit of different forms and degrees. The main characteristic of Catholic integralism was the idealization of the Christian state (and

though it is always somewhat unfair to judge past generations by present standards, one may well speculate whether the history of the twentieth century might not have been different had the Roman Catholic Church decided to advocate human rights and democracy after Vatican I (1870).[11]

The stumbling block in the relationship between Roman Catholicism and modern political culture was the right to religious freedom. The Declaration on Religious Freedom *Dignitatis humanae* (1965) of Vatican II marks the final point of this controversy. It was drafted by an American Jesuit, John Courtney Murray, who had experienced religious pluralism in a country where Catholics had always been a minority. His theological reconciliation of the right to religious freedom with the Roman Catholic tradition represents a major intellectual achievement as well as the basis for the implementation of the agenda of Vatican II. Without it dialogue with other Christians, as well as with non-believers and adherents of other religions, would not have become possible.

But why had this path not been taken earlier? Apart from the difficulty of accepting the loss of political power, there were fundamental theological questions that needed to be solved. The first one of these was: Can those who do not belong to the Church be saved, or are they condemned forever? If the latter were the case, the toleration of other creeds would not be an act of respect, but one of truly monstrous negligence. As strange as this may seem today (which shows that an immense change of mind has taken place), for most of history this was the central question. I would like to draw the following comparison. Doctors who use methods not in accordance with medical standards and who might therefore harm their patients are not granted permission to practice. Thus, in order for Catholicism to accept religious freedom, it had to be clear that membership in the Catholic Church was no precondition for salvation; in other words, the *extra ecclesia non est salus* principle had to be refuted. Although widely

---

the homogenous Christian society of the Middle Ages). This was accompanied by an acute sense of cultural and moral crisis, viewing modernity as an age of decay. Cf. Oswald von Nell-Breuning, *Modernismuskrise: Lexikon für Theologie und Kirche*, Bd. 7 (Freiburg: Herder, 1962), pp. 367ff.

11. The Political Catholicism since the end of the nineteenth century that led to a rather powerful Catholic presence in the political life of countries such as Austria, Germany, and Belgium thus lacked a theological foundation. Seen in retrospect, this accommodation to the modern pluralist state on pragmatic grounds only was also one of its weaknesses.

spread, this exclusivist position was never undisputed. Eminent theologians like St. Augustine (354-430) — despite his rather pessimistic views on salvation in general — distinguished between the visible and the invisible Church. This position obviously accords better with God's goodness and freedom. The idea that it is not formal faith in Christ and membership in the Church that are decisive for salvation, but personal deeds, is biblically well founded. Central New Testament passages such as that on the Last Judgment (Matt. 25:36-43) and the hymn of love of St. Paul (1 Cor. 13:13) unequivocally state that love is superior to faith.[12]

The second theological question is of a rather different nature: Can the Church accept religious pluralism in the political community on theological grounds? The solution put forward in *Dignitatis humanae* is quite simple: the dignity of the religious choice of the individual must have priority over the realization of ecclesiastical truth claims at the state level. The argument was not really new: already in the early Church some theologians pleaded for religious freedom.[13] What is more important, it had always been theologically undisputed that nobody may be forced into embracing a specific faith. Besides the obvious fact that theological principles are often disregarded in political practice, the problem was the limitations that arose from the political thinking of the time. In this case, the individual's freedom of conscience was overruled by the right of the state to impose a uniform creed on its citizens. The other limitation imposed was that either a change of religion or deviation from the official faith (e.g., heresy) was prohibited. The Declaration on Religious Freedom changed the perspective by affirming that the freedom to opt for a religion, as well as the right to change it, are to be guaranteed by the state, which "in its legal order has to recognize the right of religious freedom as a civil right," with restrictions being justified only to protect the common good (*Dignitatis humanae* 2, 7).

Giving up its claim to being a state religion freed the Roman Catholic

---

12. With regard to this question cf. Josef Ratzinger, *Das neue Volk Gottes* (Düsseldorf: Patmos, 1969), pp. 339-62. The current Pope states here that this dogmatic tenet — like separate biblical sentences — should be understood within its context and in relationship to other tenets. Cf. also Walter Kern, *Außerhalb der Kirche kein Heil?* (Freiburg: Herder, 1979); Medard Kehl, *Die Kirche. Eine katholische Ekklesiologie*, 2 Aufl. (Würzburg: Echter Verlag, 1993).

13. Cf. the Latin church father Tertullian (150-230), *Liber ad scapulam*, Patrologia Latina 1, 777.

Church from a heavy historical burden and paved the way for its active participation in the political arena through education and civic as well as political involvement. It enabled it to become a global advocate of religious freedom, a task it has performed ever since on a truly impressive scale. Thanks to the untiring efforts of Pope John Paul II (1978-2005), it contributed decisively to the overthrow of authoritarian and totalitarian regimes worldwide in the 1980s and 90s. The theologically founded position of the Magisterium on human rights, together with the commitment of Catholics ready to defend these truths even when confronted with the threat of persecution, had decisive political impact. This is important today in communist states such as China, as well as in countries under dictatorships, especially in Africa and Latin America. To cite but one example: the Bishops' Conference of Zimbabwe recently issued a pastoral letter to be read in all churches of the country condemning the human rights violations of President Mugabe. The leader of this courageous opposition is Archbishop Pius Ncube, who took his inspiration from the Orange Revolution in the Ukraine — a successful example of political globalization.

Civil rights require citizens to make responsible use of these rights. Religious liberty as a public right thus corresponds with the duty of the person to search for the truth and follow it according to his or her conscience. Since freedom is the core value of liberal modernity, I would say a few words on this concept. Anti-modern skeptics of all stripes tend to confuse the modern notion of freedom with arbitrariness. This is a misinterpretation: at the public level liberty rights require a high ethos not only on the part of the state, but also from citizens, who are called to respect others as equal human beings. At the private level the Enlightenment idea of autonomy does not mean that one may do as one pleases. The *autos*, i.e., the person, must decide which laws *(nomoi)* he is to follow in private life. These norms should be conceived in such a way as to be universally acceptable. The problem of this "categorical imperative" as a modern form of Golden Rule morality is not arbitrariness, but the high demands it makes on the individual as a responsible agent. Moreover, it does not take into account that existential freedom is always limited under earthly conditions. It may increase or diminish according to one's lifestyle and choices. It is in this sense that St. Paul speaks of men without righteousness as being slaves of sin (Rom. 6:6). Thus, inner freedom is obviously different from freedom of choice and, according to Christian belief, will be completed in the final communion with God.

Religious freedom as a civil right is intended to enable the individual to act in accordance with conscience without having to fear grave legal and social consequences. The deference that the state pays to conscience as the ultimate arbiter in religious matters recognizes it as the "inner sanctuary in which man communicates with God" (*Gaudium et spes* 17). Because of its sanctity it may command unconditional obedience, which also takes priority over a person's duty to obey social and even ecclesiastical norms. "We must obey God more than men" (Acts 5:29). This emphasis on the individual's conscience, which has been called a Protestant principle, is in fact common to all Christian traditions. Thus, John Henry Newman, one of the most eminent theologians of the nineteenth century, who converted from Anglicanism to Roman Catholicism after a long and painful inner struggle, writes at the end of his treatise on conscience: "I add one remark. Certainly, if I am obliged to bring religion into after-dinner toasts (which indeed does not seem quite the thing), I shall drink — to the Pope, if you please, — still, to Conscience first, and to the Pope afterwards."[14] The audacity of this "monotheistic revolution" (Peter Berger), which holds that man is responsible only to God, can be fully appreciated only if one is aware of its inherent potential for abuse. In order not to become a license for immorality, freedom of conscience as a legal right requires from the individual and civil society a firm commitment to its education. This shows that the right to religious freedom and human rights in general are not only a precious, but also a precarious invention of modernity, which cannot guarantee social peace by itself. The mere coexistence of different creeds and worldviews would lead to social disintegration without the willingness of their adherents to actively cooperate. The increase in pluralism due to immigration, urbanization, and individualization therefore requires intensive efforts to achieve value consensus through public dia-

14. John Henry Newman, *A Letter Addressed to the Duke of Norfolk on Occasion of Mr. Gladstone's Recent Expostulation on Certain Difficulties Felt by Anglicans in Catholic Teaching*, vol. 2 (1875), www.newmanreader.org/works/anglicans/volume2/gladstone/index/html, p. 261 (20/07/2007). The whole letter argues against Anglican allegations that the Pope stands above conscience. "Did the Pope speak against Conscience in the true sense of the word, he would commit a suicidal act" (p. 252). "In the true sense of the word" means the theological proposition that one has to follow one's conscience must not be confused with a position that considers all judgment of conscience as *objectively* right, which would in essence be a relativist position. Cf. Josef Ratzinger/Benedict XVI, *Werte in Zeiten des Umbruchs. Die Herausforderungen der Zukunft bestehen* (Freiburg: Herder, 2005), p. 101.

logue. It also calls for the training of citizens to engage in rational argumentation about their religious and moral beliefs, as well as the common good. Because of its long historical experience and the high value it has always placed on religious and moral rationality, Roman Catholicism could contribute to clarifying issues and even act as a mediator in these processes.

Theological Reflection as a Resource:
The Affirmation of Religious Truth and Its Limits

Both relativists and fundamentalists have difficulties, to say the least, with theological and ethical rationality. If truth does not exist, it is futile to search for it, and extreme relativists may even reject rational argumentation altogether, opting for irrationalism.[15] Fundamentalists, for their part, regard reasoning in theological and moral matters as superfluous and even harmful, as something that fosters ambiguity and sows doubt in matters that are clear for all those of good will and firm faith. In his controversial speech at the University of Regensburg in September 2006, Pope Benedict stressed this need for rational argumentation in matters of faith and morals, and warned against loosening the link between faith and reason.[16] This would do grave damage, since faith without reason is blind and easily leads to irrational violence, whereas reason without faith becomes shallow and can degenerate into a worldview void of sense and moral firmness. Both reduce the chances for universal discourse on religious and ethical questions at a time when it is particularly needed. Christian theology, for which God is *logos* — which means *word* as well as *reason* — can be a corrective in this situation by taking up the argument against epistemological reductions that exclude religious and moral truth claims from rational dis-

15. Surrealism after World War I represented the negative climax of modern irrationalism, glorifying even destruction and violence. Similar tendencies can be observed today, even if they have not yet gained prominence.

16. Cf. www.vatican.va/holy_father/benedict_xvi/speeches/2006/september/documents/html. For critical reactions cf. Knut Wenzel (Hg.), *Die Religionen und die Vernunft. Die Debatte um die Regensburger Vorlesung des Papstes* (Freiburg: Herder, 2007). The criticism was mainly directed against the Pope's insinuating that primarily the Catholic tradition has the resources for bridging the gap between faith and reason, whereas Islam and Protestantism tend to separate them.

course.[17] This happens when truth is limited to the rationality typical of natural science, i.e., to quantifiable facts discovered by experiment and open to falsification. The predominance of this type of rationality over all other forms of knowledge leads to religious and ethical matters being confined to the realm of emotion and subjective preference, thus paving the way for moral relativism and religious skepticism.[18] It weakens the capacity to consider moral alternatives, weigh different positions, and creatively interpret one's own traditions. In short, it consigns the entire area of discourse on human and social matters to oblivion.

There are, however, not only those who, like Pontius Pilate, skeptically ask "What is truth?" There are also those who use it as a weapon or means of coercion. Monotheistic religions in particular have gravitated towards asserting absolute truth claims, which has often been accompanied by intolerance and violence in the name of God. The flip side of Greek rationality, which lies at the foundation of Western theology, was its overzealous belief in the capacity of human reason with regard to the divine, i.e., in theological matters. The fights over dogmatic truth that resulted from this (and were carried into politics) represent the barbarian backside of Christian history. Theological reasoning therefore has to include the commitment to a non-violent proclamation of truth. Moreover, it requires intense reflection on its specific nature. As Aristotle remarked, it would be senseless to demand the same type of certainty from ethics as one does from mathematics.[19] The same holds true for theology, and to an even greater extent. Its certainties are of a nature completely different from those of the empirical world. I would, therefore, like to suggest three characteristics of theological truth that are interrelated: its historical and anamnetic character, its dialogical and communicative character, and its transcendental character.[20]

---

17. Max Weber has called this the "disenchantment" of the world, which he describes as follows: "The final and most sublime values step back from public life, either into the realm of a mystic *Hinterwelt* or into the brotherliness of direct human relations." Max Weber, *Wissenschaftslehre* (Tübingen: Mohr, 1988), p. 612 (translation IG).

18. A far-reaching consequence of the limitation of rationality to the objects of the natural world has been a serious impoverishment in the realm of culture. Since facts do not convey meaning, they are of no value for making sense of the world and the universe, and they teach nothing about social values and norms for human interaction.

19. Aristotle, *Nichomachean Ethics* (I 1: 1094b-1095a11).

20. The following sequence does not denote an order of precedence.

First, theological rationality is historical and anamnetic.[21] An existential characteristic of human life is its temporality. All our activities and thinking take place within a specific time and place, and are bound by the limitations this entails. Historicism concluded that since there can be no *absolute* truth in history, there is no truth at all. As a reaction to this, Catholic theology tended to assert religious truth as being ahistorical. Another way to cope with the insecurity resulting from a heightened sense of historical relativity was the neo-traditionalist invention of an idealized past. By overemphasizing the value of tradition for the Christian faith, it became overly fixed on the past. If anything, however, Christian hopes are directed towards the future, as suggested by the intense expectations of the early Christians of the *parousia,* the advent of the Lord at the end of time. This already indicates that temporality in Christian theology (as in Judaism) acquires a new poignancy: the belief that the transcendent God reveals himself in history makes it the place of his deeds and self-communication.[22] What is most incredible about this revelation in history is that Jesus was a fairly unimportant preacher in Judea — a distant corner of the Roman empire — who was crucified by the political and religious authorities of the time. If anything, this story should inspire a good degree of modesty and guard against religious hubris and the glorification of power and wealth. The centrality of history for the Christian faith is reflected in the importance it gives to memory. Thus, in the celebration of the mass, the passion and resurrection of Jesus Christ until his Second Coming are commemorated. This shows the Church as being embedded in history and in fundamental solidarity with all human beings who are on the same pilgrimage.[23]

21. Cf. Johann Baptist Metz, *Memoria passionis. Ein provozierendes Gedächtnis in pluralistischer Gesellschaft,* 2. Aufl. (Freiburg: Herder, 2006).

22. The historical dimension was rediscovered by the French *Nouvelle Théologie* in the first half of the twentieth century. From there it found its way into the documents of Vatican II, especially the Pastoral Constitution *Gaudium et spes,* with its notion of the Church as being on a pilgrimage through time. Its main proponent was the Dominican theologian and expert on medieval theology Marie-Dominique Chenu, who first expounded his ideas against ahistorical neo-Thomist theology in his book *Le Saulchoir. Une école de théologie* (Paris: Étiolles, 1937).

23. Cf. the first passage of *Gaudium et spes* 1: "The joys and the hopes, the griefs and the anxieties of the human beings of this age, especially those who are poor or in any way afflicted, these are the joys and hopes, the griefs and anxieties of the followers of Christ" — and finishes this first article "That is why this community [e.g., the church] realizes that it is truly linked with mankind and its history by the deepest of bonds."

Man is *homo viator*, and his perception of truth therefore necessarily remains fragmentary: "At present we see indistinctly, as in a mirror, but then face to face. At present, I know partially, then I shall know fully, as I am fully known" (1 Cor. 13:12). Absolute comprehension is impossible under the conditions of contingency. Although this fact may seem trivial, it should engender existential and intellectual humility. Moreover, it has strong anti-ideological and anti-fundamentalist consequences. The German theologian Johann B. Metz speaks of an "eschatological reservation" *(eschatologischer Vorbehalt)*, which means that all absolute claims to truth, be they political or religious, become ideological in character because the full truth will only be revealed in the *eschaton*.

Anamnetic theology is, however, also confronted with the remembrance of the atrocities committed by religious communities in history. Faith traditions that take history seriously must therefore be mindful of the need for repentance. The persistence with which Pope John Paul II insisted on the "cleansing of memories" demonstrates the practical consequences of this not only for the individual, but also for the Church as a whole. One of the most innovative and courageous acts of his pontificate was to solemnly ask forgiveness for the sins committed by the Church, in the mass on Ash Wednesday in 2000. This was a concrete manifestation of its "ministry of reconciliation" (2 Cor. 5:18-19). The idea was not to pass judgment on former generations, who may have lacked the insights we have today, but to make it clear that all violent and inhumane acts committed or condoned by the Church in the past, by the hierarchy as well as the laypeople, were against the moral standards of the Christian faith. Even if historical injustices can never be undone, asking for forgiveness as a symbolic act acknowledges the wrong done and opens new ways for cooperation in the future. These considerations do not exhaust the relevance that "religion as memory" (D. Hervieu-Léger) has for the present situation. If one should have to indicate one single reason that furthers both relativist and fundamentalist tendencies, it would have to be modernity's deeply ingrained prejudice against all tradition, which views the past mainly as a dark background against which the grandeur of modern achievements shines even brighter. This *amnesiac* character of modernity cuts it off from the resources it indispensably needs for understanding itself, and particularly from those of its Christian heritage.[24]

24. This point has been made frequently in recent years by the German philosopher

Second, the old dictum *lex orandi, lex credendi* (the rule of prayer is the rule of faith) indicates that theological rationality is rooted in prayer, both private or liturgical. Man's ability to address God, to praise him and complain to him, to thank him and plead before him, and even to doubt him, distinguishes him from all other creatures.[25] The fact that the Christian faith acknowledges man as *capax Dei* (capable of perceiving God), and not only as an *animal rationale,* shows it to be deeply rooted in personal communication. It would be impossible to speak *about* God if we were not able to speak *to* him. Addressing God as a personal *Thou* and as *Our Father* — as in the main Christian prayer — is the basis for all theological reflection. Personal communication, however, creates existential certainties that are fundamentally different from that of the natural world of objects. It is founded in the experience of the trustworthiness, goodness, and loyalty of the Other. Since personal truth needs time to unfold, faith and the reflection on it are a lifelong learning process that normally begins in the family and the local church community, and is fostered by reading the scriptures and participating in the liturgy. These elements complement each other in the light of one's personal experience.

Third, probably the most important characteristic of faith reflection is that its "object" — God — is a supreme mystery that by far transcends human comprehension. Our theological language, therefore, is always far more inadequate in divine matters than it is adequate. Acknowledging this simple and self-evident fact could immunize theology against all forms of religious positivism. There would have been fewer conflicts over religious differences if people had kept in mind the fact that our ignorance in divine matters by far exceeds our knowledge of them.[26] A famous story in the history of theology shows St. Augustine walking along the seashore, reflecting

---

Jürgen Habermas, who is himself an agnostic. Cf. his widely discussed speech "Glaube und Wissen," *Frankfurter Allgemeine Zeitung,* October 15, 2001, p. 9; English version: "Faith and Knowledge," in *Equalvoices* no. 7 (November 2001), www.eumc.eu.int/publications/ equalvoices/ev07/ev07-4_en.htm (accessed July 20, 2007).

25. This intense doubt in God's existence, and especially in his goodness in view of the evil in the world, is found in many biblical books, most profoundly in the Lamentations of the prophet Jeremiah and in the prayer of Jesus on the cross (Matt. 27:46). The difference between this existential doubt and the methodological doubt applied in natural science is obvious.

26. This strong statement against positivism in matters of religion was made at the Fourth Lateran Council (1215). Cf. Heinrich Denzinger, *Enchiridion symbolorum definitionum et declarationum de rebus fidei et morum,* ed. Peter Hünermann, 37th edition (Freiburg: Herder, 1991), no. 806, p. 361.

on the mystery of the Holy Trinity. When he saw a child trying to bail out the sea with a nutshell, he understood that his intellectual endeavors were much of the same kind as the attempts of this child. The theological pursuit of religious truth must be accompanied by the humble insight that the truth of God is unfathomable and infinitely greater than human reason.

Since the Bible is the basis of all theology, these questions about the nature of theological rationality are also part of the debate over its interpretation. Modern rationality confronted biblical exegesis with two main questions: Did the events related in the Bible happen *exactly* as described? And: How can past events acquire existential relevance for the reader? The first question echoes the modern, matter-of-fact approach to reality. The second mirrors a view of history for which the past is simply passé.[27] Gottfried E. Lessing, the poet of the German Enlightenment, spoke about the "ugly moat" separating the time of Jesus Christ from ours. Since neither facts nor past events can convey religious meaning, they cannot give answers to the question of faith as such. Fundamentalists who insist that the biblical stories are factual reports thus miss the point. Even if we happened to have reliable documentary films on the life of Jesus and his apostles, this would be of little avail for our faith.

In the Dogmatic Constitution *Dei Verbum* (1965), the Roman Catholic Church recognized the validity of historical-critical exegesis and the hermeneutical approach to the scriptures as important tools for understanding the texts and for interpreting them in their historical context. However, there remains a dialectical tension between the central truths of faith and the stories in which they are clad. The "middle of the scriptures," i.e., their central message, is that God revealed himself in history in order to save each and every human being, and that Jesus Christ is his ultimate word. The recognition of this intention, central to the texts, is the key to any meaningful interpretation of the events described and the parables related. In this sense there is a "hierarchy of truths," as the Decree on Ecumenism states (*Unitatis redintegratio* 11). The gist of the Christian faith is then expressed in an amazing variety of personally colored stories written by different authors. The differences between them can and must not be har-

---

27. Historical science today no longer views history as an objective sequence of facts, but as their interpretation, which depends on a certain *Vorverständnis* (Hans-Georg Gadamer) that depends on the individual and the community in which this interpretation takes place.

monized, neither with regard to the facts nor to the different perceptions of the life and teaching of Christ.[28] This makes the theory of verbal inspiration obsolete. The authors of the books of the New Testament were not, so to speak, divine secretaries taking dictation from God word by word. They wrote the texts according to their own religious experience and personal abilities, and their work reflects the knowledge of the times and its literary culture.

Summing up: the importance of rational argumentation in matters of faith is increasing at a time when different religions and faith traditions are interacting on a daily basis, both nationally and globally. To regard religious convictions and moral issues as matters of subjective preference is not helpful in this situation. It rather leads to the isolation of communities of faith and furthers distrust and possibly conflict. It is therefore vital to find ways and means to rationally argue about religious and moral matters. This is not an easy task. It requires respect for the other as well as sensitivity to the specific character of religious truth, particularly its historical and therefore fragmentary quality. This realistic modesty, indispensable in matters of the divine, is the only attitude that does justice to God's transcendence. It is also the only way to avoid a hardening of religious positions. The service of theology should, after all, be to teach men to marvel at the greatness of God and proclaim him as the source of love and peace, thus furthering unity and not conflict.

Roman Catholicism: Public Religion in a Global Age

The preceding sections demonstrated the acceptance of religious pluralism as one of the preconditions for the participation of the Roman Catholic Church in the political life of democratic societies. They also showed that its traditions of theological and moral reasoning may help prevent fundamentalist oversimplifications at a time of religious resurgence. The final part of this paper poses the question of how Roman Catholicism may contribute to civility, nationally and internationally, in a more concrete manner. Since this is an extremely broad subject I will focus on three issues: the

28. The well-meaning attempt of a Greek monk in the second century to harmonize the biblical writings in the so-called *Diatessaron* was rejected because the plurality of the scriptures is essential to the faith.

rational affirmation of moral truth in the private and public spheres, the Church's commitment to issues of global justice, and the practice of dialogue as a contribution to non-violent conflict resolution in civil societies.

Concerning the first issue: some time ago, the German legal scholar Ernst-Wolfgang Böckenförde formulated what has been discussed since then as the "Böckenförde Paradox": Liberal institutions rest on moral foundations they cannot create or re-create by themselves, but must assume as given.[29] The implications of this are clear: the moral resources indispensable for social life both nationally and globally must be generated outside the political and economic spheres. The public square needs individuals who not only have the capacity to argue rationally about the good and just but are willing to do so and thus bring their vision of the common good into the political process. This dependency on moral agents is the weak side of liberal societies. Seen in this context, the call for firm values in private and public life, which is high on the agenda of all fundamentalist movements, be they nationalist or religious, reveals its fundamental vulnerability. The erosion of moral rationality and practice, therefore, engenders feelings of uncertainty in large parts of the population, even if this is celebrated as liberation by a few postmodern intellectuals.

The largest institutions that create the moral capital needed in liberal societies are the churches. This is indeed their first and foremost contribution to civil life. To act decently in private, professional, and public life is neither simple nor trivial. It requires that one be educated to exercise right judgment as well as the willingness to act accordingly. Even if Christian religious instruction in its varied forms may not always produce the expected results, it would be cynical to think that Christians — who are taught at each service to love their neighbors, forgive those who harm them, and practice non-violence and justice — would go home and do the opposite. Moreover, a rationally acting *homo Christianus* will take into account the great benefits promised for right behavior and the serious sanctions threatened for their violation. The biblical writings make it clear that Christian practice and the efforts to further true humanity and love in private and social life are not a supplement to the creed, but the confirmation of its authenticity.

---

29. Ernst Wolfgang Böckenförde, *Die Entstehung des Staates als Vorgang der Säkularisation;* Ernst Wolfgang Böckenförde, *Staat, Gesellschaft, Freiheit. Studien zur Staatstheorie und zum Verfassungsrecht* (Frankfurt: Suhrkamp, 1976), pp. 42-64, p. 60.

This is the practical side, but there is also theory. An epistemological position is needed for which both the good and the just are discernible with reasonable certainty. If moral values are but the expression of subjective preferences, emotions, or interests, arguments about justice simply veil power struggles and morality becomes a matter of personal lifestyle. Theories that deny the rational status of ethics are currently gaining ground, weakening the consensus on social norms. This is the case with meta-ethical and postmodern theories, which hold that ethical questions cannot be discussed rationally at all, as well as with biological ethics, which considers moral norms to be nothing more than an illusion since human behavior is determined so as to further the fitness and progress of the human race. However, there has also been a substantive revival in secular ethical theory since the 1970s. The main difference between it and Christian ethics is that the latter considers the morals of the individual to be the basis of social norms and institutions.[30] As C. S. Lewis once remarked comparing Christian to secular ethics, the former focuses on the condition of each ship, while the latter is primarily concerned with the formation of the fleet. But obviously, good ships are needed to make a good fleet.[31] This shows that private and public morals are intimately linked, with the latter being based on the former. Catholic moral theology has always strongly emphasized individual ethics because of its conviction that "the imbalances under which the world labors are linked with that more basic imbalance which is rooted in the heart of man" (*Gaudium et spes* 10). This requires that people be educated to reflect on moral issues — an ability that, according to Hannah Arendt, is the basis of all civility.[32] Perhaps the most serious deficiency of modern anthropology is that it underestimates this

30. To illustrate this position further: the first sentence of John Rawls's *A Theory of Justice* (originally published in 1971), which decisively contributed to the ethical renaissance, defines justice as "the first virtue of *institutions*." This shows the preeminent position accorded to the political and institutional order, the task of which is to guarantee justice independently of the ever-unreliable moral behavior of human beings. Or, as Immanuel Kant wrote, "a good state can also be created by a group of devils, if only they have (practical) reason" (*Zum ewigen Frieden*, BA 59f., translation IG). Although one might justifiably doubt the validity of this statement, who would want to live in such a state?

31. C. S. Lewis, *Mere Christianity* (1952) (San Francisco: HarperSanFrancisco, 2000), p. 71.

32. Hannah Arendt regards the loss of the ability of self-reflection as a sign of the twentieth century and a reason for its political catastrophes. Cf. her *Responsibility and Judgment* (New York: Schocken, 2003).

need for moral education, and, moreover, largely ignores human fallibility. It thereby reduces our understanding of ourselves. Christian ethics, which takes the life-destroying consequences of sin seriously, is much more realistic in this respect.

But besides the exclusion or underestimation of individual ethics in the secular ethical discourse, there is another pitfall Christian and secular ethics need to avoid, which is to reduce them to a system of norms to be followed. This way its true focus, which is the moral development of the person, gets lost from sight. The aim of morality, and ethics as the reflection on it, is to make men and women more human by ordering and deepening their relationship to each other. This ultimately — according to Christian faith — also leads to a more profound relationship with God, the love of the other and of God being inseparable. Christian ethics is there to help people find and maintain a Christian lifestyle that encompasses all areas of social interaction. This aim was realized in the moral philosophy of Thomas Aquinas in a way that is still exemplary. The importance it assigns to ethics is shown in the fact that he dedicates the largest part of his *Summa theologica* to moral issues. His writings contain a wealth of moral discernment that reveals the impoverishment of present ethical discourse in which the replacement of virtues by norms is accompanied by the tendency to reduce morality to a few central issues. Such a shift in emphasis away from the person as a moral agent to norms lies at the heart of present culture wars. One way to overcome these polarizations would be to realize that Catholic moral traditions are much richer and also more balanced. To take but one example: sexual ethics — which are at the center of current public discussions on morals — are treated in Thomist ethics in the chapters on moderation and temperance.[33] In this way its aim is made clear: Christians are to observe certain norms in this area so that they may grow in justice and love, i.e., in the respect of the integrity and feelings of others as well as of themselves. Thomas precisely formulates the relationship between justice and love in the following way: "Justice without love is cruelty; love without justice leads to dissolu-

---

33. Thomas structures his system of ethics around the three theological virtues (faith, hope, and love), the practice of which requires grace to a particular extent; and around the four so-called cardinal virtues (wisdom, justice, courage, and moderation), which he takes from classical Greek ethics. The best study in German on the subject is still that of Eberhard Schockenhoff, *Bonum hominis. Die anthropologischen und theologischen Grundlagen der Tugendethik von Thomas von Aquin* (Mainz: Matthias Grünewald-Verlag, 1987).

tion."[34] Norms by themselves formulate minimum standards.[35] If they are made the essence of moral discourse, the dimension of love as the highest Christian virtue and the culmination of Christian ethics tends to be excluded or relegated to the domain of purely personal interaction. But love should surpass justice without being oblivious to it. One of its main aims is to overcome evil through an active and — if necessary — one-sided commitment to the good: "Do not be conquered by evil. But conquer evil with good" (Rom. 12:21). The mass as the "source and culmination" of Roman Catholic spirituality shows this intimate relationship between the love of God and the love of the Other, a relationship that also embraces the whole of creation, which is to be transformed together with all of humanity.[36] For this reason there is no clear line between Christian ethics and spirituality. Christian mysticism is always inner-worldly in the Weberian sense. It has nothing to do with esoteric insights or spiritual states sought for their own sake. The criteria of its authenticity are the fruits of love that it bears. Detaching ethics from this spiritual basis ultimately causes the former to become legalistic and the latter to acquire a dualistic and pallid quality. Both spirituality and the practiced morality of Christians are essential for the credibility of the Church's arguments on moral and social issues in the public square. Nothing, after all, can do greater damage to morality than hypocrisy — the divergence between words and action.

Regarding the second issue, Roman Catholicism can make decisive contributions to a civil future through its commitment to justice, both nationally and globally. Political and economic liberalism depend on each other but are also difficult to reconcile, since liberal political institutions for their stability need a reasonable degree of social equality and the satis-

34. Thomas Aquinas, *Super Evangelium Sanctae Matthaei. Lectura,* cura P. Raphaelis Cai OP, ed. V (Turin: Marietti, 1951), p. 69.

35. Such standards are, for instance, formulated in *Gaudium et spes:* "whatever is opposed to life itself, such as any type of murder, genocide, abortion, euthanasia or willful self-destruction, whatever violates the integrity of the human person, such as mutilation, torments inflicted on body or mind, attempts to coerce the will itself; whatever insults human dignity, such as subhuman living conditions, arbitrary imprisonment, deportation, slavery, prostitution, the selling of women and children . . . all these things and others of their like are infamies indeed" (*Gaudium et spes* 27).

36. This is beautifully expressed in Pierre Teilhard de Chardin, *La Messe sur le Monde: Hymne de l'Univers* (Paris: Éditions du Seuil, 1961), pp. 15-55.

faction of basic material needs of all. Although it would be naïve to attribute the rise of fundamentalist movements to material causes alone, growing disparities in income and living conditions worldwide do play a major role in their gaining political support. Destitution, poverty, unemployment, and unfulfilled hopes for prosperity breed religious radicalism. The return to one's religious roots and the rejection of liberal Western values in this situation become ways to assert one's own dignity and protest against economic and political marginalization. Regardless of how one measures justice, the present global distribution of goods cannot be called just. The existing differences in income — and consequently in life chances — are scandalous, and moreover, create an explosive political situation. If peace, according to the words of the prophet Isaiah (Isa. 32:17), is the work of justice, the lack of it is also a great threat to global peace.

This has been the message of Catholic Social Teaching ever since its beginnings in the nineteenth century.[37] Its main aims are "a preferential option for the poor" (a term originally coined by liberation theology and then adopted by pastoral documents) as a struggle against poverty and for human dignity, and the criticism of secular ideologies, Marxism as well as liberalism. The market — and with it the market economy — are thus accepted as facts of life. At the same time, however, Catholic Social Teaching insists on the duty of the state to further the common good, i.e., to help create dignified living conditions for those who are not able to sustain themselves materially. It asserts the right to private property, but also makes it clear that material goods exist to serve all and not only a few. Catholic Christians therefore have not only the duty to be charitable, but also to support the establishment of institutions that are to contribute to a more equitable distribution. These positions represent a middle way between the above-mentioned ideologies. Marxism having lost its relevance, it remains important to point towards the limitations of liberal market economies. Though they have proven to be the best mechanism for the allocation of resources, in order to further social justice and preserve the environment, political institutions are needed that effectively pursue these

---

37. The best English introduction remains that of Donald Dorr, *Option for the Poor: A Hundred Years of Catholic Social Teaching* (Maryknoll, NY: Orbis, 1992). Cf. Ingeborg Gabriel, *Grundzüge und Positionen katholischer Sozialethik:* Ingeborg Gabriel/Alexandros Papaderos/Ulrich Körtner, *Perspektiven ökumenischer Sozialethik*, 2. Aufl. (Ostfildern: Matthias Grünewald-Verlag, 2006). The book intends to introduce readers to Catholic, Orthodox, and Protestant social ethics. An English translation is forthcoming.

aims. At a time when the nation-state is growing weaker (and along with it, its ability to exercise a corrective function), the question is: Which institutions can replace it in a globalized world and work towards a global common good? The rhetorical question of St. Augustine — "What are states without justice but big bands of robbers?"[38] — thus has to be asked anew in a world situation in which states are no longer the only or even the most important actors. The already-difficult task of ensuring that solidarity is incorporated into national institutions must in the present age be undertaken at the global level. For this, global institutions are needed that help to further justice worldwide. Through its caritative and social ministry the Church can contribute to more justice and peace — if it is outspoken enough and willing to take up these global issues. It thereby asserts the universality of social and political norms against culturalist currents that insist on their particularity. It also holds that the political and social involvement of Christians must take into account the "autonomy of earthly affairs" (*Gaudium et spes* 36). This is directed against integralist and fundamentalist ideas, which negate the complexity of social issues in modern societies and tend to disregard the way in which social, political, and economic institutions function.

A third area of particular relevance is the Catholic commitment to dialogue and non-violent conflict resolution. If pluralism — both nationally and globally — is to be more than the mere coexistence of different religious creeds and worldviews, it requires dialogue at different levels, particularly on ethical and political questions. The Roman Catholic Church after Vatican II made a key contribution to these. The essence of its commitment has been formulated in the Declaration on Non-Christian Religions *Nostra aetate*: "Ever aware of her duty to foster unity and charity among individuals, and even among nations, she [i.e., the Church] reflects at the outset on what men have in common and what tends to promote fellowship among them" (*Nostra aetate* 1). The aim is to find common ground by proceeding from what different groups already agree on. This requires respect for the other's convictions as well as competence in articulating one's positions in ways intelligible for others. What distinguishes dialogue from propaganda is the knowledge that the partner has something to contribute. To speak to each other makes sense only if one recognizes that one's knowledge and capacity to find solutions are limited and, therefore, may

---

38. Aurelius Augustinus, *Civitas Dei*, book 4, chapter 4.

be enriched by what others have to say. Dialogue thus depends on the insight of both sides that we do not own the truth, but are always striving for it and therefore need to talk to each other. It goes without saying that dialogue also presupposes reflected positions and identities. As Albert Camus wrote: "Dialogue is only possible between people who remain who they are and who speak the truth." But one's identity and convictions can be sustained and deepened only in communication — a fact that makes for the dynamism and fruitfulness of dialogue.

The three main areas in which the Catholic Church has been particularly active in theory and practice during the past decades were the dialogue with secular modernity, with other Christian churches, and with members of other religious communities. The common ground shared by secular and Christian ethics is the recognition of the supreme value of human life, its integrity and welfare, and the equality of all human beings irrespective of race, color, gender, or religion.[39] To quote Vatican II once again: "According to the almost unanimous opinion of believers and unbelievers alike, all things on earth should be related to man as their center and crown" (*Gaudium et spes* 12). As much as liberal secular and Christian positions may differ on concrete issues, there is a high degree of consensus to be found between them, the essence of which is their humanistic approach. If God's becoming man, i.e., his incarnation, is the basic tenet of Christianity, then Christianity is humanism *par excellence.* One may therefore criticize secular humanism for not being humanistic enough, but not for being too humanistic. On this common basis the differences between Christian and secular humanism can and must be discussed.[40]

Although it is of great importance, ecumenical dialogue — another main area of Catholic involvement — can only be mentioned here in brief. For the Decree on Ecumenism *Unitatis redintegratio* (1965), the ecumenical movement is the work of the Holy Spirit, progress towards unity resulting from a conversion of hearts, a better knowledge of the other's theology and traditions, and cooperation in the social area. Particularly in Europe, where confessional conflicts were one of the reasons for banishing religion

---

39. Charles Taylor has shown this in the first part of *The Sources of the Self: The Making of the Modern Identity* (Cambridge, MA: Harvard University Press, 1989).

40. Thus, the Compendium of the Social Doctrine of the Church takes integral humanism — i.e., a humanism that includes the religious dimension — as its point of departure. Cf. Pontifical Council for Justice and Peace, ed., *Compendium of the Social Doctrine of the Church* (Rome: Libreria Editrice Vaticana, 2004).

from the political sphere, peaceful cooperation between different churches is a precondition for their credibility.

Last but not least, interreligious dialogue has acquired great significance in the past decades. Its goal is not unity, i.e., it does not aim at syncretism, but the recognition of the religious and moral truths contained in other religions. The Declaration on Non-Christian Religions *Nostra aetate* (1965) opened the way for a great number of interreligious initiatives in the Catholic Church. An unprecedented event in its history was the World Prayer Meeting in Assisi (the first was held in 1986; others have followed), to which Pope John Paul II invited representatives from all world religions to pray together for global peace and justice. The main areas for interreligious dialogue are ethical (and maybe spiritual) questions where the basic consensus is by far greater and the scope for argumentation therefore larger, than in proper religious questions. This is good news. In a globalized world peace does not depend on having the same concept of God, but on having common ethical standards acceptable to all.[41] The Greek expression *dia-logou* — "through words" — connotes a form of action that is diametrically opposed to force. Therefore, as utopian as dialogue may seem at times in view of political realities, it is the only alternative to violence in a world where different faith traditions have to reach basic agreement, globally and nationally, about what is to be considered civil and humane.

The Roman Catholic Church is a huge institution. It is the only one with global administrative structures and a global government. Its sheer size, with over one billion members, makes it an important actor in world affairs; in other words, it is a "global player." But it must not be forgotten that its central structures, which have gained even greater visibility through the global media, constitute but the external representation of the world Church. Its essence is the myriad of different initiatives and institutions worldwide, be it parishes, religious, or lay congregations, each of which has its own profile as well as spiritual and social priorities. There are great regional differences between them, which also indicate that in different regional contexts different forms of action are needed to live up to the challenges of the age. Therefore, I would like to add at this point that the

---

41. This is the conclusion I have drawn from twelve years of participation in the Vienna Christian-Muslim dialogues, the proceedings of which have been published, most of them also in English and Arabic. Cf. www.univie.ac.at/ktf/sozialethik.

reflections in this paper represent a European point of view. The emphasis made by an Asian or an African Catholic would most certainly be different. As important as the positions taken by the global and local churches may be, however, what matters in the end are the (inner and outer) actions taken by Catholic Christians who practice their faith and are willing to take responsibility for it. Theological positions and magisterial guidelines can both foster or hinder this faith practice; they cannot bring it about. The importance of Vatican II lies exactly in the fact that it laid the foundations for this active involvement of Catholics in areas of particular relevance in today's world. It is a sound basis and an ongoing advantage for the Roman Catholic Church as well as of society. Despite all oscillations in ecclesiastical policy and the typical "anti-resources," such as laziness and indifference, self-sufficiency and self-righteousness, resignation and traditionalism that hinder the practical and intellectual commitment needed, it has prevented the Roman Catholic Church as a whole from falling into extremes. An idealization of the past as an era of clear Catholic identity does not do justice to the present situation. The Church — which means its faithful as well as the hierarchy — has to find solutions under the present conditions of uncertainty and risk. As the biblical metaphor goes: putting new wine in old wineskins spoils both.

One of the main challenges of the age is to sustain and spread liberal political institutions, particularly human rights and democracy. But for this it must be acknowledged that the expansion of rights only creates spaces of freedom. True respect of others cannot be guaranteed by a constitution. It requires the everyday efforts of citizens who are willing to fill these institutions with life. The motivation has to come from their own convictions: Why, after all, should I respect my neighbor as a fellow human being? The question "Can this respect of the dignity of the person be upheld without faith?" cannot be answered in the abstract. But Christian faith in the sanctity of the life of the other, whatever his personal qualities may be, is a strong foundation for this respect, on which our political system is built. It is ultimately rooted in our being created in the image of the triune God. Throughout history, this belief has stimulated the willingness to defend the dignity of the other even under difficult circumstances. This focus on the concrete person could, moreover, help debunk both idols and ideologies, which are not liberating and life-giving, but alienate human beings from themselves and their fellows.

At the intellectual level the Church can and must defend the role of reason in matters of faith and morals. This is a difficult task for a variety of reasons. These include the erosion of intellectual culture through social fragmentation, the replacement of argumentation by the often-trivial images of the media, as well as the lack of time, sheer ignorance, and confusion due to the many opinions we are confronted with in a pluralistic society. Since we live in a world that has largely been constructed by human inventions, we also have the responsibility to cope with them, asking ourselves which actions and ideas can promote further progress in civility — which is, after all, the only kind of progress that ultimately counts. The answer to modern rationalism thus must not be anti-rationalism, religious or otherwise. The warning of the present Pope should be taken seriously in this respect. It is of utmost importance for the future whether the religions will be able to bring their rational resources into play so as to find viable solutions instead of clashing with each other. This requires a creative reinterpretation of their traditions in cooperation with others, which makes dialogue so important. The belligerent relativism that proclaims the liberation from morals on the one hand, and the hardening of religious positions on the other, call for prudent reflection and moderation that is based on love.

At the same time, one must resist the temptation to become fixated on the negative sides of new developments that are taking place all over the world. There are also powerful trends towards communion between human beings, religions, and ideas. One may observe not only fragmentation, but also encouraging signs of its being overcome. To acknowledge and strengthen these, seeing them as harbingers of the world to come and signs of God's grace, is one of the noblest tasks of the Church as a sacrament of unity for mankind. This precludes any hasty opposition between humanism and Christianity. The main characteristic of the Christian God as shown by revelation is, after all, his *philanthropy,* i.e., his love for mankind. A God who does not desire the good would be nothing but an idol, and his proclamation a type of inflexible and inhumane ideology.

Catholic theology sees oneness, truth, and the good (and sometimes also the beautiful) as the transcendental qualities of life. They are its essence, and even if they are never perfectly realized in this world, they are to be furthered by Catholic Christians in every way possible. Because of its size, public visibility, and intellectual heritage, the Roman Catholic Church has a particular responsibility in this respect. The positions it takes can influence the course of events for the better. The promise of the kingdom of God, of "a new heaven and a new earth, in which justice reigns" (1 Peter 3:13), should be a strong incentive to take the action needed for a more humane future, despite the fact that the course of history is uncertain and the final outcome of present developments cannot be foreseen.

A Lutheran Approach

Peter L. Berger

NOTE: The present topic was originally intended to be dealt with in a paper by a Lutheran theologian. This paper failed to materialize. Not wanting to leave Lutheranism out of the mix of the project, I decided to venture a brief paper myself. I have no theological credentials, and what follows is a layman's effort. But, I suppose, there is a good Lutheran legitimation: the notion of the priesthood of all believers presumably extends to a believer's doing theology. But I want to make one point before I embark on this exercise: I have no doubt that a theologian will have no difficulty in showing that I have used a number of Lutheran ideas in a way that deviates sharply from their original meanings. So be it. I think that a religious tradition is not an inert object to be handed on as is from one generation to the next, but rather a living thing open to (sometimes surprising) reinterpretations. To borrow a phrase from American constitutional theory, I'm *not* a "strict constructionist" when it comes to a religious tradition. — PLB

It seems to me that the immediate effect of the Lutheran Reformation was a sense of great liberation. This was, of course, an extension of Luther's formative religious experience — a liberation from the legalistic morality of medieval Catholicism, and more directly from his self-torturing efforts to overcome his deep sense of unworthiness. (I'm not concerned here with the possibly pathological dimension of the latter.) Luther gained a conviction of joyful freedom from this experience.

Among other things, this may explain the fact that Luther is one of the very few figures in religious history with a well-developed sense of humor. (In saying this, I have no wish to gloss over some of the repulsive traits Luther developed in his later years, such as his bloodthirsty attitude to the peasants' revolt and his vicious anti-Semitic reaction to the failure of Jews to follow his originally friendly invitation to convert to the newly reformed Christianity: Lutheranism does not rest on a personality cult.) Liberation, joy, even playfulness — these are prototypically Lutheran themes. They are best expressed, not in doctrinal writings, but in hymnody and popular piety.

The Lutheran movement had to define itself in a threefold opposition: against the increasingly hostile Roman church, with its hierarchical and legalistic apparatus of salvation. Against the new legalism of the Swiss reformers, an opposition that led to the sharp division between the Lutheran and Calvinist streams of Protestantism. But also opposition against the antinomian tendencies of the so-called "left wing" of the Reformation: Lutherans had to make clear that their opposition to legalism did not imply a rejection of all objective norms of law and morality.

To maintain this threefold opposition has not been an easy balancing act. A sociologist of religion will not be surprised by the fact that, after its original charismatic phase, Lutheranism developed a legalism of its own, in a doctrinal orthodoxy that left little beyond lip service of the Christian freedom proclaimed by Luther. I suspect that this phase already began with Philip Melanchthon's valiant attempt to construct a Lutheran dogma that could maintain itself in the intellectual debates with Catholic and Calvinist theologians. This Lutheran orthodoxy then blossomed in the seventeenth and eighteenth centuries, effectively stifling the early sense of liberation. But I would also propose that the latter broke out again and again, replicating the formative experience.

In trying to define a Lutheran approach to a middle ground between relativism and fundamentalism, I will make use of a number of Lutheran ideas. They have, of course, been encased in the doctrinal formulations of Lutheran orthodoxy. But it is not in this form that they interest me. Rather, I look on them as themes, motifs, expressions of specific experiences.

Sola fide

That is perhaps the core Lutheran idea — that we are saved, not by our works, but "by faith alone." Luther hit on this while reading, or rereading, the passage in Romans 3, where the Apostle Paul writes "For we hold that a man is justified by faith apart from works of law." What Paul was writing about here concerned a Christian's view of the Jewish law. Luther transposed this to his own problem with the "law" of Catholic morality, specifically with his failure to attain perfection despite all his rigorous applications of monastic discipline. And, as Catholic critics have always pointed out, he sneaked in the word "alone" — "justified by faith *alone*." Not good scholarly practice, to be sure. But Luther was no "strict constructionist" with regard to the Bible. He was bold enough to apply Paul's core insight to his, Luther's, own problem.

It is also important to understand that "faith" here does not mean assent to a doctrinal proposition. It means trust in God's saving grace. Luther used a wordplay here — faith/*fides* is trust/*fiducia*. And in a revealing statement Luther once said "I don't know what I believe, but I know in *whom* I believe." Whether Luther intended this or not, I would interpret the *sola fide* motif as follows. Here is an understanding of faith that eschews certainty — precisely the sort of certainty that every form of fundamentalism purports to supply. At the same time it cannot be equated with any form of relativism: it is faith in a very objective understanding of reality — namely, the reality of the redemptive power of Christ. This reality is not a subjective phenomenon within our own consciousness, but it is a reality outside ourselves *(extra nos),* indeed is a cosmic reality.

Different religious traditions have sought to ground certainty in different ways. In Christian history there have been three principal ways of doing this — certainty based on an inerrant Scripture, on an infallible Church, and on an irresistible experience. The first method has been favored by various strands of conservative Protestantism, the second by a number of churches but most grandiosely in Roman Catholicism, the third by a large number of mystical or quasi-mystical movements ranging from the austere experience of a Teresa of Avila to the more mellow "strangely warmed heart" of John Wesley (not to mention the ecstatic certainty mediated by Pentecostalism, which today is exploding globally). All three methods of attaining certainty have been seriously undermined by modern forms of critical thought — biblical fundamentalism by biblical scholarship, ecclesiastical fundamentalism by church history and the sociology of religion, and the fundamentalism of experience by the psychologists who have made us cognizant of the near-infinite capacity of human beings to delude themselves. This is not the place to go into detail as to the challenges posed by these modern intellectual disciplines, except to say that they make all the more urgent an understanding of faith in the absence of certainty. What is interesting here is that Lutheranism has anticipated all three challenges and responded to them in a very distinctive way.

One more observation before I try to argue what I have just stated: some Lutheran theologians, while avoiding the term "certainty," have distinguished between "security" *(securitas)* and "certitude" *(certitudo)*, the first allegedly a bad thing, the second a good thing. It seems to me that this is having one's cake and eating it too. The distinction makes little sense. Either I know something or I don't. In the first case I don't need faith. Thus I don't need faith to know that what I see outside the window of my study is the skyline of Boston. I then have both "security" and "certitude." But when I say that I have faith in God's grace, I do need faith, because I have neither "security" nor "certitude." So much for unhelpful suggestions.

Sola Scriptura

Lutheranism insisted that Scripture, consisting of both the Hebrew Bible and the New Testament — was the only authority for Christian belief and practice — Scripture *alone*. This, of course, was making a polemical point against Rome, which (quite correctly, by the way) maintained that the biblical canon had been decided upon by the church and that the Bible comes to us via Christian (and, one may add Jewish) tradition. But that is somewhat beside the point, which was that the individual Christian had the right, indeed the obligation, to turn to the Bible for guidance in matters of belief and practice, at times pitting his or her conscience (specifically, a conscience shaped by Scripture) against the authority of the church. That, of course, is what Luther did, most dramatically in his testimony at the Diet of Worms. Luther did not intend this stance to give birth to individualism in the modern sense — his position was *not* "by conscience alone." Nevertheless, a good case can be made that an unintended consequence of the Lutheran Reformation was a new understanding of individual autonomy, and not only in religious matters.

It is all the more remarkable with what freedom Luther dealt with portions of the Bible. For example, he did not like at all the New Testament book of James, because it seemed to contradict his belief in justification by faith alone. When he undertook his historic translation of the Bible into German, he seriously contemplated throwing the book out of the New Testament. He refrained from doing so out of a reluctance to undertake unnecessarily radical measures, but clearly he regarded James as being less *Scriptura* than, say, Romans. He had one overriding exegetical principle: Did a biblical text bear witness to Christ, be it in anticipation (as in the Old Testament) or directly (as in the New)? If yes, then the text was indeed Scripture; if not, the text could be relegated to, let us say, background noise. Needless to say, this is not a principle that a modern historian would subscribe to. But it is a plausible criterion for approaching the biblical text theologically.

Such an approach obviously makes any fundamentalist notion of biblical inerrancy difficult if not impossible. I think one could clarify the difference as follows. A fundamentalist will say that the Bible *is* the Word of God. A Lutheran approach could be summed up as saying that the Bible *contains* the Word of God. This seems like a small difference. It is not. The difference is immense.

It is highly relevant in this connection to recall the fact that modern biblical scholarship originated in Germany in the nineteenth century, mostly in Lutheran theological faculties. As far as I know, this is the first case in the history of religion that the sharp scalpel of critical historical analysis was applied by scholars *to their own tradition!* I would submit that this took a lot of courage, possible only because of a Lutheran conception of freedom — which includes the freedom of the intellect. To be sure, some of these scholars became convinced that the results of their work made it difficult to remain in the church or even to remain a Christian. Thus Julius Wellhausen, the father of modern Old Testament scholarship and a professor in Berlin, wrote a very moving letter to the Prussian minister of education. In the letter he said that his lectures triggered crises of faith among some of his students, most of whom were theology students and future ministers, that he did not wish to have this effect, for which reason he respectfully requested a transfer from the theological to the philosophical faculty. (The request was denied, and Wellhausen left for another university, where his teaching could take place in a less faith-driven atmosphere.) However, most of these biblical scholars did not leave their theological faculties, did not lose their faith because of their findings, and instead tried to reinterpret the faith while acknowledging the validity of the findings. This attitude later spread beyond Lutheran circles — to other Protestants, then to Catholics, more reluctantly to Jews, hardly at all to Muslims. One does not have to be a Lutheran to reconcile faith with modern historical scholarship. But it helps.

Satis est

Article 7 of the Augsburg Confession, the most authoritative statement of the Lutheran faith, deals with the church. It states: "It is enough *(satis est)* for the true unity of the Christian church that the Gospel be preached in purity and that the holy sacraments be offered in accordance with the Gospel. And it is not necessary for the true unity of the Christian church that everywhere be observed the same ceremonies instituted by men" (my translation). This is a truly minimalist definition! Except for the preaching of the gospel, and the sacraments which constitute the gospel in another form, everything else handed on by tradition is subsumed under the heading "ceremonies instituted by men" — including the hierarchy and all the doctrinal edifice of Rome. This did not mean that all these "ceremonies" and institutions had to be thrown out at once. Indeed, the Lutheran Reformation was at first very conservative in these matters. But they *could* be thrown out — which is the crucial point here. Once again, this stance makes a church-based fundamentalism difficult: the church is not an object of faith; the gospel is the object of faith. The church is only the vehicle by which this faith is facilitated.

Even if one is unfamiliar with the development of Lutheran orthodoxy, one can note that the above lapidary formula leaves some big opportunities for a new legalism to creep back in. Who is to decide whether the gospel is preached "in purity"? Or whether the sacraments are offered "in accordance with the gospel"? Lutheran theologians of the post-Reformation era busily worked out elaborate answers, constructing a doctrine about the "marks of the church" (that is, the traits by which the true church may be recognized) that could almost compete with the intricacies of Roman canon law. Still, the Augsburg Confession continues to be *available*. Anyone tempted to base religious certainty on the church can turn to it. Again, one does not have to be a Lutheran to be free in one's attitude to the church, its ceremonies and institutions. But it helps.

Peter L. Berger

Extra nos

Already during Luther's lifetime, while the center of the Reformation remained in Wittenberg, there arose a number of independent movements generally subsumed under the label of the "Left Wing of the Reformation." Some were pacifist, some were violent in the service of utopian politics, some were simply more radical theologically than the Wittenberg coterie (once described by Paul Goodman as "a conspiracy of junior faculty in a provincial university"). Luther called these movements *Schwärmer,* a term usually translated (not very felicitously) as "enthusiasts" — it describes, pejoratively, people with wild, highly emotional ideas. What many of them had in common was a reliance on inner religious experience as the main if not the only basis of faith — precisely the third method of attaining certainty mentioned earlier in this paper. Luther disagreed with all these movements — theologically, ecclesiastically, very much politically where they became ideologies of revolutionary insurgencies. But he especially disagreed with the effort to ground faith in this or that inner experience.

This does not mean that Luther dismissed any such experience as illusionary. For example, he had a high opinion of a classical text of medieval mysticism, the so-called "German Theology." What he did dismiss was the notion that faith depended on this or any other form of ecstatic experience — the core of what he called *Schwärmerei.* In opposition to this, he used the phrase *extra nos,* "outside ourselves."

We encounter the Word of God as a reality, not within the alleged depths of our own being (which in any case Luther thought was tainted by sin), but objectively, outside ourselves, in Scripture and, even more importantly, in the living preaching of the gospel and in the sacraments. All these means of grace are hard, external facts. Scripture is a book, which we can hold in our hands. The preacher stands before us in the pulpit, a living human being. And the sacraments are equally hard, material facts — water, bread, and wine. In discussing the materiality of the Eucharist, Luther remarked that in this sacrament we can chew the body of Christ with our teeth *(manducatio oralis).* By themselves, all these facts are simply phenomena of this world, frequently exhibiting all the foibles of worldly reality — a book written by fallible men, an unimpressive cleric with bad breath, cold water, stale bread, sour wine. But the Holy Spirit, reached out to in faith, makes us find God's Word in these imperfect vehicles.

In sum, just as Lutheranism induces skepticism about all attempts to attain religious certainty by means of Scripture or church, it equally suggests skepticism about all the alleged certainties of inner experience. Three centuries after the Reformation, Søren Kierkegaard expressed a very Lutheran sensibility by describing the act of faith as a "leap" — a venturing forth toward God without any secure supports. This is not an easy form of religion. There is a German proverb that says "as a Lutheran it is difficult to live but easy to die" *("lutherisch lässt sich schwer leben, leicht sterben").*

In all of this there is also a very sober view of the Christian life. The limitations of the human condition are accepted — man is a fallen creature. The quest for perfection is futile. There are no Lutheran saints. Even the most admirable Christian is a "saint" only by virtue of God's having declared him to be such, but in this life he remains "at the same time just and sinner" *("simul iustus et peccator").* If taken to heart, here is a soberness that makes it difficult to be a fundamentalist.

"In, With, and Under"

This is the formula coined by Lutherans to describe their position on the Eucharist. It is a position midway between that of some Swiss reformers who understood the sacrament as nothing but a memorial ceremony, and the Catholic doctrine of transubstantiation, the process in which the elements of bread and wine are miraculously (though invisibly) transformed into the body and blood of Christ. The Lutheran view is that Christ is really present in the sacrament — it is not simply a memorial service, nor is it a miraculous event. But Christ is present "in, with, and under" the elements of bread and wine, which remain unchanged as phenomena of this world, transformed only in the perspective of faith.

While the formula was originally meant to apply to the Eucharist, it seems to me that it can usefully be applied as well to Scripture and the church. The Bible is a humanly produced set of documents, full of errors that scholars may explore to their hearts' content, but "in, with, and under" these human realities (so to speak) *lurks* the Word of God. The church is a human institution, like all institutions full of stupidity and wickedness, but "in, with, and under" this fallible edifice the gospel is preserved and reiterated.

Again, this formula makes it difficult to absolutize either Scripture or the church. In this sense, it too is an anti-fundamentalist formula.

"Three Uses of the Law"

Anarchy is the dark sister of freedom. The freedom of the Christian, as insisted upon by Luther, can easily morph into an anarchic relativism in which anything goes. Morally, this can take the form of antinomianism — literally, opposition to law — there are to be no external norms regulating behavior, only such norms as individuals may spontaneously generate themselves. Such a view was held by many on the "left" fringes of the Protestant movement. It is a view all too common today, perhaps most dramatically articulated by postmodernism: there are no objective criteria of truth or falsity, right or wrong. There are only different "narratives." In principle, every "narrative" is as valid as any other "narrative." (Postmodernist theorists have different ways of trying to get out of the self-destructive paradox of this view — after all, what about *their* "narrative"? But that is another story.)

The Lutheran doctrine of the three uses of the law was intended in part to protect against this type of moral relativism. The law (for our purposes here, just think of it as embodied in the Ten Commandments) has three uses. First, there is the civil use *(usus civilis),* which is instituted to maintain basic order and justice in society, with no function in the economy of salvation. Second, there is the "convicting" use *(usus elenchticus):* the law convicts us, because we are sinners who cannot possibly live up to it and are therefore dependent on God's forgiveness. And, third, there is the didactic use *(usus didacticus):* the Christian, by virtue of God's grace, is now free of the law, but it continues to serve as a guide to behavior.

One may be somewhat uneasy about this understanding of Old Testament law (I am). But the doctrine is a corrective against the notion that Christian freedom means the license to do anything one wants. In other words, just as Lutheranism has barriers against fundamentalism, it also provides these against relativism.

"Two Realms"

The quest for a middle position between relativism and fundamentalism also has political implications. Not only is it important to understand that there are secular fundamentalisms as well as religious ones, but both relativism and fundamentalism are dangers to any decent political order — relativism because it undermines the moral consensus without which a society cannot exist, fundamentalism because it balkanizes a society into hostile camps unable to cohabit peacefully with each other. The dangers are particularly great to a democratic society: because it eschews coercion, democracy is all the more dependent on moral consensus. And democracy requires precisely the sort of compromises that fundamentalists are unable to make. There is a political agenda here. Can Lutheranism be helpful to this agenda? I think it can.

For theological reasons that cannot be gone into here, Lutheranism has always made a sharp distinction between law and gospel. Unlike either Catholicism or Calvinism, it has no notion of a Christian law, nor, by the same token, of a Christian society. The distinction between law and gospel has also been expressed by the idea of the two realms. There is the realm of the gospel, which is where God is engaged in the redemption of the world. There is the realm of law, where God demands of men that they maintain elementary standards of order and justice. The two realms must not be confused. On one hand such confusion leads to the gospel being subverted by legalism (Luther would say, by "works-righteousness"). On the other hand the confusion leads to the misguided notion that, in this world, a society could be run on the basis of the Sermon on the Mount. In the realm of the law there is a different rationale, distinct from the rationale of salvation. This was pithily expressed by Luther when he said that he would rather be ruled by a just Turk than by an unjust Christian. Conversely, when Luther enjoined the Protestant princes to come to the aid of the Holy Roman Emperor (the same character who had done whatever he could to suppress Protestantism) in defense of Europe against the Turkish invasion, he went to great lengths to make clear that he did this not because the Turks were not Christians, but because they murdered, raped, and enslaved people whom the Emperor was required to defend. In other words, Luther made very clear that he was not calling for a crusade. The gospel did not need to be defended by the sword; innocent people did.

The doctrine of the two realms has often been criticized for inducing an attitude of subservience to anything done by governments. It probably had this effect at times. But that would have been a distortion of the doctrine. Governments are expected to be just; when they are not, they lose their God-given legitimacy and Christians are freed to stop their allegiance. This was quietly but very clearly expressed when congregations of the Confessing Church in Germany (the movement that resisted the Nazi attempt to take over the Protestant church) omitted the prayer for the authorities from the Sunday order of worship. To be sure, very few Germans made the step from this anti-Nazism within the church to active resistance against the Nazi regime. Some who did (Dietrich Bonhoeffer is the best known) were motivated by a very Lutheran understanding of the proper role of the state.

The doctrine of the two realms, rightly understood, is not a formula for political passivity or subservience. It is a strongly anti-utopian formula. The gospel proclaims the kingdom of God that is yet to come (though it has already been initiated in the coming of Christ). It is a distortion of the gospel to want to set up the kingdom of God here and now, be it by violent means or not. The "left wing" of the Reformation sprouted a number of movements employing violence in the service of such a utopian cause, prominent among them the inauguration of the kingdom of God in the city of Münster (which was suppressed by an alliance of Lutherans and Catholics). Alas, this was not the last such attempt. The doctrine of the two realms is a barrier against any project that promises salvation and ultimate meaning through political actions, no matter whether the project is couched in religious or secular terms. Needless to say, the horrendous totalitarian movements of the twentieth century purported to offer salvation in secular terms. By contrast, the realm of law is not to be approached in a spirit of absolute, religious, or quasi-religious commitment. Rather, it is to be approached in a spirit of prudent reason.

Max Weber, in his famous essay "Politics as a Vocation," discussed two types of ethics — an "ethic of attitude" (*Gesinnungsethik,* sometimes rendered into English as "ethic of absolute ends") and an "ethic of responsibility" *(Verantwortungsethik).* The former is guided by a set of absolute principles, to be followed regardless of circumstances. The latter guides actions in terms of a prudent weighing of likely consequences, even if the resulting course violates this or that moral principle. Weber took Tolstoy as a prototype of the former ethic. He admired Tolstoy (an admiration I don't share), but concludes that the latter is a very poor exemplar for a politically relevant actor, indeed in the final analysis is irresponsible. As a prototype of the "ethic of responsibility" Weber took Machiavelli. He cites with approval the latter's statement that, for the welfare of the city, the prince must be willing to sacrifice the eternal salvation of his soul.

I don't know whether Weber intended this, but his two ethics have a very strong affinity with the Lutheran idea of the two realms. The "ethic of attitude" is the misguided attempt to subject the realm of law to the requirements of the gospel. On the other hand, the "ethic of responsibility" is the only one that can be applied effectively by anyone who wishes to do some good in the real world — knowing full well that the consequences of his actions may escape his intentions, but daring to act in reliance on God's grace. Weber grew up in a household shaped by the culture of Lutheran pietism, although he later understood himself as an agnostic. It is not inconceivable that his ethical reasoning was influenced by this Lutheran heritage — a sort of secularized doctrine of the two realms. Be this as it may, Weber's dichotomy offers an incisive explication of the moral and political implications of this doctrine.

I have tried in this paper to suggest that the Lutheran tradition contains useful theological and moral resources for a middle position between relativism and fundamentalism. Not for a moment am I suggesting that these resources were always, or even frequently, operative in the thought and actions of Lutherans. But in that Lutheranism is not unusual. It is in the nature of every tradition to become petrified, distorted, or decayed. (Come to think of it, Weber's theory of the "routinization of charisma" gives an accurate sociological picture of this process — after the prophets always come the bureaucrats.) All the same, traditions can be submerged, lie dormant for long periods of time, but suddenly come alive again at a later moment when their genius is rediscovered.

The oldest Lutheran church in my native city of Vienna is located on a quiet street in the central district. On the wall near the altar there is a Latin inscription (not easy to find, unless one is looking for it). Thanks are expressed to the Emperor Joseph II for permitting, for the first time since the Counter-Reformation, a place for public Lutheran worship in the heart of the Habsburg capital. It is signed *"Augustanae Confessionis addicti."* Literally translated, this simply means "adherents of the Augsburg Confession." But for anyone accustomed to the English language another meaning of *addictio* suggests itself — not just an ordinary adherence, but one to which one is compelled to return. Some of us have no desire to overcome the addiction.

Pilgrim at the Spaghetti Junction: An Evangelical Perspective on Relativism and Fundamentalism

Os Guinness

"Every mind of any scope was a crossroads for all shades of opinion; every thinker was an international exposition of thought." Paul Valéry's comment on the carnival-like chaos of European thinking on the eve of World War I could be amplified infinitely in the intellectual and cultural climate of the postmodern world. Indeed, thinkers today are faced, not with a simple crossroads, but with an infinite series of spaghetti junctions, each posing multiple choices, consequences, unintended consequences, and unknown aftermaths.

Not surprisingly, the effect of such a swirling vortex of choice, change, and consequence is to entice wild swings between feelings of nausea and a desperate desire to hang on to fixed objects of certainty, however far in the past — in short, to accelerate the part-polarization, part-oscillation between relativism and fundamentalism, which the opening essays of this book have outlined so well as endemic in the conditions of our advanced modern world.

None of us who are modern are exempt from the pull of this temptation, and that of course includes Christians who identify themselves within the evangelical movement or tradition. Indeed, whether they like it or not, evangelicals usually find themselves placed squarely in the camp of one of the two extremes: fundamentalism.

That prejudice and that stereotype I protest. Unquestionably many evangelicals are fundamentalists, but a significant number of evangelicals are currently in danger of falling into the other extreme and becoming relativists. But more thoughtful evangelicals understand and articulate their faith in a way that avoids the pitfalls of both extremes. This essay is therefore a case for a more accurate and also a freer and more generous understanding of evangelicalism and its perspective on fundamentalism and relativism.

If the deepest and most universal picture of life is that of the journey, or quest, then John Bunyan's *Pilgrim's Progress* takes its place as the evangelical counterpart of other classics of Western thought such as Homer's *Odyssey*, Virgil's *Aeneid*, Dante's *The Divine Comedy*, Cervantes's *Don Quixote*, Herman Hesse's *Siddartha*, and Jack Kerouac's *On the Road*.

Yet even in such dazzling company, it would be a mistake to dismiss the simple profundity of Bunyan's story as simplistic; and to conclude that Pilgrim and those who have identified with him the most, are simple, uneducated people, as likely to be intellectually confused before the complexities of modern life as Pilgrim was spiritually and morally challenged by menaces such as Doubting Castle and Vanity Fair — in short, to believe that evangelicals are simple, uneducated believers almost certain to face the modern complexity and choose the fundamentalist response, if only out of fear of the alternative.

This prejudice does a serious injustice both to the character of evangelicalism and to the capacity of thinking evangelicals to face modern challenges and complexities thoughtfully and responsibly. Besides, the sort of prejudice that fixes the identities of individuals and groups regardless of their own understanding of themselves is a highly illiberal aspect of modern liberalism. Self-understanding and the assertion of identity are powerful and precious to groups as well as to individuals, and should be central to a liberal understanding of freedom. Identity is not in itself an argument, and there are grave dangers in identity politics, but evangelicals themselves — and not scholars, the press, or public opinion — have the right to say who we understand ourselves to be.

What then is an evangelical? And how does being an evangelical bear on the challenge of fundamentalism and relativism? The answers may be set out briefly in the following five areas, all of which bear directly on the polarization between relativism and fundamentalism.

Who We Are

What is an evangelical? The evangelical movement, in its American form, is in crisis today — not least as a result of its own remarkable growth, success, and public attention over the past few decades. And at the heart of this crisis is a growing confusion over the meaning of the term *evangelical.* This crisis has a direct bearing on the polarization between relativism and fundamentalism because a major part of the confusion stems from the fact that evangelicals are equated with fundamentalists, and therefore with the religious right.

If this crisis deepens, the confusion over the definition of *evangelical* remains unresolved, and the present drift in leadership continues, the outcome for evangelicals could be a slump into theological unfaithfulness, spiritual mediocrity, cultural worldliness and irrelevance, and an accelerated falling away among two groups that are critical to the integrity and future of evangelicalism: educated evangelicals and younger evangelicals.

Evangelicals have no pope, supreme leader, or official spokesperson, so no one speaks for all evangelicals, least of all those who claim to. I therefore speak only for myself, but as a representative of countless evangelicals who are all committed to being true to our faith and thoughtful about our calling in today's world. We acknowledge the confusions and corruptions that presently attend the term *evangelical* and the name *evangelicals* in the United States and much of the Western world today, and the concerns that this has aroused in the minds of many, both inside and outside the movement — not least because of the real or perceived extremism of the Christian right and the well-publicized scandals of certain evangelical leaders "caught with their pants down and their foot in their mouth," as it has been described.

Let me therefore state simply what I mean by evangelical, and then set out what being evangelical means for the issues raised by the polarization between fundamentalism and relativism. *To be evangelical, or to call ourselves evangelicals, is to be Christians who seek to define ourselves, our faith, and our lives according to the Good News of Jesus of Nazareth.* Evangelicals are therefore "people of the Gospel." (The Greek word for good news, or gospel, was *euangelion,* which was translated into Latin as *evangelium* and into English as the *evangel.*)

This basic definition requires a fuller explanation that goes beyond this brief essay. But defined and understood in this way, evangelicals form one of three leading traditions within the Christian church. While we fully adhere to the historic creeds of the Christian faith, along with the Orthodox and the Roman Catholics; while we stand and work with other Christians on many ethical and social issues of common concern today; and while we fully appreciate the defining principles of the Orthodox and Roman Catholic traditions, the priority of "right belief and right worship" and the "universality" of the Christian church across the centuries and the continents, we also hold to evangelical beliefs that are distinct from the other traditions in important ways — distinctions that we hold dear because we see them as matters of biblical truth, recovered by the Protestant Reformation and spreading rapidly in many parts of the world today, especially in the Global South.

Evangelicals are therefore followers of Jesus Christ, or plain ordinary Christians, in the classic and historic understanding of Christians over the last two thousand years. It is our conviction that the defining principle of being evangelical is no less deep and primary than those of the other two traditions. To be evangelical is therefore primarily and decisively theological and confessional, rather than psychological, political, or social. Evangelicalism is flexible, innovative, and adaptive, but while it has properly taken many forms in different cultures and generations, it must always be defined theologically rather than culturally. All else is potentially "cultural baggage" and a distortion.

Why the Issue Matters to Us

If evangelicals are Christians who, as "people of the Gospel," seek "to define themselves, their faith, and their lives according to the Good News of Jesus of Nazareth," there is a strong reason why the issue of fundamentalism and relativism matters: Jesus called his followers, as a matter of faithfulness, to be "in" the world but "not of" the world. In the admonition of St. Paul's letter to the church in Rome, they were to be "not conformed" to the world but "transformed" by a renewal of their minds. In the words of the Hartford Declaration, Christians who are faithful to Jesus are to be "against the world for the world."

This characteristic stance of "engagement without equation," or "adaptation without accommodation," has given the Christian church a stance in the world that is simultaneously world-affirming and world-denying. This distinctive stance has been credited as one of the sources of the culture-creating capacity of the Christian faith in history. Thus to fall for the polarized extremes represented by relativism and fundamentalism would be a severe blow to the church's effectiveness as well as its integrity.

Easily stated, this challenge to be "in, but not of" the world is not easily lived, and it is no surprise that the history of the church is also the story
of the pitfalls into which the church has fallen repeatedly in her attempt to
be faithful to this calling. In some periods, the church became so much
"in" the world that it became "of" the world, and thus worldly rather than
Christian. (On reading the four Gospels during the spiritual and moral
chaos of the Renaissance, Erasmus's friend Thomas Linacre remarked famously, "Either these are not the Gospels, or we are not Christians.") In
other periods, the church became so much "not of" the world that it was
other-worldly to the point of being, in the popular parlance, "no earthly
use."

Switching to the helpful categories proposed by Peter L. Berger in the
field of the sociology of knowledge, some Christians have erred into the
extreme of "cognitive and cultural defiance," some into the opposite extreme of "cognitive and cultural accommodation," and all too few have
achieved the faithful middle way of "cognitive and cultural negotiation."

This challenge and these dangers are at the heart of the evangelical attempt to steer a faithful course today between what we see as two extremes
in contemporary Protestantism: liberal revisionism and conservative fundamentalism. On one side, evangelicals stand over against the liberal
Protestant revisionism that has grown out of Friedrich Schleiermacher's
admirable proposal that Christians reach out to "the cultured despisers of
the gospel." In the process, some Protestant liberals have not only reached
out to the cultured despisers but joined them, and become the Protestant
echo of the spirit of the age in successive eras. (Exhorted by a fashionable
clergyman of his day, Oscar Wilde replied: "Follow you? I not only follow
you, I precede you.")

Thus in the extremes, such as Bishop John Shelby Spong of the Episcopal Church, liberal revisionists deny almost all the articles of the historic
creeds of the Christian church, but still stay on as Christian leaders — contributing to the massive crisis of authority and credibility of the church in
the modern world.

On the other side, evangelicals stand over against other Protestants
who have sought to defy the spirit of the age, but have taken their culture-
defying stance to extremes that have become sub-Christian and even anti-
Christian, and therefore undermine the evangelical impulse of living according to the good news of Jesus. (For example, compare the common
fundamentalist tactic of "demonizing" enemies with the injunction of Je-

sus that his followers "love your enemies, and do good to those who hate you.")

To be sure, the objective of the original fundamentalists — returning the church to its fundamentals — is as laudable and as Christian as Schleiermacher's goal of reaching out, and an approach that no self-respecting sports coach or academic tutor would disagree with. But since then, fundamentalism has morphed beyond its Christian roots into a world-denying stance that has become *an essentially modern reaction to the modern world*. The process has shaped not only Protestant fundamentalism but versions of fundamentalism in all the world's religions and also among secularists. (The currently popular new atheists, such as Richard Dawkins, Sam Harris, and Christopher Hitchens, have been attacked even by their fellow-atheists for being "secular fundamentalists.")

This fundamentalist overlay that is a distortion of evangelicalism is obvious — so much so that evangelicals are routinely confused with fundamentalists, and therefore equated with the Christian right. What is less obvious from outside the movement is that a large number of younger evangelicals are going in the opposite direction. Reacting against the simplistic dogmatism and narrow legalism of their fundamentalist backgrounds, and naïvely unaware of a richer, older evangelicalism, let alone the wider church and a longer history, they are throwing out baby, bathwater, and all, and heading down a path with an uncanny resemblance to the course of Protestant revisionism. (The logic and language of the Emergent Church leader Brian McLaren is often an eerie echo of John Shelby Spong.)

In sum, the issue of relativism and fundamentalism is far deeper for evangelicals than simply a matter of theory and philosophy. At its heart, it is a question of faithfulness and central to the integrity and effectiveness of evangelical faith in the modern world.

How We Come to Faith

If evangelicals are "people of the good news," it follows naturally that the story of their own coming to faith and their own passion for sharing their faith with others are central to an evangelical understanding of faith. Here again, considerable prejudice and caricatures surround the notion of faith that is supposed to be evangelical, and many presume that faith for evangelicals is both dogmatic and irrational. Dawkins, for instance, describes religious believers as "faith-heads," or people whose faith is a "delusion" because based only on "blind trust" and an intellectually suicidal "leap in the dark."

Unquestionably there are evangelicals who are proud of the charge of anti-intellectualism and who see it almost as an article of faith. Curiously, however, the criticism could be applied to both the extremes of evangelicalism mentioned above. On the fundamentalist wing are those whose faith has a dogmatic certainty that shuts out all questions and doubts, and is impervious to reason. But on the revisionist wing are those who would reject the charge of anti-intellectualism, but whose more sophisticated faith is precisely so in proportion to its abandonment of confidence in reason, according to the latest canons of postmodernism.

Against both extremes are the classical evangelicals who seek to be biblical and to make their way between false alternatives such as modernism and postmodernism, relativism and fundamentalism, by giving due weight to truth and reason, while rejecting the two equal and opposite errors of rationalism and irrationality. Such evangelicals are mainstream Christians who "think in believing and believe in thinking."

What is the thinking person's path to faith that avoids the pitfalls of both relativism and fundamentalism? It may be described best as a journey with four phases, each of which is as important intellectually as it is spiritually.

Phase One of the quest for meaning is *a time for questions,* in the sense that when a crisis, or a sense of need or longing, breaks into a person's life, that is the moment when they become a genuine "seeker." Contrary to Sigmund Freud, who dismissed a crisis-triggered faith as irrational and a form of crutch or wish-fulfillment, no one believes because of need. Rather, they *dis*believe what they believed before, because what they believed before did not answer the crisis or longing, so they become seekers, and set out to search for a more adequate position. Philosophically speaking, this first phase represents the breakdown of a previously held worldview, and therefore of its power to exclude all meanings but its own. In terms of presuppositions, the seeker is now open.

Phase Two is *a time for answers,* in the sense that the seeker consciously sets out to search for an answer, whether philosophical, emotional, or practical, to the questions raised in the first phase. This stage is essentially conceptual and comparative. All potential answers encountered are considered, weighed, and compared, but only in an "as if" way. If these answers were presupposed to be true, would they answer the questions the seeker is carrying forward on the search? Philosophically speaking, this second phase represents the consideration of potential alternative worldviews and ways of life, each of which is considered in its own terms and tested for its illuminating power.

Phase Three is *a time for evidences,* in the sense that once a seeker is attracted toward some answer, it is important to ask whether the answer can be tested as true. It is not enough for an answer to throw light on the seeker's problem, it must be shown to have sufficient weight of evidence to be accepted as true. Philosophically speaking, this third phase does not stand on its own. Facts are only facts within a framework, and evidence makes no sense without the clarifying presuppositions (supplied in Phase Two), just as alternative presuppositions will only be considered once some original presuppositions have broken down (as in Phase One).

Phase Four is *a time for commitments,* in the sense that at a certain point it is natural for seekers to commit themselves to the full consequences of that which they are now convinced is urgently needed (because of Phase One), fully illuminating (because of Phase Two), and reliably proven to be true (because of Phase Three).

In sum, such a view of faith is fully rational, but it is based on more than reason, not least for the simple reason that we humans are more than rational — faith is a fully responsible human decision that is the response of the whole person, based on the will and the emotions as well as the mind. Thus from an evangelical perspective, faith is neither rationalistic, a product of reason alone; nor is it irrational, a leap in the dark that is contrary to reason and evidence. As I said, a Christian is one who thinks in believing and who believes in thinking.

How We Hold Our Faith

The above emphasis on truth and reason may be expressed differently. For evangelicals, truth and reason may be legitimately considered philosophically and sociologically, but they are not ultimately important for philosophical and sociological reasons. At their highest, they are a matter of theology. Truth and reason matter because God is a God of truth, Jesus is the Word, or Logos, made flesh, so that any diminishing of truth or reason is a theological error as well as a philosophical and sociological error.

171

The same point applies to how evangelicals hold to their faith. If God is true, God's word is truth, and the journey to faith in God is a path grounded firmly in truth, then in the words of the early church, the believer may have confidence that "all truth is God's truth." The consequence is that faith searches for truth as an act of faith, that faith acknowledges truth wherever it is found, that faith fears no questions, that faith faces up to doubts, and that faith must always seek to give honest answers to honest questions.

In short, as the best evangelical scholarship attests, especially in fields where evangelicals are strong today, such as theology, philosophy, history, sociology, and the natural sciences, faith is both critical and self-critical.

Yet while faith is fully rational, and therefore has full confidence in the glory of reason and its God-given capacities, faith remains humble because of four major qualifications to the power of human reason.

First, as stated above, we humans are rational but we are more than rational. If we are not to create serious distortions in our thinking, we must always remember the equal place of the will and the emotions in our experience.

Second, we humans are finite, and no rational certainty can ever be achieved on the basis of our finite reason alone. Without an infinite God, as Jean-Paul Sartre used to affirm, there can only be relativism or, one might add, an overweening rationalism that rebounds into skepticism. Conversely, the possibility of absolute truth is grounded in the possibility of an infinite God — who discloses that truth to us. Thus reason plays its part in generating faith, but it is faith that plays the crucial part in guaranteeing reason. And if reason is not to overreach and become rationalism, which in turn is not to rebound into skepticism and irrationality, as we have seen with modernism and postmodernism, then reason will always have to remain within the bounds of revelation. God alone is infinite, the best minds in the world are only finite, and the greatest danger of the human mind is the overreaching that is hubris.

Third, we take seriously the biblical teaching that human sin affects the mind as well as the will and the emotions, so that we each have a proven capacity for truth-twisting as well as truth-seeking. What Freud called "rationalizing" (giving reasons other than the true reasons) and Marx called "ideology" (ideas that serve as intellectual weapons for real interests) find their parallel in the biblical notion that human pride and self-interest will distort the best of thinking and make it less rational than it pretends.

Fourth, God has not spoken on all subjects of human interest and concern, and where he has not spoken, it is a mistake to give our human thoughts more certainty and authority than they merit; just as it is to take from God's authority when he has spoken certainly. Put differently, evangelicals are aware of the error of *particularism* in moral and political thinking — giving absolute weight to a particular human way of thinking that is ours and not God's, so that we make a particular human theory or practice as uniquely Christian.

Thus while the Bible speaks authoritatively for evangelicals in all it affirms, it does not set out fully developed answers on such questions as the best way to set up government, manage an economy, plan retirement, or propose a scientific theory. In such areas it is a mistake to dub any theory uniquely "Christian." According to biblical principles, it can be said that there are ways of doing these things that are *not* Christian, but it should never be said that *one way* alone is Christian. To pretend otherwise is to fall for the mistake of particularism, to give absolute weight to what is only human and necessarily relative and provisional, and to tie Christian credibility to what is transient and bound to be surpassed and discredited.

Such a view of faith carries enormous implications for what might be called an evangelical "thought-style," the way in which followers of Jesus grow in a manner of thinking that is true to him in its style as well as its content. Christian certainty, for example, is fully rational, a way of reasoned understanding as outlined briefly in the description of the road to faith, but it is also more, much more. Christian certainty, or assurance, is a strong cord with many strands, including one part that is the knowledge that truth may be trusted because it has been disclosed rather than discovered, another part that is a conviction born of full, personal volition, and yet another part that is spiritual assurance given directly by the Spirit of God.

Or again, consider Christian humility, which in this understanding is a companion and not a rival of certainty. Respect for truth, coupled with respect for freedom of conscience and a lively sense of our own finiteness and capacity for truth-twisting, means that, unlike certain medieval Catholics and many politically correct moderns today, we reject the idea that "error has no rights." Everyone, with no exceptions, has a right to be wrong.

Yet while we seek truth above everything ("Having bought truth dear," Roger Williams wrote, "let us not sell it cheap"), and while we always grant others the right to be wrong, our duty to seek the truth is always balanced by modesty, for we too may be wrong. Arrogance is not the claim to be right, but the refusal to admit even the possibility that we might be wrong

("We have received from Divine Providence," the Emperor Constantine declared immodestly, "the supreme favor of being relieved from all error"). Thus fallibility and corrigibility are other key aspects of a Christian thought-style that is clear and certain yet humble and open to correction.

How We View the Public Square

A fifth area where the polarization between relativism and fundamentalism touches on evangelicalism today is public life, for once again evangelicals are damagingly confused with fundamentalists and the Christian right. To be evangelical is to seek to be faithful to the freedom, justice, peace, and well-being that are the heart of the kingdom of God, to bring these gifts into public life as a service to all, and to work with all who share these ideals and care for the common good. Citizens of the City of God, evangelicals join other Christians as resident aliens in the City of Man, fully engaged in public affairs, but never completely equated with any party, partisan ideology, class, tribe, or national identity.

Whereas fundamentalism was thoroughly world-denying and politically disengaged from its beginnings, names such as William Wilberforce and Lord Shaftesbury are a reminder that evangelicals have made a shining contribution to politics in general, to many of the greatest moral and social reforms in history, such as the *abolition of slavery*, and even to notions crucial in political discussion today — for example, the vital but little-known evangelical contribution to the rise of the *voluntary association* and, through that, to the understanding of such key notions as "civil society" and "social capital."

Today, however, evangelicals need to stand clear from certain conservative and fundamentalist positions in public life that are widely confused with evangelicals.

First, evangelicals repudiate two equal and opposite errors into which many of our fellow-Christians have fallen recently. One error has been to "privatize" faith, interpreting and applying it to the personal and spiritual realm only. Such dualism falsely divorces the spiritual from the secular, and causes faith to lose its *integrity* and become "privately engaging and publicly irrelevant," and another form of "hot tub spirituality."

The other error, represented by the religious left in the 1960s and the religious right since the late 1970s, is to "politicize" faith, using faith to express essentially political points that have lost touch with biblical truth. That way faith loses its *independence,* the church becomes "the regime at prayer," Christians become the "useful idiots" for one political party or another, and the Christian faith becomes an ideology in its purest form — Christian beliefs are used as weapons for political interests.

Christians from both sides of the political spectrum, left as well as right, have made the mistake of politicizing faith; and it would be no improvement to respond to a weakening of the religious right with a rejuvenation of the religious left. Whichever side it comes from, a politicized faith is faithless, foolish, and disastrous for the church — and disastrous first and foremost for Christian reasons rather than constitutional reasons.

Called to an allegiance higher than party, ideology, and nationality, evangelicals see it as their duty to engage with politics, but their equal duty never to be completely equated with any party, partisan ideology, or nationality. The politicization of faith is never a sign of strength but of weakness. The saying is wise: "The first thing to say about politics is that politics is not the first thing."

Second, evangelicals repudiate the two extremes that define the present culture wars in the United States. There are deep and important issues at stake in the culture wars, issues on which the future of the United States and Western civilization will turn. But the trouble comes from the manner in which the issues are being fought. Name-calling, insult, ridicule, guilt-by-association, caricature, negative ads, and deceptive videos have replaced deliberation and debate. Neither side talks to the other side, only about them; and there is no pretense of democratic engagement, let alone a triumph of persuasion.

All citizens and the nation itself are the losers. The incessant culture warring trivializes and distorts important issues. It demeans the participants themselves, and it becomes a vicious circle of self-fulfilling prophecy. In the bitter clash of opposing views, the truths at stake are lost and each side becomes the main argument for the other. The unsurprising outcome is a permanent hostility that is the fulfillment of the prophecies each makes about the other.

In particular, what evangelicals lament in the culture warring is not just the general collapse of the common vision of the common good, but the endless conflict over the proper place of faiths in public life, and therefore of the freedom to enter and engage public life from the perspective of faith. A grand confusion now reigns as to any guiding principles by which people of different faiths may enter the public square and engage with each other robustly but civilly.

The result is the "holy war" front of America's wider culture wars. Disputes over religion and politics in recent decades have been bitterly polarized, extremes have surfaced regularly, resort to law has become reflexive, and opponents with no arguments left have kept on trading tired insults and launching endless lawsuits. We are now at the point where no issue is too insignificant to spark a new attack, and no end is in sight to the number of possible lawsuits that may be launched or conflagrations set ablaze.

We repudiate on one side the partisans of a *sacred public square,* those who for religious, historical, or cultural reasons, would continue to give a preferred place in public life to one religion — which in almost all current cases would be the Christian faith, but could equally be the secularist faith, or one day the Muslim faith. In a society as religiously diverse as America today, for the state or federal government to continue to give any one faith a preferred or privileged position today is neither just nor workable.

Evangelicals are committed to religious liberty for people of all faiths. They are not proponents of theocracy, and they have no desire to coerce anyone or to impose on anyone beliefs and behavior that they have not persuaded them to adopt freely and that evangelicals do no not demonstrate in their own lives, above all by love.

Evangelicals repudiate on the other side the partisans of a *naked public square,* those who would make all religious expression inviolably private and keep the public square inviolably secular. Often advocated by a loose coalition of secularists, liberals, and supporters of the strict separation of church and state, this position is even less just and workable because it excludes the overwhelming majority of citizens who are still profoundly religious. Nothing is more illiberal than to invite people into the public square but insist that they be stripped of the faith that makes them who they are and shapes the way they see the world.

In contrast to these extremes, the evangelical choice is for a *civil public square — a vision of public life in which citizens of all faiths are free to enter and engage the public square on the basis of their faith, but within a framework of what is agreed to be just and free for other faiths too.* Thus every right evangelicals assert for ourselves is at once a right they defend for others. A right for a Christian is a right for a Jew, and a right for a secularist, and a right for a Mormon, and a right for a Muslim, and a right for a Scientologist, and a right for all the believers in all the faiths across this wide land.

Contrary to recent impressions, the evangelical concern is justice, not "just us." Freedom of conscience is an equal right for all. The Golden Rule of Jesus, shared widely by other faiths and systems of ethics, applies to issues that are public as well as private.

Evangelicals are especially troubled by the fact that a generation of culture warring, reinforced by the follies and perceived extremism of the religious right, is creating *a powerful backlash against all religion in public life among many educated people.* If this were to harden and become an American equivalent of the long-held European animosity toward religion in the public life, the result would be disastrous for the American republic and a severe constriction of liberty for people of all faiths. We therefore warn of the striking intolerance evident among the "new atheists," and call on all citizens of goodwill and believers of all faiths to join with us in working for a civil public square and the restoration of a tough-minded civility that is in the interests of all.

Evangelicals are also troubled by the fact that the advance of globalization and *the emergence of a global public square finds no matching vision of how we are to live freely, justly, and peacefully with our deepest differences on the global stage.* As the recent Muslim protest and riots over perceived insults to their faith demonstrate, ours is a world in which everyone can listen to what we say even when we are not intentionally speaking to everyone. So the challenges of living with our deepest differences are magnified and intensified in the age of truly global technologies such as the Internet.

As this global public square emerges, we see two equal and opposite errors to avoid: *coercive secularism* on one side, once typified by communism and now by the softer but strict French-style secularism; and *religious extremism* on the other side, typified by Islamist violence. At the same time, we repudiate the two main positions into which many are now falling. On the one hand, we repudiate all who see themselves as *progressive universalists* — those who believe their way is the only way and the way for everyone, and are therefore prepared to coerce them. Whatever the faith or ideology in question — communism, Islam, or even democracy at the point of a sword — this position leads inevitably to *conflict.*

Undoubtedly, many people would place all Christians in this category, because of the Emperor Constantine and the state-sponsored oppression he inaugurated, leading to the dangerous liaison between church and state continued in European church-state relations down to the present.

Evangelicals deplore the dangerous liaison between church and state, and the oppression that was its dark fruit. In clear contrast, evangelicals trace their heritage, not to Constantine, but to the very different stance of Jesus of Nazareth, whose good news of justice for the whole world was promoted, not by a conqueror's power and sword, but by a suffering servant emptied of power and ready to die for the ends he came to achieve. Unlike others, evangelicals do not see insults and attacks on our faith as offensive or blasphemous, but as an undeserved honor and part of the cost of our discipleship that we are to bear without complaint or victim-playing.

On the other hand, evangelicals repudiate all who act as *multicultural relativists* — those who believe that different values are relative to different cultures, and who therefore refuse to allow anyone to judge anyone else or any other culture. More tolerant sounding at first, this position leads directly to the evils of *complacency;* for in a world of such evils as genocide, slavery, and female oppression, there are rights that require defending, evils that must be resisted, and interferences into the affairs of others that are morally justifiable.

Invitation to All

As stated earlier, I do not presume to speak for all evangelicals. I speak only for myself — *yet not to myself.* This essay is therefore both a clarification of what *evangelical* means and how evangelicals view the issue of relativism and fundamentalism. But it is also an invitation to people of different faiths around the country and the world to take note of these points and to respond where appropriate.

Those who are my fellow-evangelicals, I urge to consider these points and to join in clarifying the profound confusions surrounding evangelicalism, that together we may be more faithful and true to the distinctiveness of the gospel of Jesus and its way of life.

Those who are fellow-citizens, I urge to assess the damaging consequences of the present culture wars and the unfair stereotypes of evangelicalism, and to work together on the urgent task of restoring liberty and civility in public life, and so ensuring that freedom may last to future generations.

Those who are adherents of other faiths around the world, I urge to understand that we evangelicals respect your right to believe what you believe according to the dictates of conscience, and invite you to follow the Golden Rule and extend the same rights and respect to us and to the adherents of all other faiths, so that together we may make religious liberty practical and religious persecution rarer, so that in turn human diversity may complement rather than contradict human well-being.

Those whose task it is to report and analyze public affairs, such as scholars and journalists, I urge to abandon stereotypes and adopt definitions and categories in describing evangelicals and other believers in terms that are both accurate and fair, and with a tone that you in turn would like to be applied to yourselves.

Those who are in positions of power and authority, such as legislators and policy makers, I urge to appreciate that we evangelicals are not "theocrats," "fascists," "fundamentalists," "extremists," or any of the other terms with which we are currently labeled. We seek the welfare of the communities, cities, and countries in which we live, yet our first allegiance is always to a higher loyalty and to standards that call all other standards into question, a commitment that has been a secret of the Christian contributions to civilization as well as its passion for reforms.

In sum, we who are thinking evangelicals differ decisively from both relativists and fundamentalists in both the way we come to faith, the way we hold to faith, and the way we regard other faiths. Seeking to be true to the vision of God, truth, understanding, and wisdom that we see in Jesus and discover in the scriptures, we agree with modernists on the importance of truth, but disagree that reason is ever self-justifying and self-sustaining; and we agree with postmodernists on the fallibility of human reason, but disagree that this view necessarily entails relativism about truth and skepticism about knowledge.

Having come to faith on the basis of what Socrates called an "examined life," through an examination of things revealed from elsewhere and therefore discovered rather than simply constructed, we evangelicals admit the possibility that we may be wrong, and hold ourselves always open to the challenge of being shown that we are wrong. But in the meantime — humbly, gratefully, and with the full assurance that human beings have about any human knowledge — we believe that what we trust as true will stand the test of time and disproof, and will indeed prove true, and be seen to be a sure path to the center and soul of truth, and One who is himself true and therefore to be trusted with the full weight of our lives and destiny.

Relativism and Fundamentalism:
An Eastern Church Perspective from the
"Paris School" and *Living Tradition*

Michael Plekon

Contemporary culture (and by no means only in America) appears to be in the grip of two seemingly contradictory forces. One pushes the culture toward relativism, the view that there are no absolutes whatever, that moral or philosophical truth is inaccessible if not illusory. The other pushes toward a militant and uncompromising affirmation of this or that (alleged) absolute truth . . . both formulas make civil discourse impossible, because both (albeit for opposite reasons) preclude a common and reasoned quest for moral or philosophical agreement.[1]

Images of Reconciliation

At first, taking up the task of thinking about these two very modern forces or poles in our culture — relativism and fundamentalism — from the perspective of Eastern Orthodox Christianity is daunting. After all, the rest of the culture (including many Orthodox Christians) view Orthodox Christianity in a number of images, some of which are accurate, others not so. For many, the Orthodox churches remain "the best-kept secret" of Christianity in America. Numerous times one is asked if "Orthodox" means Jewish. Some are surprised to learn that the Orthodox are Christian at all. The film of a few years back, "My Big Fat Greek Wedding," became a reference, up to a point! Also the further qualification "Eastern Orthodox" does

---

1. Peter L. Berger, "Going to Extremes: Between Relativism and Fundamentalism," at: http://www.the-american-interest.com/ai2/.

not always add clarification, especially when one considers that most Orthodox Christians in America are Westerners, Americans and not immigrants. True, there are immigrants still arriving from Russia and other eastern European countries as well as the Middle East, but it would be inaccurate to continue viewing the Orthodox churches as "immigrant churches."[2] Decades ago, John Meyendorff seriously questioned the continued use of "Eastern" to characterize the Orthodox churches in western Europe and America.

When we hear of the Orthodox Church, among the images that we will visualize most likely are the icons that are so much a part of worship and church architecture, like those from Mt. Sinai recently on exhibit at the Getty Museum in Los Angeles. The depicted faces of Christ and his mother, of the saints and angels, seem to invite the viewer into them, and suggest a different encounter even for a culture that is now image-oriented, image-driven. Equally, Eastern Orthodoxy evokes images of incense-shrouded clergy in radiant vestments, of chanting amid seas of candles on the night leading into Easter. In November 2006 many of these images were viewed internationally when Pope Benedict XVI visited Patriarch Bartholomew I in Istanbul, formerly Constantinople, seat of the Byzantine Empire long ago. They attended each other's liturgies, recited the Creed and the Lord's Prayer together, and exchanged the liturgical kiss of peace. These were scenes that recalled for some the images of Pope Paul VI and Patriarch Athenagoras I over forty years earlier, embracing and praying together, annulling the eleventh-century mutual condemnations by their churches, reconciling after almost a thousand years of schism and separation. The visits, for the universally celebrated November 30 feast of the apostle St. Andrew, patron of the city and of the Eastern churches, have been for years signs of healing. The patriarch had already visited Rome, but this was the first papal visit to the "New Rome."

Images of Division

Most would find these images welcome, as well as others from this visit, images of ecumenical healing among divided Christian communions

---

2. Orthodox churches in the U.S. did participate in the Hartford Seminary research project on denominations.

when the pope prayed with the patriarch at several liturgies and when he visited the former "Great Church" of the Byzantine Empire, Hagia Sophia, now a museum. Likewise there were images of interfaith reconciliation when, in the aftermath of the furor arising from his talk at Regensburg University, Pope Benedict visited the Blue Mosque in Istanbul, praying there with local Muslim leaders. But weeks beforehand, at Esphigmenou monastery on Mt. Athos, there were clashes, monk-to-monk combat with several injured. The conflict is an ongoing one, between monastics supporting Patriarch Bartholomew and other monastics who will not commemorate him in prayers or recognize his leadership precisely because of his reaching out to Catholics and other Christians. His ecumenical outreach is deemed heretical. A banner hangs outside this monastery: "Orthodoxy or Death!" it proclaims, hardly the joyous message many associate with Eastern Christianity: "Christ is risen!"

Within weeks of the pope's visit to Istanbul, an open letter was released from the heads of the Orthodox monasteries on Mt. Athos sternly rejecting the pope and patriarch's common prayer and the visit itself as well as that of Archbishop Christodoulos, primate of the Church of Greece to the pope in Rome. The position of the Athos abbots, also that of other traditionalist clergy, monastics, and laity, was uncompromising, insisting on the many heresies of the Catholics that continue to separate them, as well as all other Christians, from the Orthodox.[3]

From the largest church body in the Orthodox world, that of the Moscow patriarchate, there has come a mix of signals recently. On the one hand, Patriarch Alexis has supported a common stand with other traditions of faith and Christian churches over against the aggressive, sometimes hostile secularism dominating political and cultural life in Europe. His representative at the European Union, Bishop Hilarion Alfeyev, has repeatedly spoken of the close ties between the Catholic and Orthodox churches in the realm of ethics and the importance of the spiritual life. Yet the same Moscow patriarchate has aggressively intruded into local Orthodox churches throughout western Europe, most notably in the U.K. and France, calling back Christians of Russian background to their proper ecclesial home. And the Moscow patriarchate, through a number of its spokesmen, particularly Fr. Vsevolod Chaplin, has rejected Western con-

---

3. See for the text of the Athos letter: http://www.oodegr.com/english/oikoumenismos/athos1.htm.

cepts of democracy and human rights, religious and cultural diversity, as incompatible with Orthodox faith and discipline. Some of this is evident in the recently promulgated document, *The Basic Social Concept of the Russian Orthodox Church*.[4] The version of Orthodox Christianity and ecclesial model that the Moscow patriarchate church has been able to reclaim in the post-Soviet era bears an uncanny resemblance to the state-church alliance that existed before the Revolution, a union that was rejected by the majority of believers for its decadence, for its detachment from everyday life. The years of ferment and work for reform that led to the far-reaching and radical reforms of the Moscow Council of 1917-18 seem to have faded into historical mist.[5] The remarkable reckoning of a conciliar shape of the church (the Russian term used to denote this is *sobornost*), also the commitment to renewal of the liturgy, the education of clergy, the establishment of closer ties between the hierarchy and clergy and the laity — none of these have been embraced in the post-Soviet Russian church. Rather a new "union" of state, culture, and the church has been proposed, presumably making the reforms no longer necessary.

Orthodox Fundamentals or Fundamentalism?

Add to this cavalcade of images the ever-present ethnic connections. When explaining what "Orthodox" Christianity is, connections such as the following are often made: "Yes, Orthodox like 'Greek-Orthodox,' 'Russian Orthodox' . . . ," making "Orthodox" part of an ethnic identity — up until the modern period absolutely accurate, the synthesis having been the Byzantine *symphonia* of emperor-patriarch, empire-church, which be-

---

4. For the text of the Basic Social Concept see: http://3saints.com/ustav_mp_russ_english.html. Also see http://www.mospat.ru/index.php?lng=1. For an assessment of the current situation see Father Georgii Chistiakov, "Xenophobia versus Charity in Contemporary Russian Orthodoxy," *East-West Church & Ministry Report* 14, no. 4 (2006): 13-15.

5. See Hyacinthe Destivelle, *Le concile de Moscou (1917-1918)* (Paris: Cerf, 2006); Alexander Bogolepov, *Church Reforms in Russia 1905-1918*, trans. A. E. Moorhouse (Bridgeport, CT: Publications Committee of the Metropolitan Council of the Russian Orthodox Church of America, 1966); James W. Cunningham, *A Vanquished Hope* (Crestwood, NY: St. Vladimir's Seminary Press, 1981); Dimitri Pospielovsky, *The Russian Church Under the Soviet Regime 1917-1982*, 2 vols. (Crestwood, NY: St. Vladimir's Seminary Press, 1984); George T. Kosar, *Russian Orthodoxy in Crisis and Revolution: The Church Council of 1917-1918* (Ph.D. dissertation, Brandeis University, 2004).

came ethnicity-religion, a tribal cult.[6] The thread running through almost all of these cultural details however is that of an ancient quality, namely, that Orthodox Christianity is so full of ancient and holy tradition that it is somehow immune to the present and all its temptations, monstrosities, and corrosions. Of course this has not been the case, as the Russian Revolution, and before that the alienation of intellectuals from the church in Russia for the better part of the nineteenth century attest. No matter how ancient particular ideas or practices may be, it is twenty-first-century people reflecting upon them, performing them. All of tradition is living or else it is museum material. Jaroslav Pelikan's famous line is appropriate here: "Tradition is the living faith of the dead, traditionalism the dead faith of the living."[7]

There is, to be sure, much of tradition alive and well in Orthodox Christianity, and it is precisely from such "living tradition" that the normative reflections on the all-important "middle ground" we are aiming at, between relativism and fundamentalism, will be drawn. However, not *all* that claims to be tradition or is passed off as authentic tradition is authentic tradition. There is a great deal of "traditionalism," sometimes also called "neo-traditionalism" or "pseudo-traditionalism," alive and accessible in the Orthodox churches here in America and abroad. Like relativism, it is a child of modernity, a response to diversity, plurality, and freedom of speech and religion too. But it is more akin to fundamentalism, if not fundamentalist in substance. It is vocal, well supported, knows how to use the cutting edge of media technology and how to make all kinds of strategic alliances, political and cultural among others.

This is, in fact, what one can read about on countless websites, in periodicals and books about the "unchanged and unchangeable" Orthodox Christian positions on marriage, sexuality, abortion, and every other "culture war" issue imaginable.[8] Very quickly the alliance between such "traditionalist" Orthodox and the Christian right (by their definition "heretics,"

6. Alexander Schmemann, *The Historical Road of Orthodoxy*, trans. Lydia W. Kesich (Crestwood, NY: St. Vladimir's Seminary Press, 1977).

7. See Jaroslav Pelikan, *The Christian Tradition: A History of the Development of Doctrine*, vol. 2: *The Spirit of Eastern Christendom (600-1700)* (Chicago: University of Chicago Press, 1974); and Vladimir Lossky, "Tradition and Traditions," in *In the Image and Likeness of God*, trans. G. E. H. Palmer and E. Kadloubovsky (Crestwood, NY: St. Vladimir's Seminary Press, 1985), pp. 141-68.

8. http://www.ctosonline.org/ and http://www.orthodoxinfo.com/.

yet kindred spirits) is conspicuous. So too, the convergence of traditional-ist Orthodox ethics and social outlook with the political right.

It is one thing to be part of an ancient tradition. Orthodox Christians of the past and the present, whether in Greece, Syria, the Balkans, the Ukraine, or Russia, were very local. They were limited in contacts with those different from them, but where they bordered and mixed with Ro-man Catholics and Greek/Byzantine Catholics, as in the western Ukraine, they were more tolerant than combative. There were no legal or violent clashes over the use of church buildings or claims by the Orthodox Church that it was the only church with a right to exist. They did not identify and condemn those different from them as "heretics." They intermarried, fre-quented each other's churches, even here in America, and moved back and forth across jurisdictions. Their faith was intensely personal, everyday, ex-periential. Christianity always had the very human face of this priest, that neighbor. They had no inclination to tell the others that they were different and how they were wrong.

Traditionalist vocabulary and behavior is confrontational. As Anthony Giddens has put it, in describing fundamentalism, discourse is neither val-ued nor desired.[9] Reasoning differences out is rejected. Appealing to the facts of history is suspect. There is but one version of the liturgical year, the "old" or Julian calendar to follow, since Christ and the apostles and the Fa-thers followed it. There is only one version of the principal Christian lit-urgy, the Eucharist, usually in Slavonic or ancient Greek, and this version is the only authentically Orthodox way of worshiping. It is typical that often their biggest target for criticism is not those liturgically or doctrinally re-mote such as the Baptists or Pentecostals, but those most proximate — Or-thodox Christians who are "innovationist," "modernist," or "ecumenist," who use English or another local language, whose clergy say all the prayers aloud and encourage the reception of communion at each liturgy or who conduct Bible study groups. Despite the Baptists' historical practice and the growing adoption of the full immersion version of baptism, the tradi-tionalists do not accept the baptism or any other sacraments of the non-Orthodox and in some cases of other Orthodox churches. The assertion of singularity or even monopoly on true Christianity and grace is accompa-

---

9. *Runaway World* (London: Routledge, 2000). These were the Reith Lectures of 1999. For an extreme critique of religious fundamentalism see Chris Hedges, *American Fascists: The Christian Right and the War on America* (New York: Free Press, 2006).

nied by a retreat into other sectarian patterns, including distinctive clothing, the stressed difference between their practices and those of all others — e.g., their veneration of the Virgin Mary and the saints, their fasting during Lent (and other times in the year). This "timeless" possession of traditional elements guarantees them what they sing of after communion: "We have seen the true Light, we have received the heavenly Spirit, we have found the true faith. . . ."[10]

The sectarian character is further heightened by a rather deliberate critique of life and culture outside the borders of the religious community. Universities and colleges as well as public schools are suspect, and in the case of the latter small academies or home-schooling serve as alternatives. TV and film as well as the recording industry and the Internet are seen as hopelessly secular, full of ideas, values, and situations that are opposed to the faith. Unlike the Old Order Mennonites or Amish who distance themselves more geographically, traditionalists tend to distance themselves by avoidance and by alternative activities and culture. Not unlike others along the spectrum of Christianity, the traditionalists reinterpret much of church history and the scriptures' universal outreach, very public presence, and activity and tolerance of diversity.

Historically, there was notable diversity among the Christians of the Eastern churches, in language of the liturgy, music, biblical lectionaries used, details of worship and life. But thoroughly modern is the urge to insist upon an unchanging theological content to tradition and to absolute uniformity in texts and in many other aspects of liturgical and everyday life.

If one were to look around at the Orthodox Christian churches today, one would not have to venture very far to find a diverse and substantial fundamentalism in both theory and practice. To be sure, there is also a spectrum of intensity or radicalism among Orthodox Christian traditionalists, with relatively few on the very sectarian end.

About the other pole, namely Orthodox Christian relativism, in the Greek-American attorney or restaurateur, in a Lebanese physician, in a Ukrainian-American academic, or among others, both "cradle" and converts to Orthodoxy, I am sure that relativism is to be found, the "everything goes" or "Let's agree to disagree" types. But the relativism may also

---

10. See the "traditionalist" message board: http://www.beliefnet.com/boards/discussion
_list.asp?boardID=67774.

and more frequently be more of an everyday, less reflective sort. This would be neither the amorphous normlessness to be found among some Western churches and surely not the very militant variety that manifests itself in academic circles or in the media, among other locations. Frankly, from my observation over the last couple of decades, it might be hard to even call it relativism — perhaps a more tolerant, laissez-faire attitude toward those outside the boundaries of Orthodox churches. Actually, it might also be the more ordinary "folk religion," not the theology of official texts or of the institutional ecclesiastical leadership but the pragmatic, utilitarian outlook that uses religion when necessary and otherwise accepts it as part of the landscape, the furniture of one's complicated world and worldview.

Back to the Future

This would be a very cursory, perhaps selective sociological and theological scan of the Orthodox in the twenty-first century. But if one were to reverse historical direction, would the same be found? Here the picture is rather different. Without taking a great deal of time to excavate and interpret at this point, I would say that in such important, grassroots texts as the *Apophthegmata,* the sayings of the third- to fifth-century desert fathers and mothers, extremism either in ascetic practice or in prayer and belief receives consistent criticism; and more powerfully, there is the counterexample of monastic men and women who are compassionate, restrained in judgment of others, tolerant of diversity and of human frailty.[11] In both the writings and actions of some of the major church fathers such as Basil the Great and Gregory of Nyssa, among others, the same tendencies are to be found. To be sure there is no compromising the essential teachings of the Christian tradition, those in the scriptures, the liturgy, and affirmed by councils and the lives of holy people. But there is also acceptance of a wide diversity of liturgical and ecclesial forms, also forgiveness and the impulse towards reunion when there have been splits. For example, in the case of

---

11. *The Sayings of the Desert Fathers,* trans. Benedicta Ward (Kalamazoo, MI: Cistercian Publications, 1987); *The Lives of the Desert Fathers,* trans. Benedicta Ward (Kalamazoo, MI: Cistercian Publications, 1981); Laura Swan, *The Forgotten Desert Mothers* (Mahwah, NJ: Paulist Press, 2001).

Basil there is profound ecclesial understanding, a willingness to go out to those cut off from the ecclesial mainstream to reconcile them without compulsion.

Repeatedly in his writings, the lay theologian Paul Evdokimov (1901-69) cites this saying from a very early Christian text:

> He [God] sent him [Christ] out of gentleness, like a king sending his son, who is himself a king. He sent him as God, he sent him as a man to men. He willed to save man by persuasion, not by compulsion, for compulsion is not God's way of working. (*Letter to Diognetus* 7:4)

Evdokimov emphasized that this unwillingness to compel anyone was God's chief characteristic of love and respect for each human being made in his image and likeness.[12] In one of the most intriguing essays on theodicy in modern theology, Evdokimov spins out the ways in which, as his teacher Sergius Bulgakov sketched them, the loving God emptied himself in love by creating and then patiently suffering with his creation.[13]

While I think some specific canons of the Eastern churches as well as sermons of bishops and the lives of ascetics would evidence extremism of the sort we today associate with fundamentalism, in the balance, the Christian East leans in the direction of economy or indulgence *(oikonomia)* rather than rigor *(akribeia)*. Evdokimov notes this with regard to the sacrament of penance or confession, more consistently understood as healing, the restoration of a person to God and the community. He also observes the same with respect to the Eastern understanding of the "sacrament of love" — marriage — as well as monastic life.[14] Like Bulgakov, Evdokimov ultimately saw the fundamentalist extreme as incompatible with the freedom of and the absurd love of God for his freedom-endowed creatures. Hence, like Origen, Gregory of Nyssa, and others long before them, Bulgakov and Evdokimov wrote about the mercy of the *theos philanthropos,* God as the lover of humankind manifest in the restoration

---

12. *Ages of the Spiritual Life,* rev. trans. and ed. Michael Plekon and Alexis Vinogradov (Crestwood, NY: St. Vladimir's Seminary Press, 1998).

13. "God's Absurd Love and the Mystery of His Silence," in *In the World, of the Church: A Paul Evdokimov Reader,* ed. and trans. Michael Plekon and Alexis Vinogradov (Crestwood, NY: St. Vladimir's Seminary Press, 2001), pp. 175-94.

14. *The Sacrament of Love,* trans. Anthony P. Gythiel and Victoria Steadman (Crestwood, NY: St. Vladimir's Seminary Press, 1985).

of all people and things at the end of time *(apokatastasis)*.[15] And their colleague, the canonist, church historian, and ecclesiologist Fr. Nicolas Afanasiev, emphatically underscored the "power" or "rule" of love *(vlast' lyubvi)* in the ancient church over against the dominance of law and the division into clerical and lay castes of later centuries.[16]

Sources for a "Middle Ground": The "Paris School" of Émigrés

... the Fathers' writings cannot be accepted blindly as bearing dogmatic authority; they must be analyzed comparatively and critically. We must also add that the authoritative patristic tradition does not have exact boundaries in time and space. ... In other words, each historical period, not excluding our own, participates in the theological inspiration by which the authority of the Fathers' writing is established. ... The patristic tradition is not locked into some historical frame. It is not only the past but also the present and the future. And if different periods in history have their own problematics and challenges, no one is forgotten by God. The legacy of the holy Fathers, in spite of its holiness, as well as the necessity of detailed study, cannot be for us a finished task. ... To the contrary, it is necessarily a part of our task: having this talent, we must not bury it in the earth but multiply it by our own creative efforts.[17]

In the past few years I have been writing about as well as translating the work of a number of Eastern Orthodox figures, almost all of whom fled the Russian Revolution, emigrating to the West. Quite a few ended up in Paris, connected to journals such as *Put'*/The Way, edited by Berdiaev, and to the first Orthodox theological school established in western Europe, the St. Sergius Institute in Paris.[18] These include not only theologian Paul

15. *Apokatastasis and Transfiguration*, trans. Boris Jakim (New Haven, CT: The Variable Press, 1995). This was an excursus in *The Bride of the Lamb*, trans. Boris Jakim (Grand Rapids: Eerdmans, 2002).

16. Nicolas Afanasiev, *The Church of the Holy Spirit*, trans. Vitaly Permiakov, ed. Michael Plekon (Notre Dame: University of Notre Dame Press, 2007).

17. "Dogma and Dogmatic Theology," in *Tradition Alive: On the Church and the Christian Life in Our Time: Readings from the Eastern Church*, ed. Michael Plekon (Lanham, MD: Sheed & Ward/Rowman & Littlefield, 2003), p. 73.

18. See Paul Valliere, *Modern Russian Theology: Soloviev, Bukharev, Bulgakov* (Grand Rapids: Eerdmans, 2000); and "The 'Paris School' of Theology: Unity or Multiplicity" Con-

Michael Plekon

Evdokimov, Sergius Bulgakov, and Nicolas Afanasiev just mentioned but also Mother Maria Skobtsova and in a later generation Alexander Schmemann, John Meyendorff, Alexander Men, and Elisabeth Behr-Sigel.[19]

I bring these persons of faith and theological reflection to mind because like some others before them (Soloviev, Bukharev, Florensky) they were themselves *the products of the encounter between tradition and modernity*. In their youth many rejected the Russian Orthodox Church and its by-then decadence, embracing in preference — as did intellectuals before them — what they saw as the liberating thought of the West: Schelling, Hegel, and eventually, Marx. Many, like Berdiaev and Bulgakov, saw in the socialist movement what they believed to be authentic humanist reform. But all of them became disillusioned with the political versions of this growing movement in the first years of the twentieth century. With others like Pavel Florensky, Peter Struve, Simeon Frank, and Nicholas Lossky they either returned to the church or deepened their commitment and became first, the renaissance movement of religious thought, and also part of the reform movement that culminated in the Moscow Council of 1917-18. An early statement of their positions was to be found in the famous anthology *Vekhi* (1909).[20] Many eventually were forced to flee Russia for religious as well as political reasons after the Revolution, quite a few on the "philosophers' boat," in 1923.

Most then found themselves again in an intense lab of modernization in the "Russian Paris." They also found themselves divided by political and cultural loyalties while united by the Russian Orthodox Church. But in the tumultuous years after the Revolution, this was not to last. Tensions between the Moscow patriarchate and the Diaspora Russians led to several

---

ference ("La Teologia ortodossa e l'Occidente nel XX secolo: Storia di un incontro"), Seriate, Italy, October 30-31, 2004. Also Michael Plekon, *Living Icons: Persons of Faith in the Eastern Church* (Notre Dame: University of Notre Dame Press, 2002).

19. Nicolas Zernov, *The Russian Religious Renaissance of the Twentieth Century* (New York: Harper & Row, 1963); Antoine Arjakovsky, *La génération des penseurs religieux de l'émigration russe* (Kiev and Paris: Dukh i Litera, 2002); Nikita Struve, *70 ans de l'émigration russe: 1919-1989* (Paris: Fayard, 1996); Marc Raeff, *Russia Abroad: A Cultural History of the Russian Emigration 1919-1939* (New York: Oxford University Press, 1990); Michael Glenny and Norman Stone, *The Other Russia: The Experience of Exile* (New York: Viking, 1990).

20. *Signposts*, trans. Marshall S. Schatz and Judith E. Zimmerman (Irvine, CA: Schlacks, 1986).

deep divisions, lasting quite literally till the present. The metropolitan archbishop of the Russian church in western Europe, Evlogy, himself a leader in the Russian reform movement and powerful voice at the Moscow council of 1917-18, refused to acknowledge the Bolshevik government and the claim that it did not persecute the church.[21] In so doing, he found it necessary to appeal to the patriarchate of Constantinople for the legitimate status of the Russian Orthodox diocese he led in Paris and the rest of the continent. He had refused to recognize a dissident synod of Russian bishops gathered in Karlovsty. So by these actions, he found his diocese now split from both the synodal body as well as the Moscow patriarchate. Russian Paris was no longer united in one faith and church.

In his probing study of the networks among these thinkers, Antoine Arjakovsky makes it clear that there were indeed battles about tradition — what constituted the authentic tradition of the church: Could it be added to, that is, did it continue to develop in new situations, respond to new demands, or was it a kind of fortress against the acids of modernity? While some of the émigré thinkers indeed clung to a vision of a "Holy Russia," an ideal (and idealized) situation of the past longed for in the present, those we are discussing here saw this as retreatist and as a betrayal of the real tradition. Their own immersion in the skepticism of modern philosophy and science, in the criticism of modern political and social theory, had brought many of them back to Christian faith. This encounter with modernity enabled them to express Christian tradition with fidelity but beyond a primitive naïveté, as Paul Ricoeur puts it, after the demythologizing and relativizing efforts of such "masters of suspicion" as Marx, Nietzsche, and Freud (*Freud and Philosophy*).

In 1937, a number of them collaborated on an anthology titled *Zhivoe predanie* or *Living Tradition*, which gave forceful and articulate expression to their perspectives on the faith and tradition of the church in the modern world.[22]

In his distinctive confrontational and prophetic style, the philosopher

---

21. See his memoirs, *Put' moie zhizni* (Paris: YMCA Press, 1947); *Le chemin de ma vie*, trans. Pierre Tchesnakoff (Paris: Presses Saint-Serge, 2005).

22. *Zhivoe predanie: pravoslavnie v sovremennosti* [*Living tradition: Orthodoxy in the modern world*] (Paris: YMCA Press, 1937). More than half of these essays are available in translation, in the anthology *Tradition Alive*. On the significance of this volume as a statement of the creativity and openness of the Paris School see Arjakovsky, *La génération des penseurs religieux*, pp. 446-52, and Valliere, *Modern Russian Theology*, pp. 383-97.

Nicolas Berdiaev attacked the bourgeois domestication of Christianity in his contribution to the collection.[23] Berdiaev was a loud and insistent champion of the freedom given by God within the Christian tradition, a freedom of inquiry and action that resembled the very freedom of God himself. Thus, Berdiaev opposed Christianity ever being imprisoned by a political regime, an ethnic heritage, or a historical period. In the issues of the journal *Put'*, which Arjakovsky employs to track the thinking of the "Paris School," Berdiaev as editor promoted debate rather than a party line. Hence in the pages of *Put'*, as well as in the *Vestnik (Messenger)* of the Russian Christian Student Movement, Mother Maria Skobtsova challenged Fr. Sergius Chetverikov's cultural pessimism and dread of the modern world, as well as his glorification of the state-culture-church symbiosis of the past, "Holy Russia."[24] Berdiaev himself was the target of Fr. Chetverikov's criticism, for his insistence on Christianity's freedom from cultural and other confinements, and the two waged a war of essays in the pages of the journal *Put'*. Arjakovsky tracks meticulously the webs of agreement, conflict, reassessment that were spun across the Russian émigré community. As with the conversations and debate in the ecumenical Fellowship of St. Alban and St. Sergius, those in Paris left few theological issues untouched, from the relationship of the church to society and culture, to the very ways in which everyday life, that is, engagement in the world, was an authentic extension of the most sacred actions, those of the eucharistic liturgy. Especially intense were the debates that dealt with the maintenance of the church's tradition and the mandate (or not) to continue the creative work of the apostles and church fathers in the present.

In an essay in *Living Tradition* that remains till today most significant, "Dogma and Dogmatic Theology," Sergius Bulgakov presents what might be called a manifesto or summary statement of the perspective of the thinkers being highlighted here.[25] He argues very forcefully for the dynamic nature of tradition, for the church fathers being neither uniform nor infallible but rather gifted if sometimes conflicting contributors to the interpretation (and expression) of Christian faith. Bulgakov notes that theology, especially of the patristic era, employed the historical and philo-

---

23. "The Bourgeois Mind," in *Tradition Alive*, pp. 83-92.

24. See the English translation of the anthology, *Mother Maria Skobtsova: Essential Writings*, trans. Richard Pevear and Larissa Volokhonsky (Maryknoll, NY: Orbis, 2003).

25. *Tradition Alive*, pp. 67-80.

sophical disciplines of the time, using their concepts and perspectives to convey the word of God earlier gathered and put forward in the canonical scriptures. He emphasizes the education and rooting of the church fathers in their culture, then notes that contemporary teachers should be just as rooted in the disciplines of their own era. Bulgakov also rejected the stereotypical view of Orthodox Christianity as "unchanging." Tradition rather was always dynamic, filled with the Holy Spirit, constantly being revealed.

> Theology needs to be contemporary, or more precisely, to express religious thought about eternity in time . . . it follows unavoidably that relative to the development of religious thought and the expression of dogmatic opinions (and further *theologumena*) [opinions], there also exists the need to review and test already-existing revelatory dogmas — not, of course, with the purpose of "checking" them, but in order to perceive and receive them more completely. In this is fulfilled the dynamic quality of dogma: it is not only given in a pre-crystallized formula, but it is also a task for infinitely vital and intellectual exploration. We must also remember that dogmas possess a mutual transparence. They are given not as an external listing, as in a catalog or inventory, but are internally organically tied so that in the light of one dogma the content and strength of the other is revealed. This is why dogmatic theology constantly renews itself, since it should not be reckoned only as part of the record of Church tradition, where it must be accounted for in the light of historical research which studies and explains it.[26]

One should not cower from new problems or the new doctrines we may need to create because of their "newness," for to do so, Bulgakov claims, is to fall into anti-historical fundamentalism and in fact, heresy, from the perspectives of the church fathers.[27]

Not every piece of the Christian tradition is equally important, as both Bulgakov and his colleague Nicolas Afanasiev argue, contrary to fundamentalist conviction that everything is essential and that nothing can change.[28] Some elements of church tradition can lose their relevance with historical changes. Others are matters of local use and custom and were

26. *Tradition Alive*, p. 78.
27. *Tradition Alive*, p. 73.
28. "The Church's Canons: Changeable or Unchangeable," in *Tradition Alive*, pp. 31-46.

never intended to be binding universally. The philosophical terminology and concepts of antiquity do not exhaust the possible ways of expressing a dogma or a doctrine. Central to the theological project of the last decade of Bulgakov's scholarly career was the effort to explore the positive or constructive meanings, the consequences of the Council of Chalcedon's Christological dogma, stated, for reasons of theological compromise in the Greek a-privative, in the negative: Christ is God and man without confusion, division, separation, etc.[29]

In *Living Tradition* Afanasiev examined the doctrinal and historical question of whether or not the canons of the church could be changed. They can be, he concluded, in fact, they *must be* in order to deal with new situations unforeseen by the ancient councils. Afanasiev would go on in his own studies, *The Church of the Holy Spirit* and *The Limits of the Church*, to explore the relationships within the Christian eucharistic communities, the "local churches" of the first five centuries. Within these early communities he uncovered a stunning absence of clerical power in favor of communal consensus. There were no differences — ontological, theological, or sociological — between the ordained and the rest of the faithful. There was, rather, a dynamic interdependence of the members of the community that excluded law or the rule of one stratum or class over the others. It was, as he wrote, the "power," "rule," or "authority" of love that prevailed, not legal precedent or authority of office. Of course, the church departed from such initial and radical communalism in subsequent centuries. Yet for Afanasiev, even basic Christian teaching demanded careful historical analysis; otherwise the church would be reduced to either a purely spiritual or divine reality or a completely human one. Either position deviated from the authentic understanding of the church as simultaneously divine and human, like Christ himself (a good example here of the organic linkage of one doctrine with another, as noted in the text cited above).

Another fascinating essay in *Living Tradition* apropos of our search for a "middle ground" here is Cyprian Kern's discerning analysis of the Levitical and prophetic models of pastoral identity.[30] Though himself a great devotee of church tradition, Kern had been struck by the aftermath

---

29. This was the project of Bulgakov's "great trilogy": *The Comforter, The Lamb of God,* and *The Bride of the Lamb,* trans. Boris Jakim (Grand Rapids: Eerdmans, 2004, 2007, 2002).

30. "Two Models of the Pastorate: Levitical and Prophetic," in *Tradition Alive,* pp. 109-20.

of the Revolution for the Russian church, much as Mother Maria Skobt-sova and Berdiaev. The dependence upon the state and culture had made the church decadent, an institutionally top-heavy reality. No wonder that the model for the ordained clergy was the exclusive, hereditary, and power-ful Levitical priesthood of the Hebrew Bible and Temple Judaism. As Bulgakov was the promoter and producer of creative theology and Afanasiev the one to rediscover "eucharistic ecclesiology," Kern was the first to trace out the lines of a pastoral theology for the modern period, at once rooted in the church's liturgy and teaching but inspired by the cour-age of the prophets, apostles, and martyrs. Boris Sové focused on the eucharistic liturgy, which had become for many of the émigrés, especially the Paris School, the core of church life. Afanasiev was later to unearth the "eucharistic ecclesiology" of the early church, thus shaping the entire ecclesiological enterprise, even the dogmatic constitution on the church of Vatican II.[31] Sové's careful historical analysis revealed the gradual loss of the communal character of the liturgy, its devolving into strictly clerical actions passively observed by individuals. The disappearance of the altar behind icon and rood screens, the silencing of the great eucharistic prayer or anaphora, the reduction of reception of communion to a yearly event — all were features of Russian liturgy even in the early twentieth century, defended vigorously too by some. But almost from the start of theological reflection and writing in exile, even thinkers who disagreed violently on other issues were united in the centrality of the Eucharist and the necessity of frequent communion and active communal participation in the liturgy. Still later, Alexander Schmemann, an heir to this eucharistic renewal and revival, would bring it to America — and not to the Orthodox churches alone.

In his contribution, historian George Fedotov echoed, intentionally or not, his colleague Afanasiev's insistence on the need for careful historical analysis and the use of history's lessons.[32] Fedotov argues for the church's being shaped by the modern world and its thinking (as well as vice versa), what he had found in his painstaking research on the holy women and

---

31. "The Eucharist in the Ancient Church and Contemporary Practice," at: http://www.holy-trinity.org/liturgics/sove-eucharist.html.

32. Fedotov's studies of the saints in the Russian tradition and the specifically Russian hagiography, *The Russian Religious Mind*, 2 vols. (Cambridge, MA: Harvard University Press, 1966) and *A Treasury of Russian Spirituality* (New York: Sheed & Ward, 1950), were seminal and remain classics.

men in the Eastern church. Though not a part of this anthology, Paul Evdokimov, a student of those we have already mentioned, later seconded their conclusions in his discerning look at the historical and changing forms of the spiritual life as well as the historical specificity (in the modern period) of the personality of the most popular of Russian saints, Seraphim of Sarov.[33]

Today, as noted, traditionalist/fundamentalist voices condemn the search for unity among the divided Christian churches — the ecumenical movement — as perhaps the greatest heresy of the era or of all time. While such would, to most outside such circles, appear counterintuitive, the need for absolute certainty and the exclusive possession of the same by one's own community were and remain strong impulses. A great deal but not all of the present Eastern Orthodox fundamentalism stems from the catastrophic shattering of bonds of unity after the Russian Revolution. Yet, of course, the makings of such divergence were present beforehand as some embraced and sought to find their places in modernity and others condemned and fled it. In his essay in *Living Tradition*, Lev Zander vigorously argues for reconciliation among the churches.[34] He identifies ecumenical work as the work of the Spirit and an integral impulse in the history of the church — the healing of divisions. Quite radical for the time yet still challenging to us today, he affirmed ecumenical work as a continuing Pentecost, borrowing this image from his friend and colleague Fr. Bulgakov, and in the same vision as Bulgakov had (also attributed to Paul Evdokimov) one must see all believers as "Christ-bearers" to each other and to the world, though members of divided churches.

Zander as well as Bulgakov, Zenkovsky, Kartashev, and other contributors to *Living Tradition* were members of the first-ever ecumenical fellowship established between Orthodox Christians and members of non-Orthodox churches. In the case of the Fellowship of St. Alban and St. Sergius it was primarily Anglicans, although some Methodists, Presbyterians, and others took part in Fellowship activities of prayer, study, conversation, and publication of their work. Brandon Gallaher has documented and shown the depth to which Bulgakov, Zernov, Kartashev, Evgeny Lampert, and Zander pursued the question of the sharing of the

---

33. "Holiness in the Tradition of the Orthodox Church," in Plekon/Vinogradov, *In the World, of the Church*, pp. 95-154.

34. "On the Essence of Ecumenical Participation," in *Tradition Alive*, pp. 223-40.

Eucharist among divided Christians in the Fellowship.[35] They realized that in so doing, they were exploring the very issue of how the great schism of 1054 might be appropriately healed, what "unity in the faith" might mean and look like. They proposed, in a way startling to this day, that such unity was simultaneously both maximal and minimal, and this not only on the basis of doctrinal and sacramental unity but also from the historical precedent of the reconciling of separated ecclesial communities in the ancient period.

The Russian émigrés were welcomed in western Europe and assisted from the start by other, non-Orthodox Christians. The YMCA through John Mott helped in the purchase of the property, a former Lutheran church, that became St. Sergius Theological Institute.[36] The YMCA also helped with the startup of the Russian Christian Students' Association as well as the YMCA Press, which published the writings of the émigré thinkers, most notably those being examined here. Paul Anderson and Donald Lowrie represented Anglican assistance to émigré clergy and to St. Sergius Institute. Berdiaev and many of the contributors to this *Living Tradition* collection as well as others like Mother Maria Skobtsova, Nadezhda Gorodetsky, and Myrrha Lot-Borodine knew and conversed with the likes of Jacques Maritain, Emmanuel Mounier, Gabriel Marcel, Louis Massignon, and Etienne Gilson, to name but a few important figures. Period photos show Bulgakov, Zander, Zenkovsky, and Afanasiev in meetings of their own Fraternity of Holy Wisdom, in meetings of the Russian Christian Students' Association, and of the humanitarian-oriented Orthodox Action group. Most of these same individuals appear in photos and at conferences with future archbishop of Canterbury Michael Ramsay, with Bishop Walter Frere, Susanne de Dietrich, future Ecumenical Patriarch Athenagoras I, and Evelyn Underhill, among others.[37]

---

35. *Catholic Action: Ecclesiology, the Eucharist and the Question of Intercommunion in the Ecumenism of Sergei Bulgakov*, MDiv thesis, St. Vladimir's Seminary, 2003. Also see his "Bulgakov's Ecumenical Thought [Part I]," *Sobornost* 24, no. 1 (2002): 24-55 and "Bulgakov and Intercommunion [Part II]," *Sobornost* 24, no. 2 (2002): 9-28.

36. Alexis Kniazeff, *L'Institut Saint-Serge* (Paris: Beauchesne, 1974).

37. There are several locations for these photos. A number of those featuring Fr. Bulgakov and scenes of the Fellowship meetings are at http://www.geocities.com/sbulgakovsociety/. Still others featuring Mother Maria are at http://incommunion.org/contents/mother-maria and in Sergei Hackel, *Pearl of Great Price: Mother Maria Skobtsova 1891-1944* (Crestwood, NY: St. Vladimir's Seminary Press, 1981).

Clearly what we see here is the recognition of Christian unity that had existed before the schism, one that transcended national and political lines and was seen by the ecumenical movement as the situation that could be recovered in the modern era.

Again in *Living Tradition,* church historian A. V. Kartashev argued for the freedom of theological work over against ecclesiastical authority, a bold challenge both to the pre-revolutionary Russian church and some of the rigidity of Diaspora communities. Basil Zenkovsky took on the cosmic aspects of Christian faith and thought, and future bishop Cassian Bezobrazov argued for the use of many disciplines in the interpretation of the scriptures, including historical analysis and philosophy in the heritage and history of the church. Ivan Lagovsky's essay, "The Return to the House of the Father," defended not only Bulgakov's use of the figure of Sophia/Divine Wisdom in his explorations of God's relationship to creation; he also argued for exactly this freedom and creativity in theological expression on the basis of the ongoing presence of the Spirit in the experience of the Christian community. The entire *Living Tradition* anthology in fact was premised upon the Pauline claim that "the letter kills but the Spirit gives life" (2 Cor. 3:6).

> The way to God lies through love of people. At the Last Judgment I shall not be asked whether I was successful in my ascetic exercises, nor how many bows and prostrations I made. Instead I shall be asked, Did I feed the hungry, clothe the naked, visit the sick and the prisoners. That is all I shall be asked. About every poor, hungry and imprisoned person the Savior says "I": "I was hungry and thirsty, I was sick and in prison."[38]

Mother Maria Skobtsova, recently made a saint by the Ecumenical Patriarchate and her Paris archdiocese, did not contribute to the *Living Tradition* volume but was to be found in numerous other publications as an essayist.[39] She earlier had published poetry before the Revolution and continued in this genre as well as in drama. Engaged in her youth in the politi-

---

38. Hackel, *Pearl of Great Price,* p. 29.

39. On Mother Maria, see the previously cited Sergei Hackel biography, the Orbis anthology, and the French-language version with Hélène Arjakovsky Klépinine's biographical sketch. Also edited by her is a collection of the letters between her father while in the concentration camps and her mother, *Et la vie sera amour* (Paris/Pully: Cerf/le sel de la terre, 2005).

cal activity that culminated in the Revolution, she was almost executed by both the Red and White armies. Twice married and divorced, the mother of two daughters and a son, she eventually was received into monastic life with metropolitan Evlogy's encouragement. Her "monastery was the world," as the metropolitan Evlogy once put it, and she returned to the diaconal work of early monastic figures about whom she had written. She opened several hostels for the homeless, the elderly, and the sick in Paris and its suburbs. But having started out as a rising poet in the circle of Alexander Blok and the group around Merezhkovsky, her years of service to the poor and suffering did not exclude a continuing career as a writer.

She not only put into practice the works of loving-kindness highlighted in the twenty-fifth chapter of the Gospel of St. Matthew — "Whatsoever you do for the least of my brethren you do for me" — she also conducted a literary attack on fundamentalism among the Russian émigrés. She sought to historically debunk the idea of a mythical, idealized "Holy Russia" by following the lead of the historian and hagiologist George Fedotov. The authentic lives of holy people in the past provided apt models for Christian action in the present. And such service of the brother or sister in need was for her the "liturgy after the liturgy," or the "liturgy outside the church building," the "sacrament of the neighbor."[40] Even as the deacon or priest censes all the icons of Christ, the Mother of God, and the saints of the past in the church building during the liturgical services, the "living icons" — the Christian faithful present there — are also censed because they are those called to do the work of Christ in the world. In a powerful essay, she assesses several different "types" of religious existence, in the end identifying only one of radical love and care for the neighbor as that truly reflecting the gospel.

Mother Maria, like Fr. Sergius Bulgakov, her mentor, saw the world not only as God's good creation, certainly not as evil and to be escaped or shunned, but as the arena of or room of the Spirit's work. As Arjakovsky notes, they saw it as already touched by, inhabited by the kingdom of God. In seeking to "church" all of life *(votserkovenlie zhizni)*, they were grounded in the tension of the New Testament to "save the world, not condemn it," and to be in the world, though not of it.[41] This is a dialectic of

40. Pevear/Volokhonsky, *Mother Maria Skobtsova: Essential Writings*, pp. 81, 183-86.

41. Alexis Kniazeff, "L'ecclésialisation de la vie," in *La pensée orthodoxe*, 4 (Lausanne: L'Age d'Homme, 1987), pp. 108-35.

being at once both redeemed and yet in need of redemption, a realization often thought to be heralded first in the Reformation by Luther and Melanchthon but really echoing all the way back to apostolic writers such as Irenaeus of Lyons and later Ambrose of Milan.

The point here is not to claim that the contributors to *Living Tradition* and their essays exhaust the outlook of the Paris School. Each of the thinkers noted here had their own projects, and among them all there were disagreements and differences as well. Afanasiev, though interrupted by World War II, was committed to working back through church history to the ecclesiological vision and shape that existed in the first centuries. Bulgakov was enormously productive. He completed a monumental trilogy on the "the humanity of God," dealing with the Holy Spirit, Christ, and the church as the "bride of the Lamb" and the last things, eschatology. In his work in the Fellowship of St. Alban and St. Sergius he wrote an essay on what still unified the otherwise divided churches, "By Jacob's Well," a piece that is both poignant and challenging today.[42] So many others, such as Constantin Mochulsky, Vladimir Lossky, and George Florovsky, though differing sometimes sharply, could also be described as wanting to be in dialogue with, in fact, participants in the life and action of the church in the modern world.

Those of the next period — Frs. Alexander Schmemann, John Meyendorff, Elisabeth Behr-Sigel, and Fr. Alexander Men — would again in their own distinctive ways encourage an openness to the world, an attitude toward it that did not shrink from prophetic witness and criticism but also embraced the world as God's good creation, the subject of Christ's redeeming love and the arena of the Spirit's constant work. The church was present in the world "for the life of the world," as in the Johannine title of Fr. Schmemann's best-known book.[43] Decades after his death, selections from the journals he kept the last years of his life have riveted readers, both here in America and in Europe, and have caused a stir of response even in Russia.[44]

---

42. In *Tradition Alive*, pp. 55-66. Also see Michael Plekon, "Still by Jacob's Well: Sergius Bulgakov's Vision of the Church Revisited," *St. Vladimir's Theological Quarterly* 49, nos. 1 & 2 (2005): 125-44.

43. Alexander Schmemann, *For the Life of the World: Sacraments and Orthodoxy* (Crestwood, NY: St. Vladimir's Seminary Press, 1971).

44. *The Journals of Father Alexander Schmemann 1973-1983*, trans. and ed. Juliana Schmemann (Crestwood, NY: St. Vladimir's Seminary Press, 2000). Also see *My Journey with Father Alexander* (Montreal: Alexander Press, 2006).

John Meyendorff would borrow the *Living Tradition* title for an anthology of his own essays, recognizing the early collection's spirit and substance.[45] Meyendorff's bold commentary was collected in a number of volumes.[46] Elisabeth Behr-Sigel for decades published essay after essay on the ways toward holiness, both in the past and in the present.[47] To these she added a series of radical pieces on the place of women in the church, and through all these writings she too argued for the church's encou~ter with the world, perhaps a witness against it for things such as hatred and torture but never a rejection of it. Having had Fr. Bulgakov as her confessor Elisabeth Behr-Sigel also shared his ecumenical vision and fervor, and her work resounds with the passion for unity of the churches that characterized the earlier figures. Fr. Alexander Men's life ended with an ax blow to the back of his head on the morning of September 9, 1990. Before that martyr's death, both before *Glasnost* and after, he was a tireless teacher. Whether one looks at his catechetical talks on the Creed, his handbook on prayer and liturgical life, his volumes on the world religions or the New Testament, in these the encounter between tradition and modernity is without fear or condemnation, with compassion but without compromise.[48] In a collection of his comments from various lectures gathered by his disciples after his death, the clear rooting in tradition and the liberating possibilities of this are evident.

Christianity is not an "ideology," an abstract doctrine or fixed system of rituals. The Good News entered the world as a dynamic force, encom-

---

45. *Living Tradition* (Crestwood, NY: St. Vladimir's Seminary Press, 1978).

46. *Vision of Unity, Witness to the World* (Crestwood, NY: St. Vladimir's Seminary Press, 1987).

47. *Discerning the Signs of the Times: The Vision of Elisabeth Behr-Sigel*, ed. Michael Plekon and Sarah Hinlicky (Crestwood, NY: St. Vladimir's Seminary Press, 2001); *The Ministry of Women in the Church,* trans. Stephen Bigham (Crestwood, NY: Oakwood/St. Vladimir's Seminary Press, 1991); *Alexandre Boukharev — un théologien de l'église orthodoxe russe en dialogue avec le monde moderne* (Paris: Beauchesne, 1977); *Lev Gillet — The Monk of the Eastern Church,* trans. Helen Wright (Oxford: Fellowship of St. Alban and St. Sergius, 1999); *Prière et sainteté dans l'église russe* (Paris: Cerf, 1950; rev. ed. Bellefontaine, 1982); *The Place of the Heart,* trans. Stephen Bigham (Crestwood, NY: Oakwood/St. Vladimir's Seminary Press, 1992); Elisabeth Behr-Sigel (with Kallistos Ware), *The Ordination of Women in the Orthodox Church* (Geneva: World Council of Churches, 2000). Also see Olga Lossky, *Vers le jour sans déclin: Une vie d'Élisabeth Behr-Sigel (1907-2005)* (Paris: Cerf, 2007).

48. Alexander Men, *The Son of Man,* trans. Samuel Brown; *Orthodox Worship: Sacrament, Word and Image;* and *Seven Talks on the Creed,* trans. Colin Masica (Crestwood, NY: Oakwood/St. Vladimir's Seminary Press, 1998, 1999).

passing all sides of life, open to everything created by God in nature and in human beings. It is not just a religion which has existed for the past twenty centuries, but is a Way focused on the future. . . .[49]

Fr. Men led discussion groups with the members of his parish outside Moscow.[50] He published under various pseudonyms, trying to provide basic understanding of not only Orthodox faith and practice but the wider sweep of religious traditions in history. He became a missionary of sorts to intellectuals and students seeking what had been denied them in the Soviet era.[51] Hence his lines about the stance of a Christian in culture and society:

a Christian . . . recognizes the line dividing tradition — the spirit of faith and learning from "traditions," many of which are associated with folklore and are impermanent accretions to religious life . . .

. . . respects the ritual forms of devotion without forgetting for a moment that they are secondary in comparison with love for God and other people

. . . knows that liturgical rules and canon law have changed over the centuries and cannot (and should not) remain absolutely unaltered in the future

. . . experiences the divisions among Christians as a sin which is common to all and a violation of Christ's will; believes that in the future this sin will be overcome not by a sense of superiority, pride, complacency or hatred but rather through a spirit of brotherly love without which the Christian calling cannot be fulfilled

. . . is open to all that is valuable in all Christian denominations and non-Christian beliefs

. . . sees all that is beautiful, creative, and good as belonging to God, as the secret activity of Christ's grace

. . . does not consider reason and science to be enemies of faith . . . faces all the problems of the world, considering that any of them can be evaluated and made sense of in the light of faith

49. *Christianity for the Twenty-First Century: The Prophetic Writings of Alexander Men,* ed. Elizabeth Roberts and Ann Shukman (New York: Continuum, 1996), p. 68.

50. Alexander Men, *About Christ and the Church,* trans. Alexis Vinogradov (Crestwood, NY: Oakwood/St. Vladimir's Seminary Press, 1996).

51. For an overview of Fr. Men's life and work see Yves Hamant, *Alexander Men: A Witness for Contemporary Russia,* trans. Stephen Bigham (Crestwood, NY: Oakwood/St. Vladimir's Seminary Press, 1995).

. . . looks upon the life of society as one of the spheres where the principles of the Gospel can be applied

. . . believes that history is moving forward through trials, catastrophes and struggle towards the future kingdom of God which transcends history. . . .[52]

Tragic as it is to say, Fr. Alexander Men's death does not now seem so unexpected, in light of what he so boldly had written for years and then said night after night — in small gatherings after vespers, in large auditoriums and university lecture halls. Such a middle ground, such a mediation between tradition and our time is, in ways, even more threatening than the extremes of fundamentalist rhetoric or relativistic compromise.

Conclusion: The Paris School and *Living Tradition* Decades Later

The aim here has not been to become so deeply entwined with the figures, debates, and details of early twentieth-century Russian Orthodox theology but rather to see that some of the Russian émigré thinkers *recognized alternatives to extreme positions when modernity encounters religious tradition.* They were well aware of the choices made by the Karlovtsy Synod, later known as the Russian Orthodox Church Outside Russia (ROCOR), to violently condemn the Paris School and the writers in *Living Tradition* and those aligned with them as heretical, "without grace," outside Christianity and the church. On not a few websites one can read the same judgment today. However, the fundamentalists of Russian Orthodoxy back then also decided to distance themselves from Western culture, politics, and society, existing as a remnant or enclave, awaiting the fall of the Soviet regime, the return of the monarchy and "Holy Russia," the seamless unity of church and state they idealized. While what we might call relativism was perhaps not as fully in bloom in the early decades of the twentieth century, surely there had been in the Russian context a radical rejection of both traditional religious and political traditionalism in favor of political and cultural secularism or even cultic experimentation. One thinks here of theosophy and Madame Blavatsky, of the Symbolist poets and other artistic circles. Later there would be the Soviet ideology and its vision of a new man and new proletarian order.

---

52. Roberts/Shukman, *Christianity for the Twenty-First Century*, pp. 69-73.

Michael Plekon

The collaborators in *Living Tradition* and others in the Paris School aligned with their vision were committed to precisely what the title of their collection expressed, namely a tradition that was not fossilized or reduced to rules and formulae, a particular style and time frame after which all development ceased. It is important to recall that from 1905 onward, efforts to reform the Russian church were taking place in earnest, including a survey of the country's episcopate, all of this culminating in the Moscow Council of 1917-18 which introduced profound reforms at all levels, really a return to ancient forms. In his magisterial study of this council, Hyacinthe Destivelle emphasizes the assembly's reappropriation of an ancient conciliar ecclesiology and the creation, consequently, of a conciliar institutional form for the Russian church. Due to the Revolution's ferocity, these were never implemented in Russia but became the blueprint for Orthodox churches in the exarchate of western Europe based in Paris, in the former diocese of Sourozh in the U.K., in the churches of Finland and Japan, and in the Orthodox Church in America (OCA).

If we look back at the Paris School, the contributors to *Living Tradition* and related figures, their writings and lives, many of the issues that seem to be crucial to a "middle ground" between the extremes of relativism and fundamentalism are addressed. Bulgakov, but also Afanasiev, among others, underscore that the Christian tradition's essential elements are not to be confused with many later, historically specific points of view. Themselves shaped by careful social and historical analysis, Bulgakov's perspectives on doctrine and Afanasiev's on ecclesiology both reveal discernment of how the church over time developed structures, expressed its teaching, and sought to reform what was problematic and to adapt to new and different cultural situations. Others, like Mother Maria Skobtsova, Schmemann, and Meyendorff, were able to describe the varieties of religious existence over the centuries, to discern in them realities like the Byzantine *symphonia* between state and church that later degenerated into intolerable conditions for the church.

The experience of the Russian Revolution and exile from it to the West thrust many of these individuals into a new and very different context, one where their Orthodox tradition was a minority phenomenon. However, welcomed by brother and sister Christians from the Protestant and Catholic churches, materially assisted in establishing a theological school and publishing house, helped in both youth and social ministry as well, the Eastern Christians recognized the gospel and Christ in these Westerners from whom they had been canonically divided for centuries. They came to respect the freedom of religion as well as the religious diversity that marked Western societies. To be sure, some were repulsed by all this diversity and freedom and retreated into a cult of "Holy Russia" and a sectarian exclusivity and isolation. But those profiled here thought otherwise, became leaders in the burgeoning ecumenical movement, and even took courageous action during World War II. Bulgakov condemned the Fascists' use of coercion and violence, especially the Nazis' organized anti-Semitism that produced the Holocaust. Mother Maria and her son Yuri, her chaplain Fr. Dimitri Klepinin, and her treasurer Ilya Fundaminsky all died in Nazi concentration camps, turned in to the Gestapo for sheltering Jews and other targets of Nazi terror in her hostels.

The fundamental theological outlook of these Orthodox presented here was part of the *ressourcement,* the "return to the sources" of Christian tradition but not for its own sake. Rather, as the very title of their anthology indicated, they understood tradition to be invaluable precisely because it was living, because it kept addressing the world and culture, seeking to use the language that could be understood, seeking to comprehend, with the "mind of Christ," what the problems but also the hopes of men and women were in the twentieth century, specifically for the demands of that time. They did not choose the option that some of their fellow Orthodox Christians elected, namely of defining all that was occurring as evil, as inimical to the Christian tradition. In her luminous study of the period just prior to the Russian Revolution, Vera Shevzov sketches the decadence and stagnation of Russian church life but is quick to also point to the signs of life, of spiritual health and renewal in popular devotion, in chapels and in the veneration of the Mother of God that could not be controlled or encompassed by the "official" structures of the "synodal" Russian apparatus.[53] Contrary to even present-day critics who charge that even the massively supported reforms of the 1917-18 Moscow Council were evidence of modern, secular, Western contamination — dangerous "Protestant" or "democratic" influences, Shevzov traces the gradual growth of lay assertiveness and identity. When many of the bishops indicated the great need for reform at every level — that of the national church, of the theological schools, and of the parishes —

---

53. Vera Shevzov, *Russian Orthodoxy on the Eve of the Revolution* (Oxford: Oxford University Press, 2004).

in response to the questionnaire in 1905, they were expressing the already strongly held desires of many clergy and laity. The council that was to meet more than a decade later already had its foundation earlier. The rediscovery of the church as *sobornost'*, as a conciliar or communal reality, cannot be dismissed as social or political thinking alien to the Orthodox Church. The Moscow Council itself sought to maintain both the conciliar presence of representatives of the clergy, laity, and monastic communities along with the bishops as the chief pastors, by also maintaining the bishops' ability to veto the actions of the council as well as work along and approve such decisions. Hyacinthe Destivelle calls this compromise a *via media* between "conciliarist" and "episcopalist" groups within the council.[54]

But Vera Shevzov shows that conflicting ideas about the church as a community of love versus a rule-guided organization led by the bishops (and to a much lesser extent the rest of the clergy) had been a matter of debate since much earlier, over fifty years earlier, in the writings of Alexei Khomiakov and a different Bulgakov, the metropolitan of Moscow Makarii, also between lay theologians and canon law specialists Papkov and Berdnikov.[55] Later these would continue to reverberate in the Paris School I have looked at and in others — Afanasiev, Sergius Bulgakov, George Florovsky, and Vladimir Lossky.

Should we not realize — it would be an important part of an effort to create "middle ground" — that some of the polarizations that divide us are not new, but have been a matter of discussion for decades? We are but the current participants. And I think it also would be useful to recognize that there is very often significant overlap or agreement despite basic contrasts in positions. For example, none of the theologians I have mentioned, or that Shevzov noted, argued against an ordained ministry — bishops, priests, deacons — or the sacraments or that there is a communal dimension in the church or a significance in the local church, most often the parish, in the individual Christian's experience. Sergius Bulgakov, a key player himself at the Moscow Council, argued that the conciliar model was neither episcopal/clerical nor populist hegemony but all members united in their baptism, in their belonging to the community of faith. Such a middle course is the "rule of Love" *(vlast' lyubvi)*, as Nicolas Afanasiev insists in

---

54. Destivelle, *Le concile de Moscou*, pp. 100-109.

55. Shevzov, *Russian Orthodoxy on the Eve*, pp. 27-45.

his pioneering effort to recover the "eucharistic ecclesiology" of the first five centuries or so.[56]

For me, in the end, the results or consequences are more important than theoretical intricacies. The best examples of Orthodox churches facing modern cultural and social situations come when such a middle ground is pursued, one faithful to the ecclesiology of the Christian tradition, one in which there is neither a clericalist elite nor an extreme democratic process. So I would point to the moment in the 1960s when then Pope Paul VI and Ecumenical Patriarch Athenagoras I embraced, prayed together, put aside the anathemas or condemnations of the eleventh century as one consequence. Also when the Faith and Order document of the World Council of Churches, *Baptism, Eucharist and Ministry,* consciously or not took the lead of Sergius Bulgakov's discerning and courageous claim that many elements of unity still existed among the divided churches. The presiding of Cardinal Walter Kasper at the funeral liturgy of Brother Roger of Taizé was yet another, as was the recent visit of Pope Benedict XVI to Istanbul. In a less internationally conspicuous way, the work of Archbishop Anastasios (Yannulatos) of Tirana in rebuilding Albania — not just the church but the educational, health, and cultural life, is another example of "living tradition" at work.[57] Ecumenically open to not just other Christians but to Muslims and people of no faith tradition, the archbishop is able to deal with the aftermath of the Hoxha regime without condemning modern culture or aligning himself with regressive political visions or exclusive ethnic issues. Back home in the U.S., in a way reminiscent of Mother Maria Skobtsova, radical writer Sara Miles has colorfully described her own eucharistic conversion experience at liturgy one morning in an Episcopal church.[58] Her encounter with Christ in receiving holy communion that day led to a new and different life for her. Not only did she become a member of a church community but a leader in it as well. She founded in the parish a weekly food pantry — a project of feeding the hungry, and along the way she documents many other discoveries about partisan politics and faith, about precisely finding a middle ground in which Christians who disagreed could remain in community with each

56. Afanasiev, *The Church of the Holy Spirit,* especially ch. 8, "The Rule of Love."

57. Jim Forest, *The Resurrection of the Church in Albania* (Geneva: World Council of Churches, 2001).

58. Sara Miles, *Take This Bread* (New York: Ballantine, 2007).

other. She came to understand that in a time where polarized politics dominates the media and penetrates relationships, the reality of sharing Christ's love requires just such "middle ground," where divergent perspectives and people have space and respect in the eucharistic assembly as opposed to yet further fragmentation. My own experience as an associate parish priest tells me Sara Miles's experience is indeed crucial. To somehow be the Body of Christ, the "bread for the life of the world" in many different ways, we have to reject the urges to sectarian and divisive actions. The more we know about the Christian communities of the distant as well as the more recent past, the better we will see that such unity in diversity is not only possible but necessary for living out the gospel. In a time of decadence and stagnation, St. Seraphim of Sarov radiated the Spirit and the love of Christ to all who came to visit him. No questions about jurisdictional membership or theological and political positions were asked. They could be dealt with later; the point was to be part of the Body. One could point to others who despite the conditions did likewise: Angelo Roncalli who became Pope John XXIII, monk and writer Thomas Merton, lay theologian Elisabeth Behr-Sigel.[59]

For the thinkers I have put forward here, "living tradition" meant a recovery of the sacredness of the world and of the human person because of God's becoming one with these in the Incarnation. This was Sergius Bulgakov's principal project, tracing out in his last books the consequences of what Soloviev called the "humanity of God" *(Bogochelovechestvo)*.[60] Bulgakov, as did Afanasiev, Kartashev, Fedotov, Mother Maria, Evdokimov, and the rest, saw it as necessary to honor the earthly, the human as well as the divine realities. Being good historians as well as theologians was for them being faithful to the Incarnation. Bulgakov sought to emphasize this by his constant reflection on the presence and activity of God's Wisdom in the world, what he called "sophiology." For these Orthodox Christians the "churching" of life was no rejection of the value of culture and society but

---

59. See Peter and Margaret Hebblethwaite, *John XXIII: Pope of the Century* (New York: Continuum, 2005); Michael Mott, *The Seven Mountains of Thomas Merton* (New York: Houghton Mifflin, 1994); Olga Lossky, *Vers le jour sans déclin: Une vie d'Élisabeth Behr-Sigel (1907-2005)* (Paris: Cerf, 2007).

60. In the final book, *The Bride of the Lamb*, the conciliar understanding of the church and the world are brought together in the eschatological vision, the view of the "last times," of all restored to communion with God in the New Jerusalem of the New Testament's Book of Revelation/Apocalypse.

rather an effort to recover the Christian sense of love and action — "for the life of the world."[61]

I think many of the "middle ground" traits — a sense of what is central and peripheral to the tradition, the ability to inquire, to criticize and doubt, recognition of and respect for those outside one's communion or tradition of faith, genuine love for the world, for society and culture as the creation of God and what he seeks to redeem, even if the world too must be challenged prophetically — surely all these are evident in the thinking of these Eastern Church figures I have presented here. Perhaps we will not find every detail in accord with what we as Western Christians are accustomed. However, their contribution remains a valuable one, not just for their own period but for a pattern of how "living tradition" can be a middle ground for ours as well.

---

61. *For the Life of the World* was the title of American Orthodox theologian Alexander Schmemann's most widely read book, an essay on the liturgy and mission in the world.